RAND McNALLY

the road atlas

DELUXE MIDSIZE

CONTENTS

Photo Credits: ©Mary Lu Laffey/Rand McNally 2 (#1&2), 3 (#1,2&3), 6 (#1,2&3), 7 (#1); ©Nathalie Stassheim/Rand McNally 4 (#1&2), 5 (#1&2); © Dreamcatcher Sailing Charters 4 (#3); ©Laurie Borman/Rand McNally 8 (#1&2), 9 (#1,2&3); ©Rand McNally 10 (#1,2&3), 11 (#1&2); ©Getty Images 12 (#1), 14 (#1), 15 (#1), 177 (#1), 191 (#1).

Copyright ©2008 by Rand McNally & Company. All rights reserved.
Published in U.S.A.
Printed in U.S.A.
Library of Congress Catalog Number: 92-060588

For licensing information and copyright permissions, contact us at licensing@randmcnally.com

If you have a question or even a compliment, please visit us at go.randmcnally.com/contact or e-mail us at consumeraffairs@randmcnally.com

or write to:
Rand McNally Consumer Affairs
P.O. Box 7600
Chicago, Illinois 60680-9915

1 2 3 BN 08 07

Travel Information 2008

Maps and Indexes

State & Province Maps

BEST of the Road

Each year our editors drive five new road trips to share with you those special things we call Best of the Road™.

Simply Irresistible

Santa Barbara to Monterey, California

Driving north and west from Santa Barbara to Monterey, this route follows the El Camino Real Road and CA 1 as it wends its way through the core of coastal California. Following this course, the ocean is always on your left so you can't lose direction. But with the beauty that surrounds you, you may lose your heart south of San Francisco. Sunsets anchored by acres of blooming flowers are rivaled only by those setting over rolling vineyards, or melting into mammoth rock formations along the shore. Romance doesn't linger in the air, it permeates it. Along the way, you'll discover plenty of reasons to pull over into a small village, stroll along a sandy beach, or be mesmerized by the mystique that dusk brings to Monterey's Cannery Row.

Paseo Nuevo

Best known: Stearns Wharf in Santa Barbara and the flower seed fields of Lompoc; the charming Danish village of Solvang and the festivals found at Paso Robles; Hearst Castle; the wind-blown cypress trees and fog-laden cliffs that mark the coastline along the Big Sur.

See map on pg. 127

EDITOR'S PICKS

Paseo Nuevo (Santa Barbara)

Foodies and oenophiles know about Santa Barbara, but so should shoppers. Shopping at its best can be found along the winding pedestrian walks at this outdoor mall anchored by major retailers and Santa Barbara's main thoroughfare, State Street. Small shops offer wares from crystal, jewelry, and children's clothing like This Little Piggy Wears Cotton, to souvenirs, books, and flowers. The area brims with fountains, colorful arches, and casual al fresco dining spots like Pierre Lafond Paseo, a deli that serves wraps, sandwiches, soups, and salads. A classic grilled chicken Caesar Salad is generous enough for two. $8.95 on the luncheon menu.
de la Guerra and State St., (805) 963-2202

Clairmont Lavender Farm (Los Olivos)

Walk through rows of lavender plants on this five-acre farm and then watch as 100-percent organic lavender oil is made using a copper still. The distilling demonstration is free. Once a horse farmer, the owner switched passions to flowers and grows enough product to stock a boutique of all things lavender—essential oils, candles, sachets, and personal products like shampoos and conditioners for people and pets, too. Shampoos for both start at $14.
2480 Roblar Ave., (805) 688-7505

tangent (San Luis Obispo)

Grab a chair at this tasting room before 5:30 p.m. or miss prime sunset seating. Outdoor tables, chairs, and chaises are lined up every day at the restored Independence Schoolhouse-turned-tasting room for tangent's crisp Pinot Gris and Sauvignon Blanc wines and Baileyana's, its sister brand, Pinot Noirs and Syrahs. The schoolhouse, now painted a creamy yellow, is set in the 2,500-acre Edna Valley, part of the Central Coast appellation. Tastings are $5. Open daily, 10 a.m. to 5 p.m.
5828 Orcutt Rd., (805) 269-8200

17-Mile Drive (Pacific Grove)

Located in the Del Monte Forest, this private toll road curves between the Pacific Ocean and multi-million-dollar estates and world-famous golf courses. Open sunrise to sunset, there's ample time to park the car, walk along the shoreline, even picnic. Pull-offs have intriguing names like #12 Spy Glass Hill or #17 the Ghost Tree, which is near Pescadero Point. The Point posts signs warning of "large unexpected waves that will sweep people off their feet." To visitors, just the sight of the Pacific crashing against the rocks does that trick. Enter at Pacific Grove gate. It's $9 per car—free if you ride in on a bicycle. At pull-off

#16, the Lone Cypress perches on rocks. The symbol of Pebble Beach, the wind-swept tree is estimated to be more than 250 years old.
CA 1 at Pebble Beach, Pacific Grove, (831) 624-3811

From Scratch (Carmel)

Breakfast service at this warm, friendly, and family-owned restaurant starts at 8 a.m. Arrive early and grab a newspaper as the locals do before heading toward their regular table. You'll want a paper to read as your order may take some time; it could be 20 minutes. From Hollandaise sauce to bakery goods, menu items are made fresh and from scratch. A fire in a stone fireplace foils the coastal morning chill for patrons wishing to dine inside; later in the day, an arbor protects outside diners from the warm California sun. Breakfast specialties include Roquefort Quiche and made-to-order omelets. Lunch service starts at 11 a.m. and offers Monte Cristo sandwiches that are grilled, not fried. Average price of an entrée: $9.
3626 The Barnyard Shopping Village, (831) 625-2448

MORE GREAT STOPS

Lompoc:
Mural tour, Lompoc Valley Chamber of Commerce
111 South St., (805) 736-4567
www.lompoc.com

Monterey:
Sea Harvest
Fish Market and Restaurant
598 Foam St., (831) 646-0547

Paso Robles:
Holiday Inn Express Hotel and Suites
2455 Riverside Dr.
(805) 238-6500

San Luis Obispo:
Muzio's Grocery and Deli
870 Monterey St.
(805) 543-0800

Santa Barbara:
Franciscan Inn
109 Bath St., (805) 963-8845

For more romantic travel:

ARIZONA, Scottsdale: At the end of one of the 325 days of cloudless skies, stop what you are doing and catch the sunset as it melts over Camelback Mountain. Then watch as the stars light up the desert sky. *(480) 421-1004; www.experienceScottsdale.com*

CALIFORNIA, San Francisco: Ride a cable car to Ghirardelli Square and then share a chocolate bar while you stroll along Fisherman's Wharf. San Francisco is considered the most romantic of American cities. *(415) 391-2000; www.onlyinsanfrancisco.org*

NEW YORK, Niagara: See the majestic falls from the U.S. side at Prospect Point. Lovers might even catch a rainbow in the mist. *(716) 282-8992; www.niagara-usa.com*

PUERTO RICO, San Juan: Old San Juan's winding, narrow streets lined with pastel buildings exude romance. Visit the adjacent wharf to watch cruise ships glide in and out of the bay. No passport required. *(800) 866-7827; www.gotopuertorico.org*

SOUTH CAROLINA, Charleston: Visit Middleton Place, home of America's oldest landscape gardens (c. 1741) where the flowers, like love, bloom year-round. *(800) 868-8118; www.charlestoncvb.com*

North by Northwoods

Bayfield to Eagle River, Wisconsin

This drive through Wisconsin's Northwoods begins in Bayfield, perched on Lake Superior. Heading south, silky-smooth roads cut through forests once logged nearly bare but now nurtured, as densely green as they ever were. Pack the kids' gear to hike or ski the woods, listening for bird calls. Fish or kayak the waters—eagles may join the family. Ojibwe culture reveals time-honored ways to respect the woods while living in them. The Northwoods offer stops where everyone wants to get out of the car. The journey ends in Eagle River, nestled among a 28-lake chain.

Copper Falls State Park

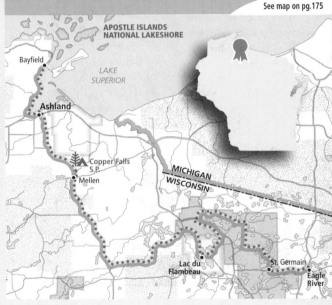

Best known: Apostle Islands National Lakeshore cruises; Bayfield's Old Rittenhouse Inn; Lake of the Torches resort/casino in Lac du Flambeau; all things snowmobile, including the Snowmobiling Hall of Fame in St. Germain.

See map on pg.175

EDITOR'S PICKS

Dreamcatcher Sailing Charters (Bayfield)

Slip between the silent, wooded Apostle Islands aboard sailboats *Esprit* or *Dreamcatcher*. Captain John Thiel charts a course and offers tidbits about lake and island ecology while kids take the wheel and adults trim the jib. Island day trips ($110/person) feature craggy-shoreline exploration by dinghy and lunches of fresh turkey, ham, and hummus on locally baked bread, all washed down with Bayfield's signature apple cider. On the return leg of an afternoon sail ($55/person), the sun sinks toward Bayfield, warming your face as the hull slices through the swell. No worries—a 5,000-lb. keel keeps the boat upright. *City Dock, (715) 779-5561; (800) 262-4176*

Blue Vista Farm (Bayfield)

Northern Wisconsin: snow, lakes, and . . . agriculture with a view? On Blue Vista's slopes, soak up Lake Superior before plunging once more into raspberry canes heavy with plump red fruit ($3.25/lb.). Half-high bushes and dwarf trees invite toddlers to pick their fill of Patriot blueberries and Honeycrisp apples ($2.25/lb., $6/peck). Pick flowers, too. Ball-shaped dahlias, swaying sunflowers, and 300 other varieties grow well given the elevation and southern exposure. Purchase them fresh or dried, even arranged, in the shop tucked into the big red barn's fieldstone foundation. Dried Nigella buds, hanging from the support beams, go for $4/bunch. *34045 County J, (715) 779-5400*

Copper Falls State Park (Mellen)

High above the Bad River gorge, Civilian Conservation Corps-built log fences line the Doughboys' Trail. It was named for the WWI veterans who returned to the Northwoods and cleared the original loop. The current 1.7-mile trail winds through second-growth forest. It's quiet one minute then roaring the next when the Bad River or its tributary, Tyler Forks, plunges over outcroppings of lava on its way to Lake Superior. A disabled-access trail, broad with minimal rise, leads to the park's best outlook, a deck overlooking Brownstone Falls, where Tyler Forks rushes over a precipice to meet the Bad. On Sundays, visitors are treated to a pancake breakfast in the CCC-era concession cabin ($5.95/person). *36764 Copper Falls Rd., (715) 274-5123*

Wa-swa-goning (Lac du Flambeau)

Forest sounds—underbrush rustlings, nuthatches calling, leaves whispering—surround as you tread the path between re-created Ojibwe villages at this cultural exhibit. Small group tours can last 2.5 hours as volunteers explain how the Ojibwe used forest resources to survive outdoors, year-round. Birch bark roofs shed rain from bulrush-sided summer wigwams. Underground tubes carved from birch pipe in air to fuel fires, keeping windproof winter wigwams toasty. The trail ends at the sun-lit log gift shop—no electricity here—where locally made Ojibwe crafts (you're on the Lac du Flambeau reservation) are sold. A startlingly real duck decoy costs $35. *2750 County H, (715) 588-2615*

Chanticleer Inn (Eagle River)

Entire families return to the lakeside inn year after year; Jake and Sue Alward, the innkeepers, greet them by name. Even the chef has been there 30 years and counting. He dresses succulent 8-oz. filet mignon in green peppers, mushrooms, onions, and peppercorns ($27.95). Kids go for the pasta dishes (baked cheese ravioli: $14.50) or classic kids' menu items such as chicken strips ($5.95). Their elders enjoy an array of surf and turf, including a local favorite: walleye pike fillet ($17.95). Wood paneling glows in soft light, the rattle and crush of ice escapes from the bar, two leather sofas gather by the fireplace. Dining room tables overlook Voyageur Lake. *1458 E. Dollar Lake Rd., (715) 479-4486*

Northwoods Children's Museum and Discovery Store (Eagle River)

Even when it's not raining, kids, parents, and grandparents riffle through costumes in the dress-up attic, choose sundries in the old-time general store, and arrange furniture in the pioneer cabin. Twenty activity stations offer hands-on opportunities for families to learn together. If you really liked the catapult in the medieval castle, you can buy it ($20) and the other figurines at the store, which stocks all the activity station toys and then some. Check for events like July's Badger Mining Adventure: Kids uncover minerals common in Wisconsin. *346 W. Division St., (715) 479-4623*

MORE GREAT STOPS

Bayfield:
Apostle Islands Outfitters
10 S. Broad St.
(715) 779-3411

Ashland:
Northern Great Lakes
Visitor Center
29270 County G
(715) 685-9983
www.nglvc.org

Lac du Flambeau:
George W. Brown, Jr. Ojibwe
Museum & Cultural Center
603 Peace Pipe Rd.
(715) 588-3333
www.ldfojibwe.com

Lac du Flambeau:
Dillman's Bay Resort
13277 Dillman's Way
(715) 588-3143
www.dillmans.com

Eagle River:
Farmer's Wife Restaurant
1100 US 45 S.
(715) 479-7428

{ **For more family travel:** }

ARKANSAS, Murfreesboro: Pickings aren't slim at Crater of Diamonds State Park, the only place in the world where visitors may keep any diamonds they find. More than 75,000 sparklers have been uncovered in this 37-acre field. *(870) 285-3113; www.craterofdiamondsstatepark.com*

CALIFORNIA, Palm Desert: The 1,200 acres at The Living Desert zoo and botanical garden are home to more than 125 species of desert-dwelling animals, including meerkats, cinereous vultures, and Gila monsters, as well as 1,000 varieties of plants representing 10 desert ecosystems. *(760) 346-5694; www.livingdesert.org*

KENTUCKY, Louisville: Order your name on a wooden bat when starting a 30-minute tour of the Louisville Slugger Museum & Factory. It'll be finished when the tour is. Everyone receives a mini-bat (nonpersonalized) at tour's end. *(877) 775-8443; www.sluggermuseum.org*

MARYLAND, Tilghman: The *Rebecca T. Ruark,* a working 1886 skipjack, sails from Tilghman Island with waterman Captain Wade Murphy, Jr., as your two-hour tour guide. He invites kids and parents to take the helm. *(410) 886-2176; www.skipjack.org*

MICHIGAN, Grand Rapids: More than 550 carnivorous plants, the Venus flytrap included, inhabit the Carnivorous Plant House at the Frederik Meijer Gardens and Sculpture Park. The Children's Garden offers five acres of themed walkways through Midwest wild-life and geology. *(888) 957-1580; www.meijergardens.org*

Discover America's Past

Historic Jamestowne to Yorktown, Virginia

Curving its way through forested land with nary a billboard or telephone pole in sight, the Colonial Parkway connects America's Historic Triangle of Williamsburg, Jamestown, and Yorktown. Built by the Civilian Conservation Corps in the 1930s, the parkway serves as a time tunnel that leads travelers to the historic reenactment areas in Tidewater Virginia where freedom was won and America began.

The Revolutionary City

EDITOR'S PICKS

The Revolutionary City (Colonial Williamsburg)

Introduce yourself to Thomas Jefferson and debate the cost of personal freedom with other patriots or loyalists as part of a three-day program called "Revolutionary City." Each interactive two-hour presentation (such as "Citizens at War") re-creates the confusion on the streets in the colonies as the idea of independence is realized. Join the revolution and march behind a fife and drum corps with the people who made it happen.
Duke of Gloucester Street, (800) 447-8679

Riverfront Discovery (Jamestown Settlement)

Climb on board a replica of the *Susan Constant,* flagship of the three ships that carried colonists, supplies, and livestock to Virginia 400 years ago—but watch your head. The belowdecks quarters are much more cramped than today's passenger ships. Visit with a 17th-century Englishman as he loads and fires a matchlock musket, watch a Powhatan char a cypress tree to make a dugout canoe, and talk with settlers about their lives at James Fort.
VA 31 and Colonial Parkway, (888) 593-4682

Yorktown Battlefield (Yorktown)

Walk reconstructed berms and original cannon lines built during the siege of Yorktown, which was led by General George Washington. Be sure to stop at the Moore House, often called the historic house that no one remembers. Unheralded Moore House was the location of British surrender negotiations. Ranger-led or self-guided auto tours end at Surrender Field, where the redcoats laid down their arms on October 19, 1781, signaling the end of the Revolutionary War.
Colonial Parkway, (757) 898-2410

Best known: The elegant architecture of Colonial Williamsburg, the world's largest living history museum; 1607 fort at Historic Jamestowne; Surrender Field at Yorktown; tri-cornered hats and costumed interpreters; replicas of the *Susan Constant, Godspeed,* and *Discovery;* the legend of Pocahontas, and the campus of the College of William and Mary.

See map on pg. 172

Gabriel Archer Tavern at Williamsburg Winery (Williamsburg)

Fifty acres of vineyards provide a spectacular view for lunch or a weekend dinner. If you like to dine al fresco, this is the spot; the terrace is sheltered by a wisteria arbor. The French Country Platter of assorted patés, meats, cheeses, and breadstuffs serves two for lunch ($13) and reflects food choices of the 18th century.
5800 Wessex Hundred, (757) 229-0999

Abbey Stone Theatre at Busch Gardens Europe (Williamsburg)

The seats fill quickly for "Emerald Beat," a musical production of Celtic and contemporary Irish song and dance. While the rhythm and clacking of tap shoes entice the audience to get up and dance, clapping along has to do. Twenty members of Dublin-based O'Shea's School of Irish Dance perform fast-paced tapping and traditional Irish step dancing.
One Busch Gardens Blvd., (800) 343-7946

Riverwalk Landing (Yorktown)

Sun, shop, and dine in Yorktown along the shores of the York River. Shake off the sand from a morning at the beaches along Water Street before browsing the galleries and gift shops at the Landing. There's fine dining and fun food at Nick's Riverwalk Restaurant. Nick's houses three venues including The Rivah Café, which offers a menu of sandwiches from burgers ($8.50) to crab cakes ($9.50).
323 Water St., (757) 875-1522

MORE GREAT STOPS

Historic Jamestowne:
The Archaearium
Colonial Parkway
(757) 229-9776

Williamsburg:
Aromas Coffeehouse
Bakeshop & Café
431 Prince George St.
(757) 221-6676

Williamsburg:
King's Arms Tavern
Duke of Gloucester St.
(757) 229-2141

Yorktown:
Yorktown Waterfront Beach
423 Water St.
(757) 890-3500

Yorktown:
Yorktown Victory Center
VA 120
(757) 887-1776

For more travel through history:

FLORIDA, St. Augustine: Among the most intriguing of St. Augustine's Spanish-period structures are the Castillo de San Marcos, the Basilica of St. Augustine, and the San Agustin Antiguo or Spanish Quarter—a re-creation of an 18th-century Spanish Colonial village. *(800) 653-2489; www.getaway4florida.com*

ILLINOIS, Springfield: For those harboring a desire to have met Abraham Lincoln, a visit to The Abraham Lincoln Presidential Library and Museum is as close as you'll get. In two buildings, it houses the world's largest collection of Lincoln-related documents and artifacts. *(217) 782-5764; www.alplm.org/home.html*

OKLAHOMA, Oklahoma City: The Oklahoma City National Memorial remembers those who lost their lives in the bombing of the Alfred P. Murrah Building on April 19, 1995. The outdoor memorial is open 24 hours a day. *(405) 235-3313; www.oklahomacity nationalmemorial.org*

OREGON, Astoria: The 2,000-acre Lewis and Clark National Historical Park commemorates the arrival at the Pacific Ocean of the Lewis and Clark Expedition in mid-November 1805. Located at the mouth of the Columbia River, it includes the spring, the canoe landing, and a reconstruction of Fort Clatsop, where the expedition wintered. *(503) 861-2471; www.nps.gov/lewi*

PENNSYLVANIA, Gettysburg: Preserved on 5,989 acres, Gettysburg National Military Park is the site of the largest battle of the Civil War. Licensed Battlefield Guides lead two-hour tours; self-guided auto tours stop at key field exhibits and monuments. *(717) 334-1124; www.nps.gov/gett*

High Tide, Low Stress, Big Adventure

Prince Edward Island and the New Brunswick coast, Canada

Trailside Inn and Café

From pastoral green fields and gentle dunes on Prince Edward Island (PEI), across the Confederation Bridge and along New Brunswick's Bay of Fundy coast, this highly scenic drive means low stress and light traffic. Big adventures abound, including climbing PEI lighthouses and kayaking along national parks to hiking along Canada's version of the Appalachian Trail in New Brunswick's Fundy National Park. You can even drive across the ocean floor at low tide to visit Minister's Island. Just be sure to sneak back to the mainland before the tide captures your car!

EDITOR'S PICKS

Trailside Inn and Café (Mount Stewart, PEI)

Along the 270-km (168-mi.) Confederation Trail, which runs from Tignish to Elmira, the Trailside Inn and Café is housed in a former barn and filled with antiques. It offers four rustic accommodations above the café; tasty fare including chowder and seafood seasoned by herbs picked from the garden outside; and Canadian talent, entertaining on the very intimate stage. Rent bikes by the hour or day to explore the nearby bird sanctuary or to wheel along the trail. *109 Main St., (888) 704-6595*

Best-known: Tour Anne of Green Gables house in Cavendish, PEI; listen to bagpipers at the College of Piping in Summerside, PEI; watch for whales and seals all along the PEI coastline; walk around Hopewell Rocks at low tide in New Brunswick's most-photographed spot; sample smoked salmon and seafood shops just outside Saint Andrews, New Brunswick.

See map on pg.189

East Point Lighthouse and Welcome Centre (East Point, PEI)

If the welcome centre's manager Nadine Cheverie seems to know everything about East Point, it's because she grew up here and loves the place. She'll take you up the steps to the top, for a view of cormorants diving and seals playing where the tides of the St. Lawrence and the Northumberland Strait meet in an X shape. If you go to the lighthouse at the other end of the island, you can collect a certificate proclaiming you've been tip to tip. *Rte. 16, (902) 357-2718; (902) 687-3489 October through May*

Lennox Island Ecotourism Complex (Lennox Island, PEI)

Drive over a small bridge into the heart of native Canadian Miq'mak culture on this Miq'mak-owned island. Try geocaching; stroll one of the island's three looped nature trails; taste Mik'maq traditional bread, local oysters, and seafood at the Minegoo Café. Hear about the history from the locals, such as how lightweight and insect-resistant their birch bark wigwams and canoes were. Up to 14 people can stay overnight in the hostel for just $20 CN ($17.60 US). *Rte. 163, off Rte. 12, (866) 831-2702*

Fundy National Park (Alma, NB)

The world's highest tides—as much as 12.2 m (40 ft.) between high and low tides—are the star attraction. Many spectacular hiking trails range from moderate to challenging in difficulty, offering Bay of Fundy views. You can even hike and camp on along the Fundy Trail—Canada's version of the Appalachian Trail—without any houses or roads to disturb your reverie. *Highway 114, (506) 887-6000*

Seascape Kayak Tours (Deer Island, NB)

Bruce Smith runs the original kayaking outfitter for the Canadian Pasamaquoddy Bay area. Guides teach about the high tides and local sea creatures such as lobster, crab, seals, and whales, as kayakers glide through water on 2-hour, 3-hour, or day-long adventures. *40 NW Harbour Branch Rd., (506) 747-1884; (866) 747-1884*

Ovenhead Salmon Smokers (Bethel, NB)

Not all smoked salmon tastes the same, and Ovenhead proves this point with a very smoky, not-too-sweet version of the local specialty. Cold-smoked under maple chip fires, the salmon can be bought at the smokers' headquarters on Ovenhead Road. The menu is simple: smoked salmon, salmon jerky, and salmon paté. *101 Ovenhead Rd., (506) 755-2507*

MORE GREAT STOPS

Winsloe, PEI:
PEI Sweater Shop
Rte. 10
(902) 621-0185

North Rustico, PEI:
Outside Expeditions
Kayaking Tours
370 Harbourview Drive
(902) 963-3366
www.getoutside.com

Saint Andrews, NB:
Fairmont Algonquin Hotel
184 Adolphus St.
(506) 529-8823
www.fairmont.com

Saint Andrews, NB:
Van Horne Estate on
Ministers Island
(506) 529-5081;
(800) 561-0123
www.gnb.ca/0007/Heritage/
ministers.asp

Blacks Harbour, NB:
Grand Manan Car and
Passenger Ferry
Wallace Cove Road
(506) 662-3724
www.coastaltransport.ca

{ For more adventurous travel: }

CANADA, Alberta, Jasper: Strap on some crampons and gently tread over frozen ice flows, past waterfalls stopped by cold temperatures in Jasper National Park's Maligne Canyon. Hikers can hear the water rushing underneath their feet, and sheer granite cliffs rise up on either side. *(780) 852-5595; www.jasperadventurecentre.com*

FLORIDA, Tierra Verde: Fort De Soto Park routinely wins accolades for its sparkly white sand beach, but the marked 2.25-mile recreational canoe trail is the secret gem here for the adventurous. Experienced kayakers may prefer to paddle the 10 miles around Mullet Key. *(727) 464-3347; www.pinellascounty.org/park*

HAWAII, Moloka'i, Kalaupapa: Ride a mule along 26 switchback turns, down 2.9 miles of the world's highest sea cliffs to the Kalaupapa National Historical Park. Home to a former leper colony (only a few elderly residents remain), the real scare is how people with the disease were abandoned here starting in 1866. *(800) 567-7550; www.muleride.com*

UTAH, Springdale: Long, deep canyons and massive granite cliffs define the landscape of Zion National Park. Serious hikers relish the strenuous challenge of Walter's Wiggles on the trail up to Angels Landing, a 1,488-ft. elevation gain to 5,790 ft. on the five-mile round trip. *(435) 772-3256; www.nps.gov/zion*

WEST VIRGINIA, Beckley: Rafters head straight into whitewater exploring the New River Gorge National River or the Gauley River National Recreation Area. Rafting runs from gentle, family friendly sections of the upper New River to full-out rapids on the lower New and Gauley Rivers. *(800) 252-7784; www.class-vi.com*

Culture in Cowboyland

Fort Worth, Texas to Tulsa, Oklahoma

Water Taxi,
Oklahoma City

You'll find nary a tumbleweed on the route from Fort Worth to Tulsa. This drive—which passes through both green countryside and busy metropolises as it curves north, then east—is peppered with a surprising number of sleek museums, fine dining, and bijou-filled boutiques. From brimming arts districts to Art Deco architecture, the sights along this drive testify that culture and cowboys are more than compatible.

EDITOR'S PICKS

Best known: Fort Worth Stockyards National Historic District; Sixth Floor Museum at Dealey Plaza, Dallas; National Cowboy and Western Heritage Museum and the Oklahoma City National Memorial, Oklahoma City; the Philbrook Museum of Art and the Gilcrease Museum, Tulsa.

Kimbell Museum (Fort Worth, TX)

Museums as well respected as the Kimbell can be vast and wearying. But this gem of a collection, with works by Fra Angelico, El Greco, and others, is small enough to manage in an afternoon, with time left over for a game of Frisbee on the lawn, a snooze beside the outdoor fountain, or a bite in the award-winning restaurant. Admission is free.
3333 Camp Bowie Blvd., (817) 332-8451

Cierra Furniture (Dallas, TX)

Where does owner Tim Heard find the Mexican, Moroccan, traditional African, and Indian housewares, furniture, and art that fill this rabbit warren of a store? "He shops the world," a salesperson says. See (and buy) the fruits of his travels: Red Moroccan drinking glasses etched with gold go for $10 each, while $12 milagros crosses from Mexico line an entire wall.
2920 N. Henderson Ave., (214) 887-8772

See map on pg. 160 (OK) or pg. 169 (TX)

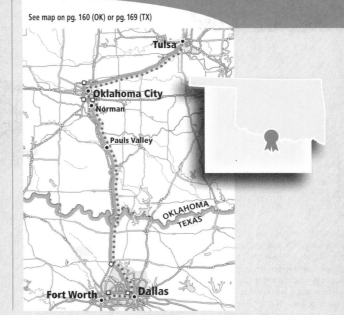

DeGolyer Garden Café (Dallas, TX)

This chic, friendly lunch spot, with white tablecloths and classical music playing on the patio, offers a bit of refined repast in the midst of the Dallas Arboretum's flowery profusion. One entrée: crustless tea sandwiches (cucumber, egg salad, and chicken salad) nestling against each other ($8). During the winter holidays and in the spring, visitors can splurge on high tea (which includes both tea sandwiches and dainty desserts) for $30.95 per person.
In the Dallas Arboretum, 8525 Garland Rd., (214) 515-6512

Bedre Fine Chocolate (Pauls Valley, OK)

Despite its Swedish name (it means "better"), this business is owned by Oklahoma's Chickasaw Nation—more evidence that chocolate is the universal language. Tours include the chance to watch liquid chocolate flow Willy Wonka-style before it solidifies into dark chocolate espresso crème Oklahoma Black Gold Bars ($3.50 each) and other treats that honor the area's heritage. Baskets of samples await in the gift shop.
2001 W. Airline Rd.,
(405) 207-9320 or (800) 367-5390

Water Taxi (Oklahoma City, OK)

A shallow, lovely canal winds through the city's historic Bricktown entertainment district (named for its WWI-era deep red brick buildings), and $6.50 grants all-day access to the small boats that glide along it. In the evenings, blues music from neighboring nightclubs drifts over the water. The round-trip ride takes about 40 minutes, but you're welcome to hop on and off throughout.
Buy tickets at dock below Mickey Mantle Boulevard,
(405) 234-8294

Tulsa Gathering Place (Tulsa, OK)

With an hour's notice, glass artist Sarah Diggdon will help visitors to this small shop and studio make their own glass flower to take home. For $25, they'll learn how to swirl or "gather" glowing-hot liquid glass onto a metal rod and shape it into a delicate blossom to keep. Works for sale include vases as bright and flowery as the blooms they're meant to hold ($20 and up).
19 E. Brady, (918) 582-4527

MORE GREAT STOPS

Dallas, TX:
Tom Tom Asian Grill
3699 McKinney Ave.
(214) 522-1237
www.tomtomasiangrill.com

Fort Worth, TX:
Lone Star Wines
140 E. Exchange Ave.
Ste. 108
(817) 626-1601

Norman, OK:
Fred Jones Jr. Museum of Art
555 Elm Ave.
(405) 325-4938
www.ou.edu/fjjma

Oklahoma City, OK:
Panaderia la Herradura
2235 SW 14th St.
(405) 232-3502

Tulsa, OK:
Linnaeus Teaching Garden
2435 S. Peoria Ave.
(918) 746-5125
www.tulsagardencenter.com

{ **For more cultural travel:** }

CANADA, Québec, Montréal: Vacationers don't have to go to Europe to have a French vacation. French is the official language of Québec. Montréal boasts a deep connection with its French forebears as a stroll through Old Montréal's narrow lanes attest.
(514) 873-2015;
www.tourism-montreal.org

LOUISIANA, Baton Rouge: To experience working life at a 19th-century plantation, visit Louisiana State University's Rural Life Museum. It re-creates plantation life using 28 buildings filled with artifacts and tools of the day.
(225) 765-2437; rurallife.lsu.edu

MINNESOTA, Minneapolis: While in Minneapolis, home to the acclaimed Guthrie Theater for regional productions, theater fans also can head to Hennepin Avenue for touring Broadway shows.
(888) 676-6757; www.minneapolis.org

NEW MEXICO, Santa Fe: A major culinary and art capital, Santa Fe is a repository of Spanish and Native American culture. Many top spots are within a short stroll of the Palace of the Governors, one of four facilities of the Museum of New Mexico.
(505) 955-6200; www.santafe.org

NORTH DAKOTA, Stanton: Knife River Indian Villages offers a glimpse of life for the Hidatsa Indian tribe on the northern plains before the advent of explorers, fur traders, and settlers. The Hidatsa may have arrived in this area as long ago as the early 1300s.
(701) 745-3300; www.nps.gov/knri

Road Work

Road construction and road conditions resources

Road closed. Single lane traffic ahead. Detour. When you are on the road, knowledge is power. Let Rand McNally help you avoid situations that can result in delays, or worse.

There are ways to prepare for construction traffic and avoid the dangers of poor road conditions. Read on:

1. Use the state and province websites and hotlines listed on this page for road construction and road conditions information.

2. Go to randmcnally.com/roadconstruction for current U.S. and Canadian road construction information.

❋ **Road Conditions**

⚒ **Road Construction**

● **Both**

United States

Alabama

www.dot.state.al.us/docs ●

Alaska

511 ●
(866) 282-7577 ●
(907) 456-7623 ❋
(907) 269-0450 ⚒
511.alaska.gov ●
In AK: (800) 478-7675 ❋

Arizona

511 ●
(888) 411-7623 ●
www.az511.com ●

Arkansas

(800) 245-1672 ❋
(501) 569-2374 ❋
www.arkansashighways.com ●

California

(916) 445-7623 ⚒
www.dot.ca.gov ●
www.511.org ●
San Francisco Bay and
    Sacramento areas: 511 ●
In CA: (800) 427-7623 ❋

Colorado

511 ●
(303) 639-1111 ●
www.cotrip.org ●
In CO: (877) 315-7623 ●

Connecticut

(860) 594-2650 ❋
www.ct.gov/dot ⚒
In CT: (800) 443-6817 ●

Delaware

www.deldot.net ⚒
In DE: (800) 652-5600 ●
Out of state: (302) 760-2080 ●

Florida

511 ●
www.511tampabay.com ●
www.fl511.com ●

Georgia

(404) 635-8000 ●
(888) 635-8287 ●
www.dot.state.ga.us ●

Hawaii

(808) 536-6566 ⚒
www.hawaii.gov/dot/publicaffairs/
    roadwork/ ⚒

Idaho

511 ●
(888) 432-7623 ●
511.idaho.gov ●

Illinois

(800) 452-4368 ●
(312) 368-4636 ●
www.gettingaroundillinois.com ●

Indiana

(800) 261-7623 ❋
(317) 232-8298 ❋ (12/1-3/31)
www.in.gov/dot ●

Iowa

511 ●
(800) 288-1047 ●
www.511ia.org ●

Kansas

511 ●
(800) 585-7623 ●
511.ksdot.org ●

Kentucky

511 ●
(866) 737-3767 ●
www.511.ky.gov ●

Louisiana

www.511la.org ●

Maine

511 ●
(866) 282-7578 ●
(207) 624-3595 ●
www.511maine.gov ●

Get the info from the 511 hotline

The U.S. Federal Highway Administration has begun implementing a national system of highway and road conditions/construction information for travelers. Under the new plan, travelers can dial 511 and get up-to-date information on roads and highways.

Implementation of 511 is the responsibility of state and local agencies.

For more details, visit:
www.fhwa.dot.gov/trafficinfo/511.htm.

Maryland

(800) 327-3125 ⊞
(800) 541-9595 ⊞
(410) 582-5650 ●
www.chart.state.md.us ●

Massachusetts

www.state.ma.us/eotc/ ⊥
SmarTraveler, Greater Boston only:
(617) 374-1234 ⊥

Michigan

(800) 381-8477 ●
www.michigan.gov/mdot/ ●
West and Southwest Michigan:
(888) 305-7283 ⊥
Metro Detroit: (800) 641-6368 ⊥

Minnesota

511 ●
(800) 542-0220 ●
www.511mn.org ●

Mississippi

(601) 987-1211 ⊞
(601) 359-7301 ⊥
www.mdot.state.ms.us ●

Missouri

(800) 222-6400 ●
www.modot.mo.gov ●

Montana

511 ●
(800) 226-7623 ●
www.mdt.mt.gov/travinfo/511 ●

Nebraska

511 ●
(800) 906-9069 ●
(402) 471-4533 ●
www.nebraskatransportation.org/ ●

Nevada

511 ●
(877) 687-6237 ⊞
www.nevadadot.com ●

New Hampshire

511 ●
(866) 282-7579 ●
www.nh.gov/dot/511 ●

New Jersey

www.state.nj.us/transportation/
commuter/ ⊥
Turnpike: (732) 247-0900,
then 2 ⊞ , (800) 336-5875 ⊞ ,
www.state.nj.us/turnpike/ ⊥
Garden State Parkway:
(732) 727-5929 ●

New Mexico

(800) 432-4269 ●
www.nmshtd.state.nm.us ●

New York

www.dot.state.ny.us ●
Thruway: (800) 847-8929 ⊞,
www.thruway.state.ny.us ●

North Carolina

511 ●
(877) 511-4662 ●
www.ncdotorg/traffictravel ●

North Dakota

511 ●
(866) 696-3511 ●
www.dot.nd.gov/divisions/
maintenance/511_nd.html ●

Ohio

(614) 644-7031 ⊞
www.buckeyetraffic.org ●
Cincinnati/northern Kentucky area:
511 ●, (513) 333-3333 ● ,
www.artimis.org ●
Turnpike: (440) 234-2030 ⊞ ,
(888) 876-7453 ⊥ ,
www.ohioturnpike.org ●
In OH: (888) 264-7623 ●

Oklahoma

(888) 425-2385 ⊞
(405) 425-2385 ⊞
www.okladot.state.ok.us ●

Oregon

511 ●
(800) 977-6368 ●
(503) 588-2941 ●
www.tripcheck.com/Pages/
AT511.asp ●

Pennsylvania

www.dot.state.pa.us ●
In PA: (888) 783-6783 ●
SmarTraveler, Camden/Philadelphia
area: (215) 567-5678 ●

Rhode Island

511 ●
www2.tmc.state.ri.us ●
Outside RI: (888) 401-4511 ●

South Carolina

www.dot.state.sc.us ●

South Dakota

511 ●
(866) 697-3511 ●
www.sddot.com/travinfo.asp ●

Tennessee

511 ●
www.tn511.com ●

Texas

(800) 452-9292 ●
www.dot.state.tx.us ●

Utah

511 ●
(800) 492-2400 ●
(866) 511-8824 ●
www.utahcommuterlink.com ●

Vermont

511 ●
(800) 429-7623 ●
www.aot.state.vt.us/
travelinfo.htm ●
www.511vt.com ●

Virginia

511 ●
(800) 367-7623 ⊞
(800) 578-4111 ●
www.511virginia.org ●

Washington

511 ●
(800) 695-7623 ●
www.wsdot.wa.gov/traffic/ ●

Washington, D.C.

www.ddot.dc.gov ⊥

West Virginia

(877) 982-7623 ⊞
www.wvdot.com ●

Wisconsin

(800) 762-3947 ●
www.dot.state.wi.us ●

Wyoming

511 ⊞
(888) 996-7623 ⊞
www.dot.state.wy.us ●

Canada

Alberta

(403) 246-5853 ⊞
www.trans.gov.ab.ca ●

British Columbia

(604) 660-9770 ●
www.gov.bc.ca/tran/ ●

Manitoba

(204) 945-3704 ⊞
www.gov.mb.ca/roadinfo/ ●
In MB: (877) 627-6237 ⊞

New Brunswick

www1.gnb.ca/cnb/transportation/
index-e.asp ●
In NB: (800) 561-4063 ⊞

Newfoundland & Labrador

www.roads.gov.nl.ca/
roadreport-information.stm ●

Nova Scotia

(902) 424-3933 ⊞
www.gov.ns.ca/tran ●
In NS: (800) 307-7669 ⊞

Ontario

www.mto.gov.on.ca ●
In ON: (800) 268-4686 ●
In Toronto: (416) 235-4686 ●

Prince Edward Island

(902) 368-4770 ⊞
www.gov.pe.ca/roadconditions ⊞

Québec

(888) 355-0511 ●
www.mtq.gouv.qc.ca/en/
index.asp ●
In Québec: (877) 393-2363 ⊞

Saskatchewan

www.highways.gov.sk.ca ●
Regina and surrounding areas,
areas outside of province:
(306) 787-7623 ●
Saskatoon and surrounding areas:
(306) 933-8333 ●
All other areas: (888) 335-7623 ●

Mexico

www.sct.gob.mx ●
(in Spanish only)

Numbers to Know

HOTEL RESOURCES

**Adam's Mark
Hotels & Resorts**
(800) 444-2326
www.adamsmark.com

**America's Best Inns
& Suites**
(800) 237-8466
www.americasbestinns.com

AmericInn
(800) 396-5007
www.americinn.com

Baymont Inns & Suites
(877) 229-6668
www.baymontinn.com

Best Western
(800) 780-7234
www.bestwestern.com

Budget Host
(800) 283-4678
www.budgethost.com

Clarion Hotels
(877) 424-6423
www.clarioninn.com

Coast Hotels & Resorts
(800) 716-6199
www.coasthotels.com

Comfort Inns
(877) 424-6423
www.comfortinn.com

Comfort Suites
(877) 424-6423
www.comfortsuites.com

Courtyard by Marriott
(888) 236-2427
www.courtyard.com

**Crowne Plaza
Hotel & Resorts**
(877) 227-6963
www.crowneplaza.com

Days Inn
(800) 329-7466
www.daysinn.com

Delta Hotels & Resorts
(888) 778-5050
(877) 814-7706
www.deltahotels.com

**Doubletree Hotels
& Guest Suites**
(800) 222-8733
www.doubletree.com

Drury Hotels
(800) 378-7946
www.druryhotels.com

Econo Lodge
(877) 424-6423
www.econolodge.com

Embassy Suites Hotels
(800) 362-2779
www.embassysuites.com

Exel Inns of America
(800) 367-3935
www.exelinns.com

Fairfield Inn by Marriott
(800) 228-2800
www.fairfieldinn.com

Fairmont Hotels & Resorts
(800) 257-7544
www.fairmont.com

**Four Points Hotels
by Sheraton**
(800) 368-7764
www.fourpoints.com

**Four Seasons
Hotels & Resorts**
(800) 819-5053
www.fourseasons.com

Hampton Inn
(800) 426-7866
www.hamptoninn.com

Hilton Hotels
(800) 445-8667
www.hilton.com

**Holiday Inn
Hotels & Resorts**
(800) 465-4329
www.holidayinn.com

Homewood Suites
(800) 225-5466
www.homewood-suites.com

Howard Johnson Lodges
(800) 446-4656
www.hojo.com

Hyatt Hotels & Resorts
(888) 591-1234
www.hyatt.com

**InterContinental
Hotels & Resorts**
(888) 424-6835
www.intercontinental.com

Jameson Inns
(800) 526-3766
www.jamesoninns.com

Knights Inn
(800) 843-5644
www.knightsinn.com

La Quinta Inn & Suites
(800) 642-4271
www.lq.com

Le Meridien Hotels
(800) 543-4300
www.lemeridien.com

Loews Hotels
(866) 563-9792
www.loewshotels.com

MainStay Suites
(877) 424-6423
www.mainstaysuites.com

Marriott International
(888) 236-2427
www.marriott.com

Microtel Inns & Suites
(800) 771-7171
www.microtelinn.com

Motel 6
(800) 466-8356
www.motel6.com

Omni Hotels
(888) 444-6664
www.omnihotels.com

Park Inn
(888) 201-1801
www.parkinn.com

Preferred Hotels & Resorts
(800) 323-7500
www.preferredhotels.com

Quality Inns & Suites
(877) 424-6423
www.qualityinn.com

Radisson Hotels & Resorts
(888) 201-1718
www.radisson.com

**Ramada Inn/
Ramada Limited/
Ramada Plaza Hotels**
(800) 272-6232
www.ramada.com

Red Lion Hotels
(800) 733-5466
www.redlion.com

Red Roof Inns
(800) 733-7663
www.redroof.com

**Renaissance Hotels
& Resorts**
(800) 468-3571
www.renaissancehotels.com

Residence Inn by Marriott
(800) 331-3131
www.residenceinn.com

The Ritz-Carlton
(800) 241-3333
www.ritzcarlton.com

Rodeway Inn
(877) 424-6423
www.rodeway.com

Sheraton Hotels & Resorts
(800) 325-3535
www.sheraton.com

Signature Inns
(800) 526-3766
www.signatureinns.com

Sleep Inn
(877) 424-6423
www.sleepinn.com

Super 8 Motel
(800) 800-8000
www.super8.com

Travelodge Hotels
(800) 578-7878
www.travelodge.com

WestCoast Hotels
(800) 325-4000
www.westcoasthotels.com

Westin Hotels & Resorts
(800) 937-8461
www.westin.com

**Wyndham Hotels
& Resorts**
(877) 999-3223
www.wyndham.com

NOTE: All toll-free reservation numbers are for the U.S. and Canada unless otherwise noted. These numbers were accurate at press time, but are subject to change. Find more listings or book a hotel online at randmcnally.com.

RENTAL CAR RESOURCES

**Advantage
Rent-a-Car**
(800) 777-5500
www.arac.com

Alamo
(800) 462-5266
www.alamo.com

Avis
(800) 331-1212
www.avis.com

Budget Rent-a-Car
(800) 527-0700 (U.S.)
www.budget.com

Enterprise Rent-a-Car
(800) 261-7331
www.enterprise.com

Hertz
(800) 654-3131 (U.S.)
(800) 654-3001
(International)
www.hertz.com

National Car Rental
(800) 227-7368
www.nationalcar.com

Payless Car Rental
(800) 729-5377
(U.S., Canada & Mexico)
www.800-payless.com

Thrifty Car Rental
(800) 847-4389
www.thrifty.com

CELL PHONE EMERGENCY NUMBERS

Alabama
*47

Alaska
911

Arizona
911

Arkansas
911

California
911

Colorado
911; *277;
(303) 329-4501

Connecticut
911

Delaware
911

**District of
Columbia**
911

Florida
911

Georgia
911

Hawaii
None

Idaho
*477

Illinois
911

Indiana
911

Iowa
911; *55

Kansas
*47

Kentucky
(800) 222-5555
(in KY)

Louisiana
911

Maine
911

Maryland
911

Massachusetts
911

Michigan
911

Minnesota
911

Mississippi
911

Missouri
*55

Montana
911

Nebraska
911

Nevada
*647

**New Hamp-
shire**
911

New Jersey
911

New Mexico
911

New York
911

North Carolina
911

North Dakota
*2121

Ohio
911

Oklahoma
911

Oregon
911

Pennsylvania
911

Rhode Island
911

South Carolina
911

South Dakota
911

Tennessee
911

Texas
911

Utah
911

Vermont
911

Virginia
911

Washington
911

West Virginia
911

Wisconsin
911

Wyoming
911

Map Legend

Roads and related symbols

Free limited-access highway

Toll limited-access highway

New road (under construction as of press time)

Other multilane highway

Principal highway

Other through highway

Other road (conditions vary — local inquiry suggested)

Unpaved road (conditions vary — local inquiry suggested)

One way route; ferry

Interstate highway; Interstate highway business route

U.S. highway; U.S. highway business route

Trans-Canada highway; Autoroute

Mexican highway or Central American highway

State or provincial highway

Secondary state, secondary provincial, or county highway

County trunk highway

Toll booth or fee booth

Tunnel; mountain pass

Interchanges and exit numbers (For most states, the mileage between interchanges may be determined by subtracting one number from the other.)

Highway miles between arrows (Segments of one mile or less not shown.)

Comparative distance
1 mile = 1.609 kilometers   1 kilometer = 0.621 mile

Cities & towns (size of type on map indicates relative population)

National capital; state or provincial capital

County seat or independent city

City, town, or recognized place; neighborhood

Urbanized area

Separate cities within metropolitan area

Parks, recreation areas, & points of interest

U.S. or Canadian national park

U.S. or Canadian national monument, other National Park Service facility, state or provincial park, or recreation area

Park with camping facilities; park without camping facilities

National forest, national grassland, or city park; wildlife refuge

Point of interest, historic site or monument

Airport

Campsite; golf course or country club

Hospital or medical center

Indian reservation

Information center or Tourist Information Center (T.I.C.)

Military or governmental installation; military airport

Physical features

Dam

Mountain peak; highest point in state/province

Lake; dry lake

River; intermittent river

Desert; glacier

Swamp or mangrove swamp

Other symbols

Area shown in greater detail on inset map

Inset map page indicator

Intracoastal waterway

COOK I.   County or parish boundary and name

State or provincial boundary

National boundary

Continental divide

Time zone boundary

Population figures are from the latest available census or are Census Bureau or Rand McNally estimates.

For a complete list of abbreviations that appear on the maps, visit
go.randmcnally.com/ABBR.

©2008 Rand McNally & Company

81 GREAT Destinations

Ready for a road trip? Our North American city guide will make mapping your route and filling your vacation itinerary super easy. We've put together profiles of **81** cities in the United States, Canada, and Mexico, including detailed maps to help you get around town and suggestions for nearby excursions. For attractions, shopping, and tourism information, start turning the pages. Whether you're searching for Sue, the *T. rex* at the Field Museum in Chicago; hoping to catch a glimpse of the stars shopping along Rodeo Drive in L.A.; or looking to check out the view from atop the CN Tower in Toronto, your vacation starts right here.

DON'T MISS DRIVE

A visit to certain cities wouldn't be complete without a drive down its most famous or scenic street. Look for these routes throughout the guide for memorable moments while on the move.

DIVERSION

Even on vacation, you may want to get out of town. Many other engaging destinations are often just a short drive away. Look for these diversions and directions on how to get there inside the guide, too.

ALBUQUERQUE, New Mexico

This desert city mixes Native American and Hispanic influences with a liberal dose of modern science. Exhibits and live performances at the Indian Pueblo Cultural Center introduce visitors to the ancient ways of the area's pueblo communities, while Petroglyph National Monument is the site of ancient rock etchings. In Old Town, the National Atomic Museum tells the story of New Mexico's role in the development of modern weaponry. The climb to Sandia Crest by either road or aerial tramway leads to spectacular views and exceptional skiing. *Tax: 12.88% hotel, 6.88% sales. For local weather, call (505) 821-1111.*

Old Town Plaza

▶ SELECTED ATTRACTIONS

Albuquerque Aquarium
2601 Central Ave. NW
in Albuquerque BioPark
(505) 764-6200

Albuquerque Museum of Art and History
2000 Mountain Rd. NW
(505) 243-7255

Cliff's Amusement Park
4800 Osuna Rd. NE
(505) 881-9373

¡Explora! Science Center and Children's Museum of Albuquerque
1701 Mountain Rd. NW
(505) 224-8300

Indian Pueblo Cultural Center
2401 12th St. NW
(505) 843-7270

National Atomic Museum
1905 Mountain Rd.
(505) 245-2137

National Hispanic Cultural Center
1701 4th St. SW
(505) 246-2261

New Mexico Museum of Natural History and Science
1801 Mountain Rd. NW
(505) 841-2800

Petroglyph National Monument
6001 Unser Blvd. NW
(505) 899-0205

Rio Grande Botanic Garden
2601 Central Ave. NW
in Albuquerque BioPark
(505) 764-6200

Rio Grande Nature Center State Park
2901 Candelaria Rd. NW
(505) 344-7240

Rio Grande Zoo
903 10th St. SW in Albuquerque BioPark
(505) 764-6200

Sandia Peak Aerial Tramway
Skiing, restaurant, and tramway
10 Tramway Loop NE
(505) 856-7325

▶ SHOPPING

Coronado Center Mall
Department stores and specialty shops
6600 Menaul Blvd. NE
(505) 881-4600

Historic Nob Hill
Upscale boutiques, eclectic shops, art galleries, and restaurants
Central Ave. between Girard Blvd. and Washington St.
(505) 255-5006

Old Town
Arts and crafts shops, boutiques, and galleries
Bounded by Rio Grande Blvd., Central Ave., Mountain Rd., and 19th St.
(505) 319-4087

Santa Fe Outlets
Brand-name and designer outlet stores
8380 Cerrillos Rd.
(505) 474-4000

▶ VISITOR INFORMATION

Albuquerque Convention and Visitors Bureau
20 First Plaza NW, Ste. 601
Albuquerque, NM 87102
(505) 842-9918 or (800) 284-2282
www.itsatrip.org

Airport Information Center
Located in the lower level of the airport in the baggage claim area

Old Town Information Center
Plaza Don Luis on Romero St. NW, across from the San Felipe de Neri church

▶ DON'T MISS DRIVE

Central Avenue is old Route 66, with all of its neon, nostalgia, and distinctive architecture. Central runs through the heart of Albuquerque.

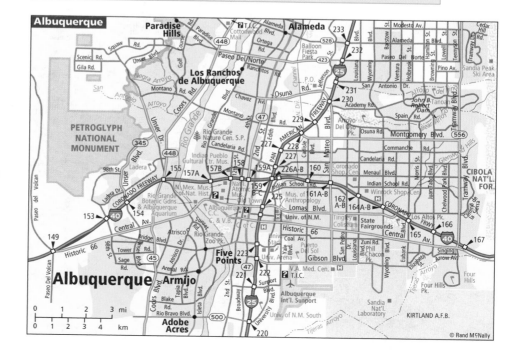

ATLANTA, Georgia

Atlanta reached the pinnacle of homegrown success when the Olympic Games were held here in 1996. Visitors can stroll through the grounds at Centennial Olympic Park. Atlanta is also home to companies such as CNN and Coca-Cola, both of which feature tours and exhibits for the public. Sites dedicated to the life of Dr. Martin Luther King, Jr. offer a more somber reflection. For old-fashioned amusements, visitors and locals head to Six Flags Over Georgia. *Tax: 14% hotel, 8% sales. For local weather, call (770) 632-1837.*

Centennial Olympic Park

▶ SELECTED ATTRACTIONS

Centennial Olympic Park
Park honoring the 1996 Olympic Summer Games
265 Park Avenue West NW
(404) 222-7275

CNN Center
Global headquarters and studio tours
One CNN Center
(404) 827-2300

Georgia Aquarium
World's largest
225 Baker St.
(404) 581-4000

High Museum of Art
1280 Peachtree St. NE
(404) 733-4444

Imagine It! The Children's Museum of Atlanta
275 Centennial Olympic Park Dr. NW
(404) 659-5437

Jimmy Carter Library and Museum
441 Freedom Pkwy.
(404) 865-7100

Martin Luther King, Jr. National Historic Site
450 Auburn Ave. NE
(404) 331-5190

World of Coca-Cola Atlanta
55 Martin Luther King Jr. Dr.
(404) 676-5151 or (800) 676-2653

▶ SHOPPING

Mall of Georgia
More than 225 stores and an amphitheater
3333 Buford Dr., Buford
(678) 482-8788

Phipps Plaza
World-class shops and fine dining
3500 Peachtree Rd. NE
(404) 262-0992 or (800) 810-7700

Peachtree Center
Specialty shops and dining
225 Peachtree St. NE
(404) 654-1265

▶ VISITOR INFORMATION

Atlanta Convention and Visitors Bureau
233 Peachtree St. NE, Ste. 100
Atlanta, GA 30303
(404) 521-6600 or (800) 285-2682
www.atlanta.net

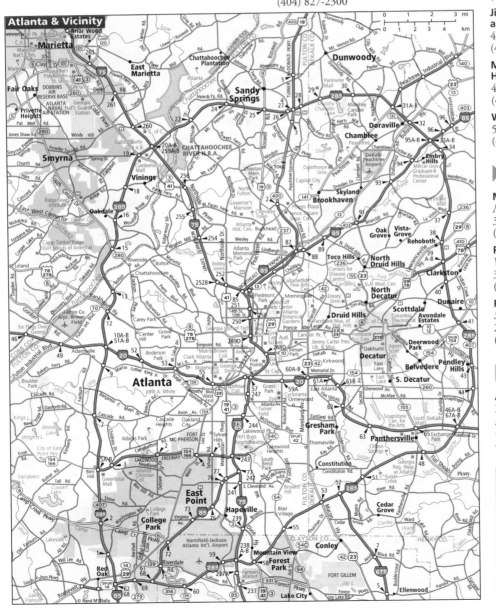

▶ DIVERSION

Stone Mountain Park is best known for its Confederate Memorial carving. The Park also has its own museums, gondola ride, and even water slides. 16 miles east of Atlanta, off US 78 at Stone Mountain. (770) 498-5690 or (800) 317-2006

ATLANTIC CITY, New Jersey

A classic seaside resort with a history going back to the mid-1800s, Atlantic City became the first "Las Vegas East" with the introduction of casino gambling in 1978. Stories of the city's early days are preserved at the Atlantic City Historical Museum, where displays include memorabilia from the Miss America Pageant. One early attraction is still open for tours—Lucy, a giant elephant made of wood. More modern amusements and rides crowd the Steel Pier. *Tax: 12% hotel, 1% hotel occupancy fee, 7% food and non-alcoholic beverage state sales tax for consumption on premises; 9% tax on alcoholic beverages consumed on premises. For local weather, call (609) 976-1212.*

Atlantic City Beach

▶ SELECTED ATTRACTIONS

Absecon Lighthouse
New Jersey's tallest lighthouse
31 S. Rhode Island Ave.
(609) 449-1360

Atlantic City Art Center on Garden Pier
Boardwalk at New Jersey Ave.
(609) 347-5837

Atlantic City Historical Museum
Garden Pier at New Jersey Ave.
(609) 347-5839

Atlantic City Miniature Golf
Boardwalk at Mississippi Ave.
(609) 347-1661

Central Pier Arcade & Speedway
NASCAR go-karts and paintball
1400 Boardwalk
(609) 345-5219

Civil Rights Garden
Seasonal garden and monument
Pacific Ave. at Martin Luther King Jr. Blvd.
(609) 347-0500

Ocean Life Center
800 N. New Hampshire Ave. at
Gardner's Basin
(609) 348-2880

Lucy the Margate Elephant
Historic building shaped like an elephant
9200 Atlantic Ave., Margate
(609) 823-6473

Steel Pier
Family entertainment, rides for kids and adults
Virginia Ave. and the Boardwalk
(609) 345-4893 or (866) 386-6659

Storybook Land
Family fun park with storybook attractions and rides
6415 Black Horse Pike,
Egg Harbor Township
(609) 646-0103

▶ SHOPPING

"The Walk," Atlantic City Outlets
Outlet stores, restaurants, and nightclubs
Michigan Ave. between Pacific and
Baltic Aves.
(609) 872-7002

Hamilton Mall
Specialty shops, restaurants, and food court
4403 Black Horse Pike, Mays Landing
(609) 646-8326

Shore Mall
Shops and restaurants
6725 Black Horse Pike,
Egg Harbor Township
(609) 484-9500

▶ VISITOR INFORMATION

Atlantic City Convention & Visitors Authority
2314 Pacific Ave.
Atlantic City, NJ 08401
(609) 449-7100 or (888) 228-4748
www.atlanticcitynj.com

Visitor Centers
The Atlantic City Expressway, two miles before Atlantic City
The Boardwalk at Mississippi Avenue
(888) 228-4748

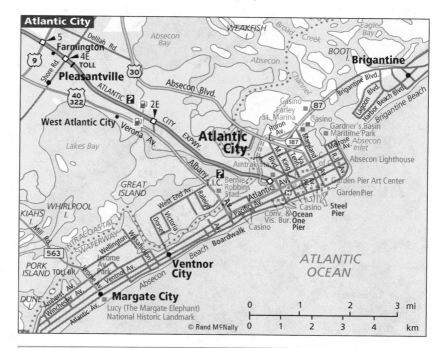

▶ DIVERSION

Step back in time and spend the day at the "Jersey Shore" as it was in the early days at Tuckerton Seaport in Tuckerton. See the lighthouse and other local landmarks. From Atlantic City, take the Garden State Parkway north to exit 50 to Tuckerton. (609) 296-8868

AUSTIN, Texas

Texas State Capitol

Austin enjoys a reputation as both a seat of state government and a powerful force in the world of popular music. Thousands trek here each year for the annual South by Southwest Music Festival. Visitors drawn to all things political will want to tour the State Capitol with its soaring marble dome as well as the Lyndon Baines Johnson Library and Museum. The Umlauf Sculpture Garden offers beauty in an all-natural setting. *Tax: 15% hotel, 8.25% sales. For local weather, call (830) 609-2029.*

DON'T MISS DRIVE

A ride down the city's famous Sixth Street places you in the middle of some 50 nightclubs and restaurants, with live music offerings of every genre and a host of colorful street characters. The Warehouse District between 4th and 6th Streets near Guadalupe also offers plenty of clubs and dining. (512) 478-0098

SELECTED ATTRACTIONS

Austin American-Statesman Bat Observation Center
305 S. Congress Ave.
(512) 327-9721

Barton Springs Pool
2101 Barton Springs Rd. at Mopac Blvd. in Zilker Park
(512) 476-9044

Elisabet Ney Museum
Sculpture studio and portrait collection
304 E. 44th St.
(512) 458-2255

Harry Ransom Center
Art museum, rare books, and manuscripts
21st and Guadalupe Sts. at the University of Texas
(512) 471-8944

Lady Bird Johnson Wildflower Center
4801 LaCrosse Ave. off Loop 1
(512) 292-4200

Lyndon Baines Johnson Library and Museum
2313 Red River St.
(512) 721-0200

Texas Governor's Mansion
1010 Colorado St.
(512) 463-5516

Texas State Capitol
1100 Congress Ave.
(512) 463-0063

Umlauf Sculpture Garden and Museum
605 Robert E. Lee Rd.
(512) 445-5582

SHOPPING

Arboretum at Great Hills
Specialty shops
10000 Research Blvd.
(512) 338-4437

Central Market
Old World marketplace grocery
4477 S. Lamar Blvd. and
4001 N. Lamar Blvd.
(512) 206-1000 or (800) 360-2552

South Congress Avenue (SoCo)
Antiques, folk art, and boutiques
S. Congress Ave., south of Town Lake to Johanna St.

West End
Art galleries and upscale antique shops
5th and 6th Sts. west of Lamar Blvd.

VISITOR INFORMATION

Austin Convention and Visitors Bureau
301 Congress Ave, Ste. 200
Austin, TX 78701
(866) 462-8784 or (800) 926-2282
www.austintexas.org

Visitor Center
209 E. 6th St.
(866) 462-8784

DIVERSION

Pack in a full day on 63-mile-long, 4.5-mile-wide Lake Travis for water sports, lakeside dining, and picnicking by the shore. From downtown Austin, travel north on Loop 1 (MoPac) to FM 2222. Go west on 2222 out to FM 620 south; Lake Travis is on the right.

© Rand McNally

BALTIMORE, Maryland

With Chesapeake Bay at its front door, Baltimore takes full advantage of all that water has to offer. The National Aquarium draws millions to its coral reef. Nearby, the Maryland Science Center's motion simulator transports visitors on virtual space walks. On the harbor's far side lies Fort McHenry, site of the War of 1812 battle during which Francis Scott Key wrote the national anthem. And food lovers can revel in soft-shell crabs (eaten whole!). *Tax: 12.5% hotel, 5% sales. For local weather, call (410) 936-1212 or (703) 260-0107.*

Baltimore's Inner Harbor

▶ SELECTED ATTRACTIONS

Babe Ruth Birthplace and Museum
216 Emory St.
(410) 727-1539

Baltimore Maritime Museum
Piers 3 & 5, Inner Harbor
(410) 396-3453

Baltimore Museum of Art
10 Art Museum Dr.
(443) 573-1700

Fort McHenry
2400 East Fort Ave.
(410) 962-4290

Harbor Cruises
561 Light St. at the Inner Harbor
(410) 727-3113

Maryland Science Center/IMAX
601 Light St.
(410) 685-5225

National Aquarium in Baltimore
501 E. Pratt St. on Pier 3
(410) 576-3800

Sports Legends at Camden Yards
301 W. Camden St.
(410) 727-1539

▶ SHOPPING

Fells Point
Antiques and collectibles
Fleet St. at Broadway
(410) 675-4776

Harborplace
Specialty shops and restaurants
200 E. Pratt St.
(410) 332-4191

Lexington Market
Fresh food market
400 W. Lexington St.
(410) 685-6169

▶ VISITOR INFORMATION

Baltimore Area Convention and Visitors Association
100 Light St., 12th Fl.
Baltimore, MD 21202
(410) 659-7300 or (877) 225-8466
www.baltimore.org

Visitor Center
401 Light St.
(877) 225-8466

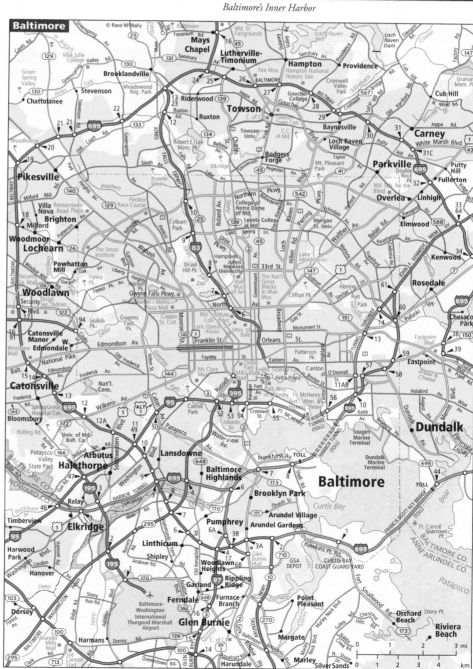

BILOXI/GULFPORT, Mississippi

A Biloxi Shrimping Trip expedition

Located at the center of the 80 miles of coast where Hurricane Katrina did maximum damage, these two Gulf Coast cities are working dutifully to clean up and rebuild. The casinos that brought Biloxi new numbers of visitors are coming back. Hundreds of homes were simply washed away, but Beauvoir, residency of Confederate president Jefferson Davis, is being repaired, and the Pleasant Reed House, built by a former slave, will be replicated near its original site. *Tax: 12% hotel, 7% sales.*

The Gulf's waters remain popular for fishing excursions and beach activity. In Gulfport, watery thrills can be enjoyed at the Gulf Islands Waterpark, while further inland, the StenniSphere allows visitors to see actual space shuttle engines and occasionally witness their testing. The Lynn Meadows Discovery Center keeps young minds engaged through role-playing activities and the ever-popular Super Colossal Climbing Structure. *Tax: 12% hotel, 7% sales.*

► SELECTED ATTRACTIONS

BILOXI

Biloxi Shrimping Trip
70-minute family shrimping excursion
693 Beach Blvd.
(228) 385-1182

Gulf Islands National Seashore
3500 Park Rd., Ocean Springs
(228) 875-9057

IP Hotel and Casino
850 Bayview Ave.
(228) 436-3000

Isle of Capri Casino Resort
151 Beach Blvd.
(228) 436-4753

Palace Casino Resort
158 Howard Ave.
(228) 432-8888

Walter Anderson Museum of Art
510 Washington Ave., Ocean Springs
(228) 872-3164

► SHOPPING

BILOXI

Edgewater Mall
Department stores and specialty shops
2600 Beach Blvd.
(228) 388-3424

Edgewater Village Shopping Center
Department stores and specialty shops
2650 Beach Blvd.
(228) 896-1631

► SELECTED ATTRACTIONS

GULFPORT

CEC-Seabee Museum
U.S. Naval base, Atlantic home of Seabees
4902 Marvin Shields Blvd., Bldg. 1
(228) 865-0480

Gulf Islands Waterpark
13100 16th St.
(228) 328-1266

Gulfport Dragway
Drag racing track
17085 Race Track Rd.
(228) 863-4408

Gulfport Little Theatre
Live performances
2600 13th St.
(228) 864-7983

Lynn Meadows Discovery Center
Children's museum
246 Dolan Ave.
(228) 897-6039

StenniSphere
Visitor Center at NASA Stennis Space Center
25 miles west of Gulfport off I-10, exit 2
(228) 688-2370 or (800) 237-1821

► SHOPPING

GULFPORT

Crossroads Mall
Department stores and specialty shops
I-10 at US 49

Prime Outlets at Gulfport
Designer outlet shops
10000 Factory Shops Blvd.
(228) 867-6100 or (888) 260-7609

► VISITOR INFORMATION

Biloxi & Gulfport Chambers of Commerce
11975 E Seaway Rd.
Gulfport, MS 39503
(228) 604-0014
www.mscoastchamber.com

Mississippi Gulf Coast Convention and Visitors Bureau
PO Box 6128
Gulfport, MS 39507
(228) 575-4297
www.gulfcoast.org

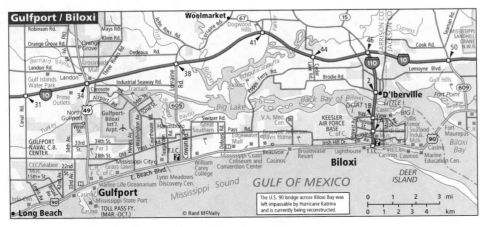

BOSTON, Massachusetts

A modern city of commerce, finance, and institutions of higher learning, Boston is inextricably linked to the Revolutionary War. A walk along Freedom Trail leads to birthplaces of the Revolution such as Paul Revere's House and the Old North Church. The city's museums include the Isabella Stewart Gardner, where works by Botticelli and Vermeer are displayed in a palatial setting, and the Institute of Contemporary Art in its new, dramatically cantilevered home by the docks. *Tax: 12.45% hotel, 5% sales. For local weather, call (617) 936-1234 or (508) 822-0634.*

Sailing in Boston

▶ SELECTED ATTRACTIONS

Boston Children's Museum
300 Congress St.
(617) 426-6500

The Freedom Trail
Self-guided historic walking tour
Tours begin at the Boston National Historical Park Visitor Center
15 State St.
(617) 242-5642

Harvard Museum of Natural History
26 Oxford St., Cambridge
(617) 495-3045

Institute of Contemporary Art
100 Northern Ave.
(617) 478-3100

continued on the next page

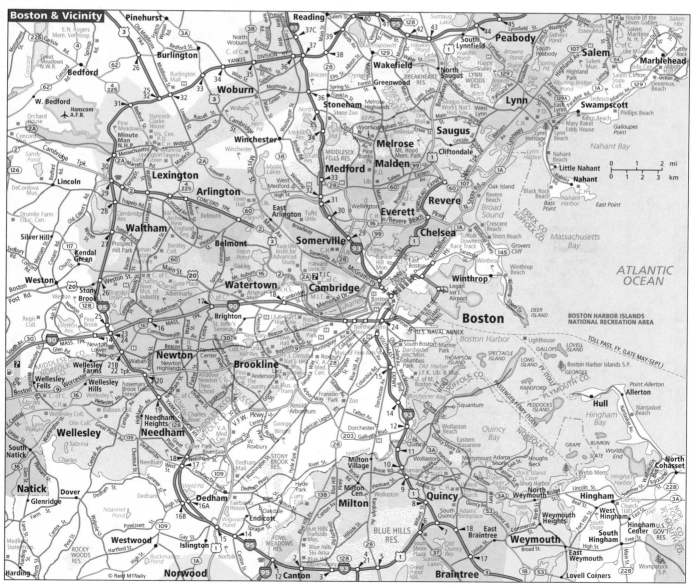

Boston attractions continued

Isabella Stewart Gardner Museum
Art museum in re-created Venetian palace
280 The Fenway
(617) 566-1401

John F. Kennedy Library and Museum
Off I-93 near Columbia Point
(617) 514-1600 or (866) 535-1960

Mary Baker Eddy Library for the Betterment of Humanity
Hall of ideas and Mapparium walk-through globe
200 Massachusetts Ave.
(617) 450-7000 or (888) 222-3711

Museum of Fine Arts
465 Huntington Ave.
(617) 267-9300

Museum of Science
O'Brien Hwy. between Storrow and Memorial Drs.
(617) 723-2500

New England Aquarium
Central Wharf off Atlantic Ave.
(617) 973-5200

Old North Church
Boston's oldest church and its historic steeple
193 Salem St.
(617) 523-6676

Skywalk Observatory, Prudential Tower
800 Boylston St., 50th floor
(617) 859-0648

USS *Constitution* Ship and Museum
At the Charlestown Navy Yard
(617) 242-5671

▶ DIVERSION

Just beyond Boston proper, connect to MA 1A and spend the day driving to Salem (perhaps with a stop at the House of the Seven Gables) and beyond on MA 127. The route hugs the rocky coast through Gloucester and beyond to Rockport and Andrews Point.

▶ SHOPPING

CambridgeSide Galleria
Riverfront mall with specialty shops and restaurants
100 CambridgeSide Place, Cambridge
(617) 621-8666

Copley Place
Department stores and designer boutiques
100 Huntington Ave.
(617) 369-5000

Downtown Crossing
Department stores and specialty shops
Washington, Winter, and Summer Sts.
(617) 482-2139

Faneuil Hall Marketplace
Restaurants, galleries, and specialty shops
Congress and State Sts.
(617) 523-1300

The Shops at the Prudential Center
Department stores
800 Boylston St.
(617) 236-3100 or (800) 746-7778

▶ VISITOR INFORMATION

Greater Boston Convention and Visitors Bureau
2 Copley Place, Ste. 105
Boston, MA 02116-6501
(617) 536-4100 or (888) 733-2678
www.bostonusa.com

Central Boston / Cambridge
© Rand McNally

BRANSON, Missouri

More than 100 different theatrical entertainments have made this Ozark Mountain town one of the most popular vacation stops in middle America. But the comedians, singers, and diverse musical sounds filling the theaters along "The Strip" aren't the only shows in town. Silver Dollar City theme park offers high-speed thrill rides in a 19th-century setting, while the new 95-acre Branson Landing features a $7 million water display amidst upscale lakefront shopping and dining. Also new is *Titanic: The World's Largest Museum Attraction*, featuring a half-scale replica of the ship, interactive exhibits, and more than 400 artifacts. *Tax: 11.6% hotel, 8.6% sales. For local weather, call (417) 336-5000.*

The Branson Strip

▶ SELECTED ATTRACTIONS

Baldknobbers Jamboree
Music theater and comedy
2835 W. MO 76
(417) 334-4528

Celebration City
Theme park with rides
1383 MO 376
(417) 338-2611

Dogwood Canyon Nature Park
2038 W. MO 86, Lampe
(417) 779-5983

Dolly Parton's Dixie Stampede
Dinner theater and horse show
1525 W. MO 76
(417) 336-3000 or (800) 520-5101

Grand Country Square
Dining, specialty shops, and family fun centers
1945 W. MO 76
(417) 335-3535

Lawrence Welk Show
Musical variety shows
1984 MO 165
(417) 336-3575 or (800) 505-9355

Ride the Ducks
City tours in land/water vehicles
2320 W. MO 76
(417) 334-3825

The Shepherd of the Hills Homestead
History and outdoor theater
5586 W. MO 76
(417) 334-4191

The Showboat Branson Belle
Show and lunch/dinner cruises
4800 MO 165
(800) 475-9370

Silver Dollar City
1880s theme park with rides
399 Indian Point Rd.
(417) 338-2611 or (800) 952-6626

Table Rock State Park
5272 MO 165
(417) 334-4704

The Tracks (Track 5)
Go-karts, mini-golf, arcade, and more
3525 W. MO 76
(417) 334-1612

White Water
12-acre water park
3505 W. MO 76
(417) 338-2611 or (800) 475-9370

▶ SHOPPING

Branson Mall
Shops, dining, and live music theater
2206 W. MO 76
(417) 334-5412

Dick's Old Time 5 & 10
Traditional dime store
103 W. Main St.
(417) 334-2410

Factory Merchants Branson
Outlet stores
1000 Pat Nash Dr.
(417) 335-6686

The Shoppes at Branson Meadows
Outlet stores
4562 Gretna Rd.
(417) 339-2580

Tanger Outlet Center
Outlet stores
300 Tanger Blvd.
(417) 337-9328

▶ VISITOR INFORMATION

Branson Lakes Area Chamber of Commerce and Convention and Visitors Bureau
269 MO 248
Branson, MO 65616
(417) 334-4136 or (800) 214-3661
www.explorebranson.com

▶ DIVERSION

Springfield, Missouri is only about 35 miles north of Branson and has a number of interesting attractions, including the first Bass Pro Shop. Also check out Wonders of Wildlife Museum and Aquarium, Wilson's Creek National Battlefield (site of a Civil War battle), and the Dickerson Park Zoo, which has breeding programs for several endangered species. Also, Fantastic Caverns offers ride-through cave tours. Springfield CVB: (417) 881-5300 or (800) 678-8767

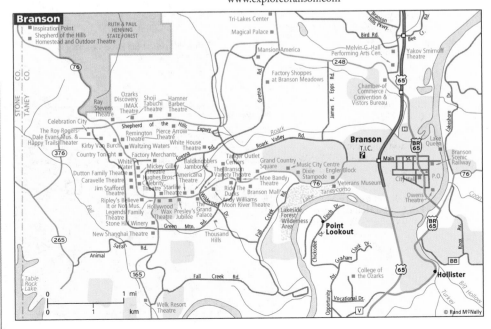

CALGARY, Alberta, Canada

Eau Claire Festival Market

Calgary occupies the western edge of the Canadian plains, the commercial center of a vast empire of cattle ranches, wheat farms, and oil and gas fields. Each year, hundreds of thousands attend the Calgary Stampede, one of the largest rodeo events in the world. For sweeping views of the mountains and plains, visitors ride to the observation deck and restaurant at the top of the Calgary Tower. The daring find even bigger thrills at Shaw Millennium Park, which offers the largest free outdoor skate park in the world, and at Canada Olympic Park, where visitors can take a turn on the luge. *Tax: 4% provincial room tax, 1% destination marketing fee, 6% goods and services tax.*

SELECTED ATTRACTIONS

Aerospace Museum
4629 McCall Way NE
(403) 250-3752

Butterfield Acres Children's Farm
Family farm and petting zoos
254077 Rocky Ridge Rd.
(403) 239-0638

Calaway Park
Amusement park
245033 Range Rd. 33
(403) 240-3822

Calgary Chinese Cultural Centre
197 1st St. SW
(403) 262-5071

Calgary Stampede
Held every July, includes entertainers, cowboys, parades, chuck wagon races, and free pancake breakfasts
Calgary Stampede Park,
1310 Olympic Way SE
(403) 261-0101 or
(800) 661-1260

Calgary Tower
Views of Calgary and the Canadian Rockies
101 9th Ave. SW
(403) 266-7171

Calgary Zoo, Botanical Garden, and Prehistoric Park
1300 Zoo Rd. NE at
Memorial Dr.
(403) 232-9300 or
(800) 588-9993

Canada Olympic Park
88 Canada Olympic Rd. SW
along Trans-Canada Hwy. 1
(403) 247-5452

Canadian Country Music & Pro Rodeo Hall of Fame
1410 Olympic Way SE at
Calgary Stampede Park
(403) 261-0101

Devonian Gardens
Indoor gardens with waterfalls, playground, artwork, and sculptures
317 7th Ave. SW, 4th level
(403) 221-3782

Fort Calgary Historic Park
750 9th Ave. SE
(403) 290-1875

Glenbow Museum
Exhibits on Western settlement
130 9th Ave. SE
(403) 268-4100

Head-Smashed-In Buffalo Jump
Prehistoric archaeological site
On Hwy. 785, Fort Macleod
(403) 553-2731

Heritage Park Historical Village
Early 1900s village
1900 Heritage Dr. SW
(403) 268-8500

Inglewood Bird Sanctuary & Nature Center
2425 9th Ave. SE
(403) 268-2489

Korite Minerals and Canada Fossils
Gemstones, jewelry, and fossils
532-38A Ave. SE
(403) 287-2026

Shaw Millennium Park
Beach volleyball courts, skate park
1220 9th Ave. SW
(403) 268-2489

Telus World of Science-Calgary
701 11th St. SW
(403) 268-8300

SHOPPING

Chinook Centre
Calgary's largest shopping center, with stores, theaters, and IMAX theater
6455 Macleod Trail SW
(403) 259-2022

Eau Claire Festival Market
Boutiques, produce, restaurants, and IMAX theater
2nd Ave. and 2nd St. SW
(403) 264-6450

Kensington District
Upscale arts and crafts, retail stores, and restaurants
10th St. and Kensington Rd. NW
(403) 283-4810

Stephen Avenue Walk
Specialty boutiques and department stores
8th Ave. from 1st St. SE to 3rd St. SW
(403) 215-1570

Uptown 17th Avenue
Antiques, art galleries, and boutiques
17th Ave. between 2nd St. SW and 14th St. SW
(403) 245-1703

Willow Park Village
Outdoor mall with shops and restaurants
10816 Macleod Trail SE
(403) 215-0380

VISITOR INFORMATION

Tourism Calgary
238 11th Ave. SE, Ste. 200
Calgary, AB T2G 0X8 Canada
(403) 263-8510 or (800) 661-1678
www.tourismcalgary.com

Visitor Centers
Calgary International Airport, Arrivals Level
(403) 735-1234
Calgary Tower, 101 9th Ave. SW
(403) 263-8510

DIVERSION

Spend a day at the Royal Tyrrell Museum of Paleontology in Drumheller, 84 miles northeast of Calgary. Watch scientists restore dinosaur skeletons or sign up for an actual dinosaur dig. Take AB 2 to AB 72 (it will turn into AB 9) and head east.

CHARLESTON, South Carolina

An immaculately preserved antebellum city of restored homes and winding streets, Charleston is often regarded as the epitome of gracious living. Historic attractions abound: Charles Towne Landing, where the city first took root in the 1600s; the well-tended grounds of Magnolia Plantation, Middleton Place, and Drayton Hall; and Fort Sumter, site of the momentous events that ignited the American Civil War. On a contemporary note, the new millennium brought with it the South Carolina Aquarium, with exhibits of creatures from the state's five regions. *Tax: 12% hotel, 6.5% sales. For local weather, call (843) 744-0303.*

Middleton Place Gardens

► SELECTED ATTRACTIONS

Charles Towne Landing
State historic site and nature preserve
1500 Old Towne Rd.
(843) 852-4200

Charleston IMAX Theater
360 Concord St. at Aquarium Wharf
(843) 725-4629

Charleston Museum
Regional history museum
360 Meeting St.
(843) 722-2996

Cypress Gardens
Swamp tours, aquarium, and butterfly house
3030 Cypress Gardens Rd., 24 miles north off US 52, Moncks Corner
(843) 553-0515

Drayton Hall
18th-century plantation
3380 Ashley River Rd.
(843) 769-2600

Fort Sumter National Monument
Boats leave from locations at Liberty Square and Patriots Point complex
(843) 883-3123

Gibbes Museum of Art
135 Meeting St.
(843) 722-2706

Heyward-Washington House
18th-century house museum
87 Church St.
(843) 722-2996

Magnolia Plantation and Gardens
Oldest major public garden in America
3550 Ashley River Rd.
(843) 571-1266 or (800) 367-3517

Middleton Place
18th-century plantation
4300 Ashley River Rd.
(843) 556-6020 or (800) 782-3608

Old Exchange and Provost Dungeon
Customs house and Revolutionary War prison
122 E. Bay St.
(843) 727-2165 or (888) 763-0448

Patriots Point Naval and Maritime Museum
40 Patriots Point Rd., Mt. Pleasant
(843) 884-2727

South Carolina Aquarium
100 Aquarium Wharf
(843) 720-1990

► SHOPPING

Citadel Mall
Department stores and specialty shops
2070 Sam Rittenberg Blvd.
(843) 766-8511

Historic King Street
Upscale boutiques, antique shops, and galleries
King St. north of Broad St.

Old City Market
Artisan shops and boutiques
Market St. between Meeting and East Bay Sts.
(843) 973-7236

► VISITOR INFORMATION

Charleston Area Convention and Visitors Bureau
423 King St.
Charleston, SC 29403
(843) 853-8000 or (800) 868-8118
www.charlestoncvb.com

Visitor Centers
375 Meeting St., Charleston
22 Beachwalker Dr., Kiawah Island

► DON'T MISS DRIVE

King Street is the major road that runs from I-26 through the downtown historic district, all the way to The Battery, where cargo ships come into port. You'll see plenty of shops, restaurants, historic homes, and buildings, as well as art galleries and museums.

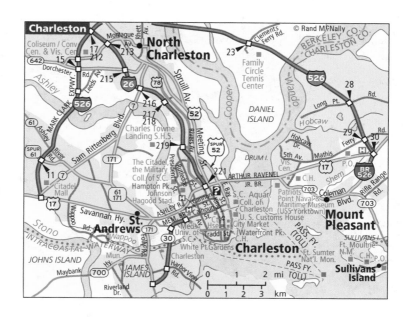

CHARLOTTE, North Carolina

Paramount's Carowinds water and theme park

The nation's second-largest financial center has been a fiscal hub since gold was discovered here in 1799. Amidst the city's glittering financial skyscrapers, the Mint Museum of Art displays a significant collection of pre-Columbian works and traditional European ceramics. Racing enthusiasts enjoy NASCAR and dirt track events as well as frequent car shows at Lowe's Motor Speedway. High-speed thrills of another kind draw huge crowds to Paramount's Carowinds theme park. *Tax: 13.5% hotel, 7.5% sales.*

DON'T MISS DRIVE

Prepare to be wowed by dream homes of nearly every architectural style on Charlotte's Queens Road West. Start your drive from uptown Charlotte, following 3rd Street east to Queens Road.

SELECTED ATTRACTIONS

Afro-American Cultural Center
401 N. Myers St.
(704) 374-1565

Charlotte Museum of History and Hezekiah Alexander Homesite
Heritage museum and Colonial-era home
3500 Shamrock Dr.
(704) 568-1774

Charlotte Nature Museum
1658 Sterling Rd.
(704) 372-6261 or (800) 935-0553

Discovery Place
Hands-on science museum, planetarium, and Omnimax theater
301 N. Tryon St.
(704) 372-6261 or (800) 935-0553

Historic Latta Plantation
Living history farm
5225 Sample Rd., 13 miles north off I-77, Huntersville
(704) 875-2312

Levine Museum of the New South
200 E. 7th St.
(704) 333-1887

Lowe's Motor Speedway
5555 Concord Parkway S., 12 miles northeast off US 29, Concord
(704) 455-3200 or (800) 455-3267

Mint Museum of Art
2730 Randolph Rd.
(704) 337-2000

Mint Museum of Craft and Design
220 N. Tryon St.
(704) 337-2000

North Carolina Blumenthal Performing Arts Center
Opera, symphony, and theater
130 N. Tryon St.
(704) 372-1000

Paramount's Carowinds
Water and theme park
14523 Carowinds Blvd., 15 miles south off I-77
(704) 588-2600 or (800) 888-4386

Ray's Splash Planet
Indoor water park
215 N. Sycamore St.
(704) 432-4729

Reed Gold Mine State Historic Site
9621 Reed Mine Rd., 30 miles east off Albemarle Rd., Midland
(704) 721-4653

SHOPPING

Concord Mills
Outlet stores and specialty shops
8111 Concord Mills Blvd., 10 miles north off I-85, exit 49, Concord
(704) 979-5000

Founders Hall
Specialty shops
100 N. Tryon St.
(704) 386-0120

SouthPark Mall
Designer stores
4400 Sharon Rd.
(704) 364-4411 or (888) 364-4411

VISITOR INFORMATION

Visit Charlotte, The Convention & Visitors Bureau
500 S. College St., Ste. 300
Charlotte, NC 28202
(704) 334-2282 or (800) 722-1994
www.visitcharlotte.com

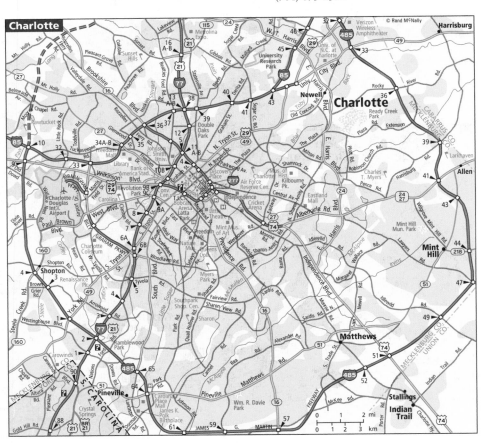

CHICAGO, Illinois

Known as the Windy City for both the challenges of its weather and the oratory of its officials, Chicago welcomes visitors with first-class architecture, renowned theater, and much-loved sports teams. Among the many museums here is the Field Museum, home of Sue, the biggest *Tyrannosaurus rex* skeleton in the world. Giant sculptures and a flashy amphitheater draw crowds to the new Millennium Park, while the joys of Navy Pier include a children's museum, the Chicago Shakespeare Theater, and a giant Ferris wheel. Countless restaurants around the city offer a taste of Chicago's famous stuffed pizza. Baseball fans head to the meccas of Wrigley Field and U.S. Cellular Field. *Tax: 15.4% hotel, 8.75% sales. For local weather, call (312) 976-1212 or (815) 834-0675.*

Shedd Aquarium

▶ SELECTED ATTRACTIONS

Adler Planetarium and Astronomy Museum
Free admission on Monday and Tuesday*
1300 S. Lake Shore Dr.
(312) 922-7827

Art Institute of Chicago
Free admission on Tuesday
111 S. Michigan Ave.
(312) 443-3600

Brookfield Zoo
8400 W. 31st St., Brookfield
(708) 485-0263 or (800) 201-0784

Chicago Architecture Foundation
Guided tours of Chicago's architectural masterpieces and neighborhoods
224 S. Michigan Ave.
(312) 922-3432 ext. 240

Chicago Botanic Garden
1000 Lake Cook Rd., Glencoe
(847) 835-5440

Chicago Children's Museum
Free admission 5 to 8 p.m. on Thursday
700 E. Grand Ave. on Navy Pier
(312) 527-1000

Chicago Cultural Center
Architectural showplace for the arts
Free admission daily
78 E. Washington St.
(312) 744-6630

Chicago Historical Society
1601 N. Clark St.
(312) 642-4600

Chicago Neighborhood Tours
Guided tours of the city's ethnic areas
Tours depart from the Chicago Cultural Center
78 E. Washington St.
(312) 742-1190

DuSable Museum of African American History
Free admission on Sunday
740 E. 56th Pl.
(773) 947-0600

Field Museum
Natural history exhibits
Free admission on Monday and Tuesday**
1400 S. Lake Shore Dr. at Roosevelt Rd.
(312) 922-9410

John Hancock Observatory
875 N. Michigan Ave.
(312) 751-3681 or (888) 875-8439

Lincoln Park Zoo
Free admission daily
2200 N. Cannon Dr.
(312) 742-2000

Millennium Park
Amphitheater, restaurant, fountain, sculptures, and skating rink
Bounded by Michigan Ave., Columbus Dr., Randolph St., and Monroe St.

Museum of Contemporary Art
Free admission on Tuesday evenings
220 E. Chicago Ave.
(312) 280-2660

Museum of Science and Industry
Free admission on Monday and Tuesday***
5700 S. Lake Shore Dr.
(773) 684-1414

National Museum of Mexican Art
Free admission daily
1852 W. 19th St.
(312) 738-1503

Navy Pier
Rides, museums, restaurants, IMAX theater, and family entertainment
600 E. Grand Ave.
(312) 595-7437

Peggy Notebaert Nature Museum
Free admission on Thursday
2340 N. Cannon Dr. at Fullerton Pkwy.
(773) 755-5100

Sears Tower Skydeck
233 S. Wacker Dr.
(312) 875-9696

Shedd Aquarium
Exhibits in main building free on Discount Days (call for details)
1200 S. Lake Shore Dr.
(312) 939-2438

Spertus Museum
History of Judaism and children's center
Free admission on Friday
618 S. Michigan Ave.
(312) 322-1700

continued on page 31

* *Mid-September through Mid-December*
** *Mid-September through October*
*** *Mid-September through Mid-November*

▶ DIVERSION

Depending on traffic, it usually takes an hour from Chicago's downtown to reach St. Charles, where you can explore antique stores, art boutiques, and a flea market, or take a paddlewheel riverboat cruise on the Fox River. I-90 to IL 59 south to IL 64 west to St. Charles. (630) 377-6161 or (800) 777-4373

Free every day

In Chicago, it is free day at least one day a week at most of the many museums and cultural centers that dot the city. Free day policies may change from time to time, so check before you go. Visit **www.choosechicago.com** for more information and locations:

- ABA Museum of Law
- Chicago Architecture Center
- Chicago Cultural Center
- Chicago Public Library's Harold Washington Center
- City Gallery at the Historic Water Tower
- Gallery 37 – 5th Floor Galleries
- Intuit: The Center for Intuitive and Outsider Art
- Jane Addams Hull-House Museum
- Lincoln Park Zoo
- Martin D'Arcy Museum of Art
- Museum of Broadcast Communications
- Museum of Contemporary Photography
- National Museum of Mexican Art
- Oriental Institute Museum
- Pullman Visitor Center
- Smith Museum of Stained Glass Windows

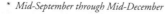

Chicago & Vicinity

© Rand McNally

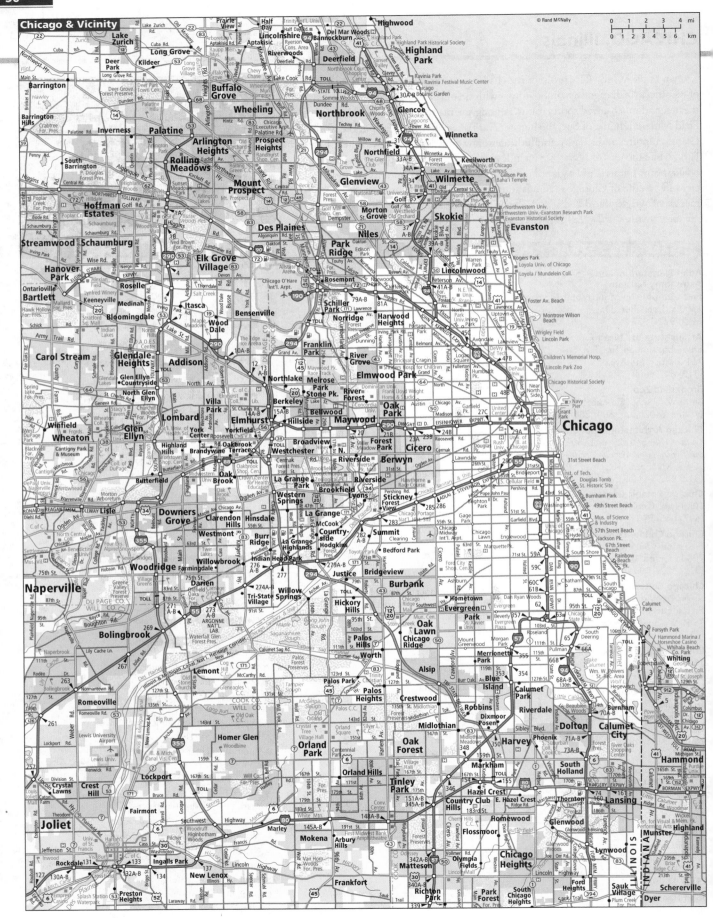

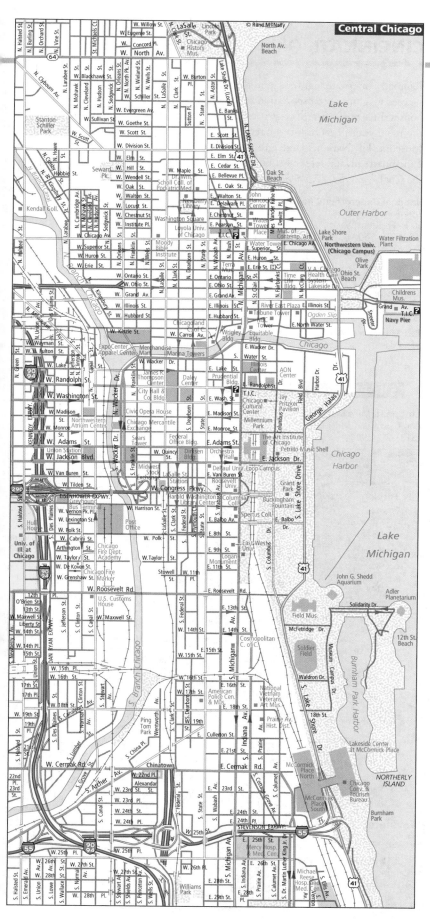

Central Chicago

The Sightseeing Scoop:

Staying in the Windy City for more than a couple of days? Consider buying a Chicago CityPass, which is good for nine days and allows you to visit the Shedd Aquarium, Hancock Observatory, Art Institute of Chicago, Field Museum of Natural History, Adler Planetarium and Astronomy Museum, and Museum of Science and Industry for one low price.

Chicago attractions continued

Swedish American Museum Center
Free admission on the second Tuesday of each month
5211 N. Clark St.
(773) 728-8111

SHOPPING

Magnificent Mile
Upscale department stores and boutiques
N. Michigan Ave. from the Chicago River to Oak St.
(312) 642-3570

Shops At The Mart
Shops and restaurants in a huge wholesale design center
222 Merchandise Mart Plaza
(312) 527-7990

State Street
Department stores and boutiques
State St. between Randolph and Adams Sts.
(312) 782-9160

Water Tower Place
Department stores and specialty shops
835 N. Michigan Ave.
(312) 440-3580

VISITOR INFORMATION

Chicago Convention and Tourism Bureau
McCormick Complex-Lakeside Center
2301 S. Lake Shore Dr.
Chicago, IL 60616
(312) 567-8500
www.choosechicago.com

Chicago Office of Tourism
78 E. Washington St.
Chicago, IL 60602
(312) 744-2400 or (877) 244-2246
www.877chicago.com

Chicago Cultural Center
77 E. Randolph St.

Chicago Water Works
163 E. Pearson

DON'T MISS DRIVE

It's been sung about and glorified on the big screen. Experience Chicago's famous Lake Shore Drive, which passes beaches, picturesque marinas, parks, and breathtaking views of the city's famed skyline.

CINCINNATI, Ohio

Taft Museum of Art

Railroads, interstate highways, and the Ohio River have all helped Cincinnati succeed as a hub of transportation and commerce. The restored Union Terminal houses three museums (history, natural history and science, and children's). Five thousand years of art history are represented at the expanded and renovated Taft Museum. The National Underground Railroad Freedom Center was inspired by Cincinnati's pivotal role in helping slaves find their way north in the years before the Civil War. *Tax: 17.5% hotel, 6.5% sales. For local weather, call (513) 241-1010.*

▶ SELECTED ATTRACTIONS

Cincinnati Art Museum
953 Eden Park Dr.
(513) 721-2787

Cincinnati Zoo and Botanical Garden
3400 Vine St.
(513) 281-4700 or (800) 944-4776

Great American Ball Park
Home of the Cincinnati Reds
100 Main St.
(513) 765-7000

National Underground Railroad Freedom Center
50 E. Freedom Way
(513) 333-7500 or (877) 648-4838

Newport Aquarium
1 Aquarium Way, Newport, KY
(859) 261-7444 or (800) 406-3474

Kings Island
24 miles north off I-71, Kings Mills
(513) 754-5700

Taft Museum of Art
316 Pike St.
(513) 241-0343

▶ SHOPPING

Cincinnati Mills Mall
600 Cincinnati Mills Dr.
(513) 671-2929

Kenwood Towne Centre
Upscale department stores and boutiques
7875 Montgomery Rd.
(513) 745-9100

Tower Place Mall at the Carew Tower
Fashion and gift boutiques
4th and Race Sts.
(513) 241-7700

▶ VISITOR INFORMATION

Cincinnati USA Convention & Visitors Bureau
525 Vine St., Ste. 1500
Cincinnati, OH 45202
(513) 621-2142 or (800) 246-2987
www.cincyusa.com

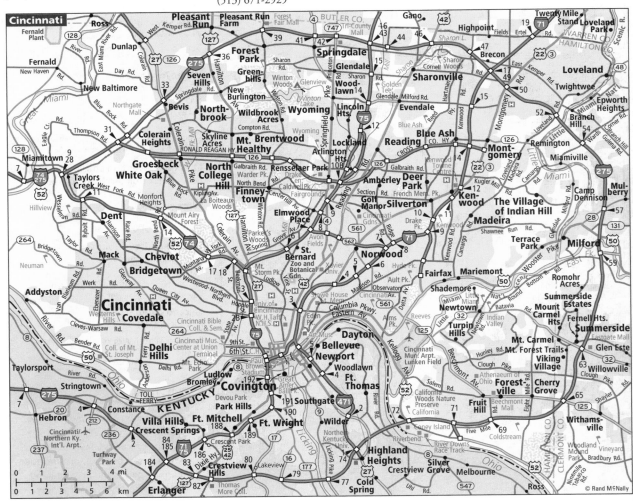

© Rand McNally

CLEVELAND, Ohio

A revitalized lakefront and riverway have helped reverse the fortunes of this Lake Erie port city. The Rock and Roll Hall of Fame and Museum draws fans from all over the world. Nearby, the Great Lakes Science Center provides its own brand of hair-raising excitement with more than 400 hands-on exhibits and demonstrations. Cultural institutions concentrated around University Circle include the Museum of Art and the Museum of Natural History. And some 600 separate species—3,000 animals in all—call the Metroparks Zoo home. *Tax: 15% hotel, 7.5% sales tax. For local weather, call (216) 881-0880 or (216) 265-2370.*

Rock and Roll Hall of Fame and Museum

▶ SELECTED ATTRACTIONS

Children's Museum of Cleveland
10730 Euclid Ave. in University Circle
(216) 791-7114

Cleveland Metroparks Zoo
3900 Wildlife Way
(216) 661-6500

Cleveland Museum of Art
11150 East Blvd. in University Circle
(216) 421-7350 or (888) 262-0033

Cleveland Museum of Natural History
1 Wade Oval Dr. in University Circle
(216) 231-4600 or (800) 317-9155

Cuyahoga Valley National Park
I-77 S to Rockside Rd. E., Valley View
(216) 524-1497

Great Lakes Science Center
Science exhibits and Omnimax theater
601 Erieside Ave.
(216) 694-2000

Jacobs Field
Home of the Cleveland Indians
2401 Ontario St.
(216) 420-4200

NASA Glenn Visitor Center
21000 Brookpark Rd. at Lewis Field
(216) 433-2001

Rock and Roll Hall of Fame and Museum
1 Key Plaza, E. 9th St. at Lake Erie
(216) 781-7625 or (888) 764-7625

The Warehouse District
Downtown along the Cuyahoga River
(216) 344-3937

Western Reserve Historical Society
Seven historic properties/museums
10825 East Blvd.
(216) 721-5722

▶ SHOPPING

The Arcade
Restored shopping center that dates from 1890
401 Euclid Ave.
(216) 696-1408

Beachwood Place
Upscale department stores and specialty shops
26300 Cedar Rd., Beachwood
(216) 464-9460

The Galleria at Erieview
Specialty shops
1301 E. 9th St.
(216) 621-9999

▶ DIVERSION

Explore the largest Amish settlement in the world about an hour south of Cleveland in Wayne and Holmes counties. The area is dotted with craft shops, farms, and flea markets. Many Swiss-style buildings remind visitors of the Swiss ancestry of Ohio's Amish.
(330) 674-3975 or (800) 362-6474

▶ VISITOR INFORMATION

Convention and Visitors Bureau of Greater Cleveland
50 Public Square, Ste. 3100
Cleveland, OH 44113
(216) 621-4110 or (800) 321-1001
www.travelcleveland.com

COLUMBUS, Ohio

Short North Arts District

More than a seat of government, Ohio's capital is a center of high-tech industrial development. It's also the home of enormous Ohio State University, which boasts an enrollment of more than 51,000. For an introduction to the joys of science, COSI Columbus (originally the Center of Science and Industry) includes more than 1,000 interactive exhibits. The city's historic German Village neighborhood offers distinctive homes, restaurants, and shops with an Old World flair, along with the Book Loft—a 32-room bookstore as long as a city block. *Tax: 16.75% hotel, 6.75% sales.*

DON'T MISS DRIVE

Travel 14 miles along High Street, which runs north to south past many of Columbus' main attractions. The drive takes visitors through several quaint suburbs and districts, past many popular sites, including the Ohio State University campus, Short North Arts District, Arena District, the Ohio state capitol building, German Village, and Brewery District.

SELECTED ATTRACTIONS

Arena District
Restaurants, bars, and nightclubs near Nationwide Arena
At Nationwide Blvd. and Front St.
(614) 857-2336

Columbus Museum of Art
480 E. Broad St.
(614) 221-6801

Columbus Zoo and Aquarium
9990 Riverside Dr., Powell
(614) 645-3550 or (800) 666-5397

COSI Columbus
333 W. Broad St.
(614) 228-2674 or (888) 819-2674

Easton Town Center
Entertainment district and shopping
I-270 and Easton Way
(614) 416-7000

Franklin Park Conservatory
Botanical gardens
1777 E. Broad St.
(614) 645-8733 or (800) 214-7275

German Village
Historic German homes
588 S. 3rd St.
(614) 221-8888

Jack Nicklaus Museum
2355 Olentangy River Rd. at Ohio State University
(614) 247-5959

Ohio Historical Center and Ohio Village
1982 Velma Ave., 17th Ave. and I-71
(614) 297-2300

Ohio Statehouse
Broad and High Sts. in Capitol Square
(614) 728-2130 or (888) 644-6123

Wexner Center for the Arts
1871 N. High St. at Ohio State University
(614) 292-3535

Wyandot Lake
Water and amusement park
10101 Riverside Dr., Powell
(614) 889-9283 or (800) 328-9283

SHOPPING

Columbus City Center
Department stores and specialty shops
111 S. 3rd St.
(614) 221-4919

North Market
Fresh produce and specialty foods
59 Spruce St.
(614) 463-9664

Short North Arts District
Galleries, unique shops, and entertainment
N. High St. between Goodale St. and King Ave.
(614) 228-8050

VISITOR INFORMATION

Experience Columbus
90 N. High St.
Columbus, OH 43215
(614) 221-2489 or (800) 345-4386
www.experiencecolumbus.com

CORPUS CHRISTI, Texas

Miles of sandy beaches along Gulf Coast barrier islands make Corpus Christi a popular vacation retreat. Before heading to ocean shores, visitors can take in downtown waterfront attractions including the USS *Lexington*, a legendary World War II-era aircraft carrier that came to be known as the "Blue Ghost." Nearby, the Texas State Aquarium invites the curious to an underwater discovery of life below the Gulf's blue waters. Fans of the late Tejano singing star Selena will find personal memorabilia such as her concert dresses on display at the Selena Museum. *Tax: 15% hotel, 8.25% sales. For local weather, call (361) 814-9463 or (361) 289-0753.*

USS Lexington *Museum on the Bay*

▶ SELECTED ATTRACTIONS

Aransas National Wildlife Refuge
70 miles north off TX 35, Austwell
(361) 286-3559

Art Museum of South Texas
1902 N. Shoreline Blvd.
(361) 825-3500

Asian Cultures Museum
1809 N. Chaparral St.
(361) 882-2641

Corpus Christi Botanical Gardens & Nature Center
8545 S. Staples St.
(361) 852-2100

Corpus Christi Museum of Science and History
1900 N. Chaparral St.
(361) 826-4650

Hans A. Suter Wildlife Area
Off Ennis Joslin St. in South Guth Park
(361) 880-3461

Heritage Park
Restored historic homes
1581 N. Chaparral St.
(361) 826-3410

King Ranch
Working cattle and horse ranch
35 miles south off US 77, Kingsville
(361) 592-8055

Lake Corpus Christi State Park
35 miles northwest off TX 359, near Mathis
(361) 547-2635

Padre Island National Seashore Visitor Center
20420 Park Rd. 22
(361) 949-8068

Selena Museum
5410 Leopard St.
(361) 289-9013

Texas State Aquarium
2710 N. Shoreline Blvd.
(361) 881-1200 or (800) 477-4853

USS *Lexington* Museum on the Bay
2914 N. Shoreline Blvd.
(361) 888-4873 or (800) 523-9539

▶ SHOPPING

Antique Strip Center
Antiques and collectibles
Everhart and Alameda Sts.

Padre Staples Mall
Department stores and specialty shops
S. Padre Island Dr. and Staples St.
(361) 991-3755

Sunrise Mall
Department stores and specialty shops
S. Padre Island Dr. and Airline Rd.
(361) 993-2900

Water Street Market
Boutiques, restaurants, and entertainment
Bounded by Water, Chaparral, Williams, and Lawrence Sts.

▶ DON'T MISS DRIVE

Ocean Drive, lined with magazine-cover homes and mansions, runs along Corpus Christi Bay. The gardens and grounds are as impressive as the houses.

▶ VISITOR INFORMATION

Corpus Christi Area Convention and Visitors Bureau
1201 N. Shoreline Blvd.
Corpus Christi, TX 78401
(361) 881-1888 or (800) 678-6232
www.corpuschristicvb.com

Visitor Centers
Downtown
1823 N. Chaparral St.
(800) 766-2322

Labonte Park
14333 I-37 at Nueces River
(361) 241-1464

On the Island
14252 S. Padre Island Dr.
(361) 949-8743

▶ DIVERSION

Padre Island National Seashore is only 15 minutes from Corpus Christi on TX 358. Birders have found the seashore to be a haven for their hobby as well as for migratory birds.

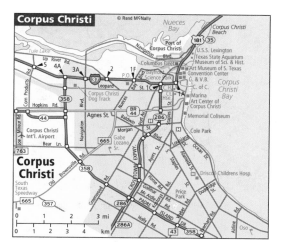

DALLAS/FORT WORTH, Texas

Dallas skyline at dusk

Sprawling Dallas rises from the Texas prairie to form the Southwest's largest center of finance and commerce. Two entertainment districts offer respite from the pressures of the boardroom: Deep Ellum is noted for funky shops and hip music clubs, while the West End features trendy restaurants and attractions. The home of the annual state fair, Fair Park also features eight different museums dedicated to women, African Americans, railroading, and other subjects. *Tax: 15% hotel, 8.25% sales. For local weather, call (214) 787-1111 or (817) 429-2631.*

Fort Worth might be known as a cowtown, but the city's wealth has brought with it a plethora of high culture. Its cultural district boasts one of the most renowned collections of museums in the nation, including the Modern Art Museum and the Kimbell Art Museum. For a taste of the West, visitors head to the National Cowgirl Museum and Hall of Fame or witness the twice-daily herding of cattle through Exchange Avenue in the Stockyards National Historic District.
Tax: 15% hotel, 8.25% sales. For local weather, call (817) 429-2631.

▶ DON'T MISS DRIVE

Main Street in Fort Worth runs from what was once "Hell's Half-Acre" through downtown's Sundance Square and the Historic Stockyards District, two of the largest entertainment districts in the city.

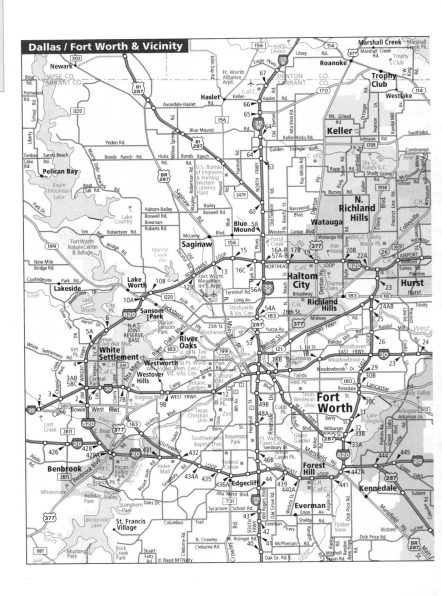

▶ SELECTED ATTRACTIONS

DALLAS

Dallas Arboretum
8525 Garland Rd.
(214) 515-6500

Dallas Museum of Art
1717 N. Harwood St.
(214) 922-1200

Dallas Symphony
2301 Flora St.
(214) 692-0203

Dallas Theater Center
3636 Turtle Creek Blvd.
(214) 522-8499

Dallas World Aquarium
1801 N. Griffin St.
(214) 720-2224

Dallas Zoo
650 S. R.L. Thornton Frwy.
(214) 670-5656

Deep Ellum Historic District
Shops, restaurants, live music, and clubs
Elm St. and Good-Latimer Expwy.
(214) 748-4332

Fair Park
State fairgrounds with nine museums
1300 Robert B. Cullum Blvd.
(214) 670-8400

Nasher Sculpture Center
Outdoor sculpture garden and center
2001 Flora St.
(214) 242-5100

Old City Park
Turn-of-the-century homes and structures
1515 S. Harwood
(214) 421-5141

Science Place
Hands-on exhibits, planetarium, and IMAX theater
1318 2nd Ave. (main building)
1620 1st Ave. (planetarium)
(214) 428-5555

Six Flags Over Texas
TX 360 and I-30, Arlington
(817) 530-6000

Sixth Floor Museum at Dealey Plaza
Exhibits about President John F. Kennedy
411 Elm St.
(214) 747-6660

West End Historical District
Shops, restaurants, and clubs
Ross at Market St.
(214) 741-7180

Women's Museum
3800 Parry Ave. in Fair Park
(214) 915-0860

▶ SHOPPING

DALLAS

Galleria Dallas
Upscale specialty stores
13350 N. Dallas Pkwy.
(972) 702-7100

continued on the next page

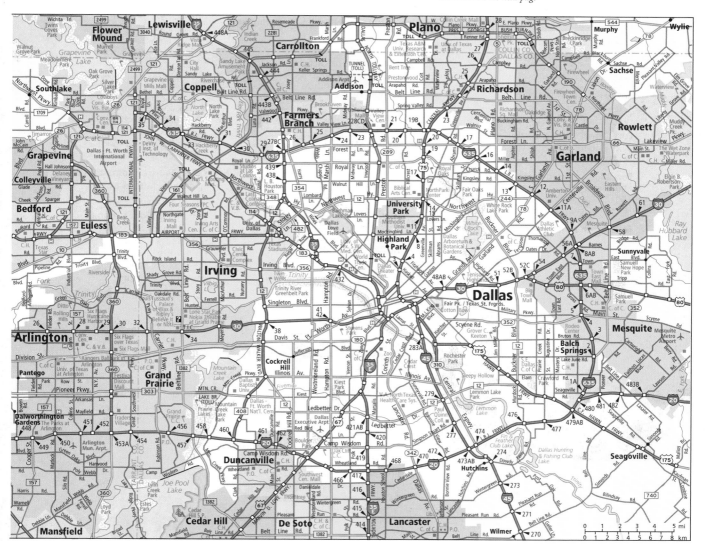

Dallas continued

Highland Park Village
47 Highland Park Shopping Village
(214) 559-2740

NorthPark Center
Department stores and boutiques
8687 North Central Expwy.
(214) 361-6345

Victory Park
Upscale boutiques, dining, and entertainment
2401 N. Houston St.
(214) 303-5572

SELECTED ATTRACTIONS

FORT WORTH

American Airlines C.R. Smith Museum
Commercial aviation museum
4601 TX 360
(817) 967-1560

Amon Carter Museum
19th- and 20th-century American art
3501 Camp Bowie Blvd.
(817) 738-1933

Ball-Eddleman-McFarland House
Original Victorian home
1110 Penn St.
(817) 332-5875

Cattle Raisers Museum
1301 W. 7th St.
(817) 332-8551

Fort Worth Botanic Garden
3220 Botanic Garden Blvd.
(817) 871-7686

Fort Worth Museum of Science and History
1501 Montgomery St.
(817) 255-9300

Fort Worth Nature Center
9601 Fossil Ridge Rd.
(817) 237-1111

Sundance Square in Fort Worth

Fort Worth Zoo
1989 Colonial Pkwy.
(817) 759-7555

Kimbell Art Museum
3333 Camp Bowie Blvd.
(817) 332-8451

Log Cabin Village
Living history in 1850s log cabins
2100 Log Cabin Village Ln. at
University Ave.
(817) 926-5881

Modern Art Museum of Fort Worth
3200 Darnell St.
(817) 738-9215

Nancy Lee and Perry R. Bass Performance Hall
4th and Calhoun Sts.
(817) 212-4200

National Cowboys of Color Museum
3400 Mount Vernon Ave.
(817) 534-8801

National Cowgirl Museum and Hall of Fame
1720 Gendy St.
(817) 336-4475

Sid Richardson Collection of Western Art
309 Main St.
(817) 332-6554

Stockyards Historic District
130 E. Exchange Ave.
(817) 624-4741

Tarantula Excursion Train
140 E. Exchange Ave.
(817) 410-3123

Texas Motor Speedway
3601 TX 114, at I-35 W
(817) 215-8500

Thistle Hill
Historic cattle baron's mansion
1509 Pennsylvania Ave.
(817) 336-1212

Vintage Flying Museum
505 NW 38th St., adjacent to
Meacham Airport
(817) 624-1935

Water Gardens
1502 Commerce St.
(817) 392-6338

SHOPPING

FORT WORTH

Camp Bowie Boulevard
30 blocks of upscale specialty shops

North East Mall
Upscale department stores and shops
1101 Melbourne Rd., Hurst
(817) 284-3427

Ridgmar Mall
Department stores, shops, and restaurants
1888 Green Oaks Rd. at I-30
(817) 731-0856

DIVERSION

Drive out to the Fossil Rim Wildlife Center, where endangered species run wild. A lodge offers overnight accommodations, and there are guided walking and mountain bike tours as well as day camps. Located in Glen Rose; take US 67 south and west to County Rd. 2008.
(254) 897-2960 or (888) 775-6742

Stockyards Station
Western shops, dining, and tours
130 E. Exchange Ave. off N. Main St.
(817) 625-9715

Sundance Square
Specialty shops and entertainment
Bounded by Belknap, Main, and 6th Sts.
(817) 255-5700

University Park Village
Upscale shops
1612 S. University Dr.
(817) 332-5700

VISITOR INFORMATION

Dallas Convention and Visitors Bureau
325 North St. Paul St., Suite 700
Dallas, TX 75201
(214) 571-1000 or (800) 232-5527
www.visitdallas.com

Dallas Tourist Information Center
Old Red Courthouse
100 S. Houston St.

Fort Worth Convention & Visitors Bureau
415 Throckmorton St.
Fort Worth, TX 76102
(817) 336-8791 or (800) 433-5747
www.fortworth.com

Fort Worth Visitor Centers
Sundance Square
415 Throckmorton St.
(817) 336-8791 or (800) 433-5747

Stockyards National Historic District
130 E. Exchange Ave.
(817) 624-4741

Cultural District
3401 W. Lancaster Ave.
(817) 882-8588

DENVER, Colorado

Colorado's capital city sits at the interface of high desert plains and the vertical rise of the Rocky Mountains. In City Park lies the Museum of Nature and Science, which features Egyptian mummies, wildlife dioramas, and dinosaur exhibits. The aquatic life of two very different river systems entertains visitors at Downtown Aquarium. Free tours of the U.S. Mint offer a look into the history of the country's currency. *Tax: 14.85% hotel, 7.7% sales. For local weather, call (303) 494-4221.*

Shops at the 16th Street Mall

SELECTED ATTRACTIONS

Black American West Museum & Heritage Center
History of African American cowboys
3091 California St.
(303) 292-2566

Colorado History Museum
1300 Broadway
(303) 866-3682

Colorado State Capitol
200 E. Colfax Ave.
(303) 866-2604

Coors Brewery Tours
13th Ave. and Ford St., Golden
(303) 277-2337

Denver Museum of Nature & Science
2001 Colorado Blvd. in City Park
(303) 322-7009 or (800) 925-2250

Downtown Aquarium
700 Water St.
(303) 561-4450

Lower Downtown Historic District (LoDo)
Bounded by Larimer St., 20th St., Wynkoop St., and Speer Blvd.
(303) 628-5428

Tiny Town
Kid-size village and railroad
6249 S. Turkey Creek Rd., Tiny Town
(303) 697-6829

United States Mint
Free tours
320 W. Colfax Ave.
(303) 405-4761

SHOPPING

16th Street Mall
Specialty shops in a pedestrian mall
Between Wynkoop and Broadway
(303) 534-6161

Cherry Creek North Shopping District
Galleries and boutiques
At 1st, 2nd, and 3rd Aves. between University Blvd. and Steele St.
(303) 394-2903

Cherry Creek Shopping Center
Department stores and specialty shops
3000 E. 1st Ave.
(303) 388-3900

Larimer Square Historic District
Specialty shops
Between 14th and 15th Sts., on Larimer St.
(303) 534-2367

VISITOR INFORMATION

Denver Metro Convention and Visitors Bureau
1555 California St., Ste. 300
Denver, CO 80202
(303) 892-1112 or (800) 233-6837
www.denver.org

DETROIT, Michigan

Arctic Ring of Life exhibit at the Detroit Zoo

The promise embodied by the 30-year-old Renaissance Center, still gleaming at the Detroit River's edge, is beginning to take shape as Detroit slowly revitalizes itself. The wealth of the nation's one-time automobile capital may be seen at historic homes such as Fair Lane, the estate of Henry Ford. Along with the Henry Ford Museum, Greenfield Village—a collection of historic buildings brought here from their original locations—celebrates both the spirit of innovation and the pastoral way of life. The high culture of the Renaissance and the Impressionist period is on view at the Institute of Arts, while Detroit's contribution to pop culture takes center stage at the Motown Historical Museum. *Tax: 6-15% hotel, 6% sales. For local weather, call (248) 620-2355.*

▶ DON'T MISS DRIVE

The Nautical Mile is a peaceful drive down Jefferson Avenue from the stately lake mansions of Grosse Pointe, passing auto family Edsel and Eleanor Ford's mansion, through St. Clair Shores' picturesque boating community, and up to Metro Beach Metropark.

▶ SELECTED ATTRACTIONS

Automotive Hall of Fame
21400 Oakwood Blvd., Dearborn
(313) 240-4000

Belle Isle Park
Conservatory and museum
Across the McArthur Bridge at the foot of E. Grand Blvd.
(313) 852-4078

Black Holocaust Museum
Located in the Shrine of the Black Madonna Cultural Center and Bookstore
13535 Livernois Ave.
(313) 491-0777

Charles H. Wright Museum of African-American History
315 E. Warren Ave.
(313) 494-5800

Cranbrook Art Museum
39221 Woodward Ave., Bloomfield Hills
(248) 645-3323

Detroit Institute of Arts
5200 Woodward Ave.
(313) 833-7900

Detroit Zoo
8450 W. Ten Mile Rd., Royal Oak
(248) 398-0900

Dossin Great Lakes Museum
100 Strand Dr., Belle Isle
(313) 833-7935

Edsel & Eleanor Ford House
Historic estate of auto baron family
1100 Lakeshore Rd., Grosse Pointe Shores
(313) 884-4222

General Motors World Museum
Interactive museum about GM
Jefferson Ave. at Beaubien St. in Renaissance Center
(313) 667-7151

Henry Ford Estate
Former home of car manufacturing magnate
4901 Evergreen Rd. between Ford Rd. and Michigan Ave. at the University of Michigan, Dearborn
(313) 593-5590

The Henry Ford
Museum, Greenfield Village, IMAX theater, research center, and auto plant tour
20900 Oakwood Blvd., Dearborn
(313) 982-6001 or (800) 835-5237

Mexicantown
Authentic restaurants and shopping
At the foot of the Ambassador Bridge, bordered by Bagley, West Vernor Hwy., 16th, and Clark Sts.
(313) 967-9898

MGM Grand Detroit Casino
1300 John C. Lodge
(313) 393-7777 or (877) 888-2121

Motown Historical Museum
2648 W. Grand Blvd.
(313) 875-2264

New Detroit Science Center
IMAX Dome Theatre, planetarium, and interactive exhibits
5020 John R St.
(313) 577-8400

Solanus Casey Center
Historic St. Bonaventure monastery, art gallery, and shrine to Detroit priest
1780 Mt. Elliott St.
(313) 579-2100

Tuskegee Airmen National Museum
6325 W. Jefferson
(313) 843-8849

▶ SHOPPING

Eastern Market
Indoor/outdoor century-old marketplace
Russell and Adelaide Sts.
(313) 833-9300

Eastland Center
Department stores and specialty shops
18000 Vernier Rd., Harper Woods
(313) 371-1501

Fairlane Town Center
Department stores and specialty shops
18900 Michigan Ave. at Evergreen Rd., Dearborn
(313) 593-3330

Grosse Pointe Village
Specialty shops and services
Kercheval Ave. between Cadieux and Neff,
Grosse Pointe
(313) 886-7474

Renaissance Center
Fine shops and boutiques
Jefferson Ave. at Beaubien St.
(313) 567-3126

The Somerset Collection
*High-end department stores and
specialty shops*
2800 W. Big Beaver Rd., Troy
(248) 643-6360

VISITOR INFORMATION

**Detroit Metro Convention &
Visitors Bureau**
211 W. Fort St., Ste. 1000
Detroit, MI 48226
(313) 202-1800 or (800) 338-7648
www.visitdetroit.com

**Convention and Visitors Bureau
of Windsor**
333 Riverside Dr. W., Ste. 103
Windsor, ON, N9A 5K4 Canada
(519) 255-6530 or (800) 265-3633
www.visitwindsor.com

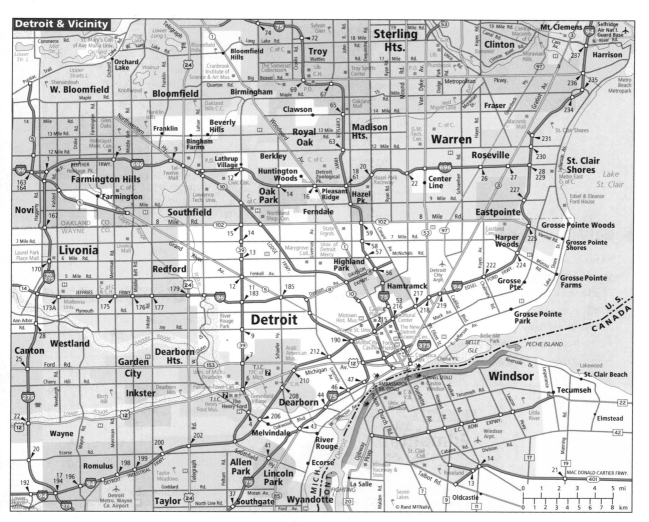

DIVERSION

Duty-free shopping and a favorable exchange rate are only minutes south of
Detroit in Windsor, Ontario, Canada. Windsor is just across the Detroit River via
the Detroit-Windsor tunnel accessed from Jefferson Avenue. Or take I-75 to the
Porter St. exit and follow the signs to the Ambassador Bridge.

EDMONTON, Alberta, Canada

Edmonton skyline

A major cross-Canada transportation hub, the capital of Alberta is noted for its extensive parklands and nearby huge oilfields. Many visitors make their first stop the West Edmonton Mall, the world's largest. This vast entertainment complex includes amusement parks, sports facilities, and a virtual reality playground. The city's other major attractions include the Telus World of Science-Edmonton, a space and science center with interactive exhibits, and Fort Edmonton Park, a living re-creation of the city in various phases of its short but remarkable history. *Tax: 11% hotel, 6% goods and services tax. For local weather, call (780) 468-4940.*

▶ SELECTED ATTRACTIONS

Alberta Railway Museum
24215 34 St.
(780) 472-6229

Art Gallery of Alberta
2 Sir Winston Churchill Square at 99 St.
and 102A Ave.
(780) 422-6223

Devonian Botanic Garden
10 km. southwest on AB 60 at the
University of Alberta
(780) 987-3054

Elk Island National Park
43 km. east on AB 16, Fort Saskatchewan
(780) 992-2950

Fort Edmonton Park
Historical park
7000 143 St. at Whitemud and Fox Drs.
(780) 496-8787

Gallery Walk
Art galleries, gift shops, restaurants, boutiques, and day spa
10411 124 St.
(780) 488-3619

John Janzen Nature Centre
7000 143 St.
(780) 496-8787

John Walter Museum
Turn-of-the-century homes of early Edmonton entrepreneur
10661 91A Ave.
(780) 496-8787

Muttart Conservatory
Horticultural display garden
9626 96A St.
(780) 496-8787

Northlands Park
Horse races and home of the Edmonton Oilers
7300 116 Ave. NW
(780) 471-7210 or (888) 800-7275

Pysanka
World's largest Easter egg
80 km. east of Edmonton on
AB 16, Vegreville
(780) 632-3100

Royal Alberta Museum
12845 102 Ave. NW at 128 St.
(780) 453-9100

Telus World of Science–Edmonton (Odyssium)
Space and science center
11211 142 St.
(780) 452-9100

Valley Zoo
13315 Buena Vista Rd.
(780) 496-8787

▶ SHOPPING

124th Street Area
Art galleries, small shops, and restaurants
124 St. from Jasper Ave. to 107 Ave.
(780) 413-6503

Edmonton City Centre
Department stores and specialty shops
102 St. and 102 Ave.
(780) 426-8444

Old Strathcona
Fashion boutiques, specialty shops, and farmer's market
Whyte Ave. between 99 and 109 Sts.
(780) 437-4182

West Edmonton Mall
Shops, restaurants, indoor amusement park, golf, dolphin lagoon, and other family attractions
8882 170 St.
(780) 444-5200 or (800) 661-8890

▶ VISITOR INFORMATION

Edmonton Tourism
9990 Jasper Ave.
Edmonton, AB T5J 1P7 Canada
(780) 426-4715 or (800) 463-4667
www.edmonton.com/tourism

▶ DIVERSION

At the Ukrainian Cultural Heritage Village, explore an open-air museum of 30 historic buildings, sample traditional Ukrainian food, or enjoy a horse-drawn wagon ride. 35 kilometers (about 21 miles) east of Edmonton on AB 16. (780) 662-3640

Edmonton

Edmonton

© Rand McNally

EL PASO, Texas

El Paso blends Native American, Spanish, Mexican, and Anglo cultures with a dose of the modern military. Worshipers attend services at three Spanish missions (still active after hundreds of years) along the Mission Trail. The Magoffin Homestead offers a peek into the lives of the first cowboy ranchers to settle here. The million-plus-acre expanse of Fort Bliss includes museums that cover its history and ongoing mission. And from downtown, trolley rides allow a quick jaunt over the river into Ciudad Juarez for authentic Mexican crafts and cuisine. *Tax: 15.5% hotel, 8.25% sales. For local weather, call (915) 533-7744 or (505) 589-4088.*

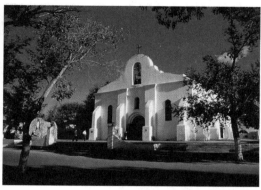

The Presidio along the Mission Trail

► SELECTED ATTRACTIONS

Border Jumper Trolleys
1 Civic Center Plaza at the El Paso Convention Center
(915) 544-0062

Centennial Museum & Chihuahuan Desert Gardens
Natural and cultural history of the desert
Wiggins Rd. at University Ave.
(915) 747-5565

Chamizal National Memorial
Exhibits, art galleries, and performing arts theater in a park
800 S. San Marcial St.
(915) 532-7273

El Paso Museum of Archaeology at Wilderness Park
4301 Transmountain Rd.
(915) 755-4332

El Paso Museum of Art
1 Arts Festival Plaza, Santa Fe and Main Sts.
(915) 532-1707

El Paso Museum of History
Santa Fe & Missouri Sts.
(915) 351-3588

El Paso Zoo
4001 E. Paisano Dr.
(915) 521-1850

Fort Bliss Air Defense/Artillery Museum
Building 1735 at Ft. Bliss
(915) 568-3390

Fort Bliss Replica Museum
Adobe fort buildings and military artifacts
Pershing and Pleasonton Rds. at Ft. Bliss
(915) 568-3390

Insights El Paso Science Museum
505 N. Santa Fe St.
(915) 534-0000

Magoffin Homestead
Historic adobe-style hacienda with original furnishings
1120 Magoffin Ave.
(915) 533-5147

The Mission Trail
Historic missions
Socorro Rd. at Zaragosa
(915) 534-0677

Tigua Indian Cultural Center
305 Yaya Ln.
(915) 859-7913

Wet 'n Wild Waterworld
12 miles north off I-10, exit 0, Anthony
(915) 886-2222

Wyler Aerial Tramway State Park
Aerial view of three states and Mexico
1700 McKinley
(915) 566-66225

► SHOPPING

Bassett Place
Department stores and specialty shops
6101 Gateway Blvd. W
(915) 772-7479

Cielo Vista Mall
Department stores and 140 retail stores
8401 Gateway West
(915) 779-7070

Sunland Park Mall
Department stores and 130 specialty shops
750 Sunland Park Dr.
(915) 833-5596

Tony Lama Factory Stores
Outlet mall
7156 Gateway E.
(915) 772-4327

► VISITOR INFORMATION

El Paso Convention and Visitors Bureau
1 Civic Center Plaza
El Paso, TX 79901
(915) 534-0601 or (800) 351-6024
www.visitelpaso.com

► DIVERSION

Drive out to the Cloudcroft-Ruidoso area in New Mexico for camping, skiing, fishing, even horse racing. It's less than 125 miles from El Paso. For Cloudcroft information: (505) 682-2733; for Ruidoso: (877) 784-3676

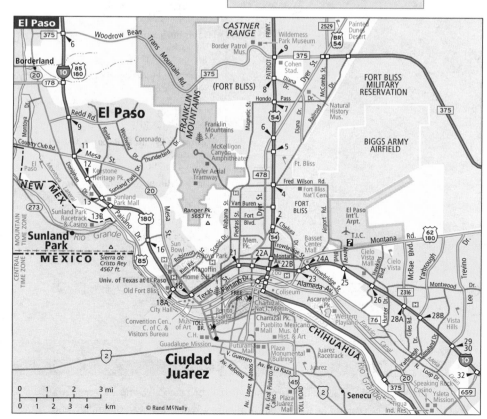

GATLINBURG, Tennessee

Ripley's Aquarium of the Smokies

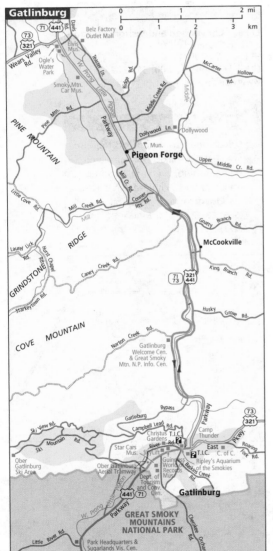

From Pigeon Forge to Gatlinburg, the road to Great Smoky Mountains National Park is awash with outlet stores, family attractions, restaurants, resorts, and motels. Gatlinburg, at the northern entrance to the park, is a hub of Southern craftsmanship. More than 100 different galleries and workshops occupy the loop through the Great Smoky Arts and Crafts Community. Dollywood's delights include live theatrical performers, a massive treehouse, and the Southern Gospel Music Hall of Fame & Museum. The Ober Gatlinburg Aerial Tramway starts on the sidewalk of downtown Gatlinburg and ferries riders to the top of Mt. Harrison, offering lofty mountain views along the way. *Tax: 12.5% hotel, 11% restaurants and attractions, 9.5% retail sales. For local weather, call (800) 565-7330 ext. 5.*

▶ SELECTED ATTRACTIONS

Arrowmont School of Arts and Crafts
Art gallery
556 Parkway
(865) 436-5860

Camp Thunder Fun Center
Go-karts, mini golf, and movies
542 Parkway
(865) 430-7223

Christus Gardens
Biblical wax museum
510 River Rd.
(865) 436-5155

Dollywood
Theme park with musical performances
1020 Dollywood Ln. off US 441,
Pigeon Forge
(865) 428-9488

Fort Fun Family Entertainment Center
Laser tag, 3D movies, and bumper cars
712 Parkway, Reagan Terrace Mall
(865) 436-2326

Gatlinburg Sky Lift
765 Parkway
(865) 436-4307

Great Smoky Arts and Crafts Community
8-mile loop of shops, studios, and galleries
100 Glades Rd., 3 miles east on E. Parkway
(US 321-N)
(800) 565-7330

Guinness World of Records Museum
631 Parkway
(865) 430-7800

Ober Gatlinburg Aerial Tramway
Ski resort, tram rides, and amusement park
1001 Parkway
(865) 436-5423

Ripley's Aquarium of the Smokies
88 River Rd.
(865) 430-8808 or (888) 240-1358

Star Cars Museum
Collection of cars used on TV and in movies
914 Parkway
(865) 430-2200

Sweet Fanny Adams Theater
Live musical comedy
461 Parkway
(865) 436-4039 or (877) 388-5784

▶ SHOPPING

Calhoun's Village
Restaurants and several small shops
1004 Parkway
(865) 436-4100

Gatlinburg Aerial Tramway Mall
Crafts, gifts, and collectibles
1001 Parkway
(865) 436-5423

Mountain Mall
Small specialty shops
611 Parkway
(865) 436-5935

The Village
Boutiques, galleries, and arts and crafts outlets
634 Parkway
(865) 436-3995

▶ VISITOR INFORMATION

Gatlinburg Chamber of Commerce
811 E. Parkway
Gatlinburg, TN 37738
(865) 436-4178 or (800) 588-1817
www.gatlinburg.com

Gatlinburg Department of Tourism and Convention Center
303 Reagan Dr.
Gatlinburg, TN 37738
(865) 430-1052 or (800) 343-1475
www.gatlinburg-tennessee.com

Pigeon Forge Department of Tourism
P.O. Box 1390-I
Pigeon Forge, TN 37868
(865) 453-8574 or (800) 251-9100
www.mypigeonforge.com

Visitor Centers
Gatlinburg Welcome Center
1011 Banner Rd. at Hwy. 441 South
(865) 436-0519

Parkway Welcome Center
520 Parkway
(865) 436-0504

Aquarium Welcome Center
Aquarium Plaza at Light #5
(865) 436-0535

▶ DIVERSION

Treasured photographs of a vacation to Gatlinburg can be taken all along a 3.5-mile stretch called the Cherokee Orchard Road. Packed with scenery, it runs between Gatlinburg and Roaring Forks.

GUADALAJARA, Jalisco, Mexico

The historic birthplace of mariachi and tequila, Guadalajara is Mexico's second largest city, an enclave of traditional values coping with modern growth. Dominated by the city cathedral's twin towers, the old city center teems with colorful fountains and buildings dating back hundreds of years. In a city crammed with museums, one of the best—the Museo Regional de Guadalajara—exhibits archaeology, history, and fine arts including paintings by Jose Ibarra and Villalpando. Those in search of exceptional quality head to Tlaquepaque, where the craftspeople are famous for their ceramics as well as metal, glass, and leather goods. *Tax: 17% hotel (15% value-added, 2% lodging), 15% value-added sales tax is usually included in the retail price.*

The Cathedral and the Plaza de Armas

▶ SELECTED ATTRACTIONS

Calandria Tour
Carriage tour of the historic city center
Tours depart from the Regional Museum outside Liberty Market or at Jardín San Francisco by Corona St.

The Cathedral
Circa 1568-1618 church and a symbol of Guadalajara
Av. Alcalde between Av. Hidalgo and Calle Morelos
011-52-33-3614-7118*

Degollado Theater
Performing arts center
Degollado St., Av. Hidalgo, and Morelos St.
011-52-33-3614-4773*

Government Palace (Palacio de Gobierno)
State Capitol building with murals by Jose Clemente Orozco
Av. Corona at Morelos
011-52-33-3668-1800*

Guadalajara Regional Museum (Museo Regional de Guadalajara)
Av. Hidalgo and Calle Liceo
011-52-33-3614-5257*

Guadalajara Zoo (Zoologico Guadalajara)
Zoo train and famous aviaries
Huentitan Canyon, Paseo del Zoologico No. 600
011-52-33-3674-4488*

Handicraft House (Casa de las Artesanias)
Blown glass, saddles, crafts, and papier-mâché
Constituyentes 21
011-52-33-3619-5402*

Lienzo Charro Jalisco
Charreadas, mariachi music, and competitions
Av. R. Michel No. 577
011-52-33-3619-0315*

▶ SHOPPING

Mercado Libertad or San Juan de Dios
Indoor market for handicrafts, clothes, souvenirs, and gifts
Calzada Independencia Sur and Av. Javier Mina

Tlaquepaque
Arts and crafts center
5 miles southwest of downtown Guadalajara

Shopping can also be found at:
Centro Magno
La Gran Plaza
Plaza del Sol
Plaza México
Plaza Pabellón
Plaza Patria
El Baratillo (flea market)
(Check with your hotel front desk for specific locations.)

▶ DON'T MISS DRIVE

Vallarta Avenue is one of the city's most beautiful streets. It brims with colorful shops and restaurants and is lined with historic monuments.

▶ VISITOR INFORMATION

Visitors and Convention Bureau at the Guadalajara Chamber of Commerce
Av. Vallarta 4095
Guadalajara, Jal. 44100, Mexico
011-52-333-122-7544

Jalisco State Tourism Ministry
102 Morelos (on Plaza Tapatia)
Guadalajara, Jal. 44100, Mexico
011-52-33-3668-1600

Mexico Tourism Board (U.S.)
(800) 446-3942
www.visitmexico.com

Number listed may or may not have an English-speaking person available.

DIVERSION

Cobblestone streets, rustic white houses, and one of the most picturesque bays in the world are only three hours away in Puerto Vallarta. Take Mexico 15 with connections to Mexico 200. Don't miss the sculptures that line the boardwalk.

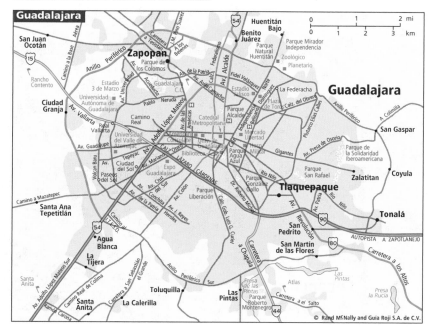

HONOLULU, Hawaii

Fire-knife dancer at the Polynesian Culture Center

The "Pearl of the Pacific" has lost none of its ability to enchant; a perfect climate, pristine beaches, and fabulous scenery induce visitors to return again and again. Hike to the 760-foot summit of Diamond Head Crater to take in the splendor of sunrise as well as 360-degree views of the island. The Bishop Museum is dedicated to telling the story of the natural and cultural history of Hawaii and the Pacific. The USS *Arizona* Memorial is a moving tribute to those who lost their lives at Pearl Harbor during the entrance of America into World War II. *Tax: 7.25-11.96% hotel, 4.17% sales, 0.55% county surcharge (Oahu only). For local weather, call (808) 973-4380 or (808) 973-5286.*

► SELECTED ATTRACTIONS

Bishop Museum
Natural and cultural history exhibits, garden shows, and planetarium
1525 Bernice St.
(808) 847-3511

Foster Botanical Gardens
50 N. Vineyard Blvd.
(808) 522-7060

► DON'T MISS DRIVE

Nu'uanu Pali Lookout overlooks forested, near-vertical 600-foot cliffs on the windward side of O'ahu and provides one of the best views on the island. From Waikīkī, take H-1 west, then take Pali Highway, HI 61, via Nu'uanu Pali Drive. Half a mile beyond Queen Emma's Summer Palace, follow signs to the lookout.

Hawaii State Art Museum (HiSAM)
Contemporary Hawaiian artists
250 S. Hotel St., (808) 586-0900

Hawaiian Waters Adventure Park
400 Farrington Hwy., Kapolei
(808) 674-9283

Honolulu Academy of Arts
Western and Asian art collections
900 S. Beretania St.
(808) 532-8700

Honolulu Zoo
151 Kapahulu Ave.
(808) 926-3191

'Iolani Palace
364 S. King St.
(808) 522-0832

National Memorial Cemetery of the Pacific
Veterans' cemetery in Punchbowl Crater
2177 Puowaina Dr.
(808) 532-3720

Polynesian Cultural Center
55-370 Kamehameha Hwy., Lā'ie
(808) 293-3333 or (800) 367-7060

USS *Arizona* Memorial at Pearl Harbor
1 Arizona Memorial Pl. off H-1 Fwy.
(808) 422-0561

Waimea Valley Audubon Center
Botanical gardens and self-guided tours
59-864 Kamehameha Hwy., Hale'iwa
(808) 638-9199

► SHOPPING

Ala Moana Center
Open-air shopping center
1450 Ala Moana Blvd.
(808) 955-9517

Aloha Tower Marketplace
Specialty stores, restaurants, live concerts, and theater
1 Aloha Tower Dr.
(808) 528-5700

Bailey's Antiques and Aloha Shirts
Hawaiiana and more than 5,000 vintage shirts
517 Kapahulu Ave.
(808) 734-7628

International Marketplace
Open-air market
2330 Kalakaua Ave.
(808) 971-2080

Royal Hawaiian Shopping Center
Specialty shops and restaurants
2201 Kalakaua Ave.
(808) 922-0588

2100 Kalakaua Avenue
High-end merchants
2100 Kalakaua Ave. at Kalaimoku St.
(808) 955-2878

Ward Warehouse
Specialty shops, restaurants, and entertainment
1050 Ala Moana Blvd.
(808) 591-8411

► VISITOR INFORMATION

Hawai'i Visitors and Convention Bureau
2270 Kalakaua Ave., Ste. 801
Honolulu, HI 96815
(808) 923-1811 or (800) 464-2924
www.gohawaii.com

► DIVERSION

Visit the "surfing capital of the world" on the North Shore of the island. The area is also home to Historic Hale'iwa Town. From Waikīkī, go west on H-1 and take exit 8-A, which will turn to H-2; then take exit 8, which becomes Kamehameha Hwy. Continue through Hale'iwa Town and on to the North Shore.

© Rand McNally

HOUSTON, Texas

Fifty miles from the Gulf and many more from the moon, Houston is both a major seaport and a familiar name in the exploration of space. The Menil Collection houses Byzantine and contemporary masterworks in a stunning building. For lighthearted entertainment, families head to Children's Museum of Houston or to the Houston Zoo, which hunkers down in the forests and trees of Hermann Park. For a trip a bit farther from home, visitors try a simulated journey to the stars at Space Center Houston. *Tax: 17% hotel, 8.25% sales. For local weather, call (281) 337-5074.*

Battleship USS Texas

▶ SELECTED ATTRACTIONS

Battleship USS *Texas*
3523 Battleground Rd.
San Jacinto Battleground State Historic Site, LaPorte
(281) 479-2431

Bayou Bend Collection and Gardens
American decorative arts collection in historic mansion
1 Westcott St.
(713) 639-7750

Children's Museum of Houston
1500 Binz St.
(713) 522-1138

Contemporary Arts Museum
5216 Montrose Blvd.
(713) 284-8250

George Ranch Historical Park
1830s stock farm with mansion and ranch house
10215 FM 762, five miles south of US 59 and Grand Parkway, Richmond
(281) 343-0218

The Heritage Society
Museum of Texas history and eight historic homes
1100 Bagby St. in Sam Houston Park
(713) 655-1912

Holocaust Museum Houston
5401 Caroline St.
(713) 942-8000

continued on the next page

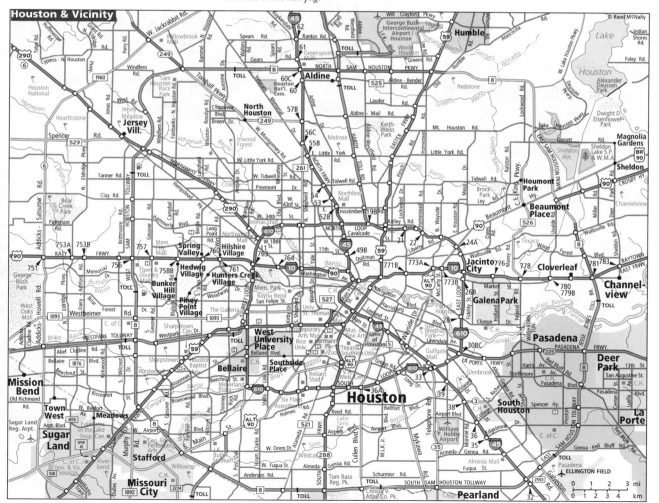

Houston City Hall

Houston attractions continued

Houston Arboretum and Nature Center
4501 Woodway Dr.
(713) 681-8433

Houston Museum of Natural Science
1 Hermann Circle Dr.
(713) 639-4629

Houston Zoo
1513 N. MacGregor Dr. in Hermann Park
(713) 533-6500

McGovern Museum of Health and Medical Science
1515 Hermann Dr.
(713) 521-1515

The Menil Collection
Art museum
1515 Sul Ross St.
(713) 525-9400

Museum of Fine Arts
1001 Bissonnet St.
(713) 639-7300

Orange Show Center for Visionary Arts
Eclectic arts center and monument
2402 Munger St.
(713) 926-6368

Sam Houston Boat Tour
Free public tour of the Houston Ship Channel
7300 Clinton Dr., Gate 8
(713) 670-2416

San Jacinto Monument and Museum of History
1 Monument Circle in the San Jacinto Battleground State Historic Site, La Porte
(281) 479-2421

Six Flags Splash Town Water Park
21300 I-45 N.
(281) 355-3300

Space Center Houston
Museum, live shows, and tram tours of NASA's Johnson Space Center
1.5 miles east of I-45 on NASA Parkway, 25 miles southeast of downtown Houston
(281) 244-2100

SHOPPING

The Galleria
Upscale boutiques, shops, department stores, and restaurants
5085 Westheimer Rd.
(713) 622-0663

Highland Village
Department stores and specialty shops
4055 Westheimer Rd.
(713) 850-3100

Houston Tunnel System
Six-mile system of underground shops and restaurants, 55 entrances

Rice Village
Boutiques, retail stores, and restaurants
Kirby Dr. and University Blvd.

Uptown Park
Designer boutiques
Post Oak Blvd. at Loop I-610
(713) 850-1400

VISITOR INFORMATION

Greater Houston Convention and Visitors Bureau
901 Bagby St., Ste. 100
Houston, TX 77002
(713) 437-5200 or (800) 446-8786
www.visithoustontexas.com

Houston Visitors Center
901 Bagby St. (Bagby and Walker Sts.)
(713) 437-5556

Bay Area Houston Visitors Center
20710 I-45, Webster
(281) 338-0333 or (800) 844-5253

DIVERSION

Washington-on-the-Brazos Historical Park north of Brenham, TX is where the treaty that declared Texas' independence from Mexico was signed. 70 miles west on US 290 to TX 105. Watch for signs.

Blast off for Houston

Space Center Houston is NASA's official visitors center. It houses actual spacecraft such as the Mercury, Gemini, and Apollo capsules and provides an exclusive tram ride through the Johnson Space Center. Visitors can make a stop at the largest IMAX theater in Texas or try to "walk in space" via state-of-the-art simulators. The Astronaut Gallery features spacesuits dating back to the first American trip into space. Hands-on exhibits encourage visitors to test their skills at landing a spacecraft or retrieving a satellite through interactive computer simulators. It's a blast, and most visitors stay all day. Located at 1601 NASA Parkway, off I-45 South, in the Clear Lake area outside of Houston. Admission is $18.95 for adults, with discounts for children and senior citizens. For information, call (281) 244-2100 or visit **www.spacecenter.org**.

INDIANAPOLIS, Indiana

The roar of racing cars will forever be associated with this metropolis of the cornfields, but Indiana's capital offers subtler charms as well. The Children's Museum boasts 100,000 items to stimulate youngsters' interests in art, science, and the world around them. The Eiteljorg Museum displays an exceptional collection of Native American and Western-themed art. It's part of White River State Park, which is where visitors also find the zoo, the NCAA Hall of Fame, and a chance to paddle through downtown on the Central Canal. *Tax: 15% hotel, 6% sales, plus a food and beverage tax of 1%. For local weather, call (317) 222-2222 or (317) 856-0664.*

Canal Walk in Indianapolis

▶ SELECTED ATTRACTIONS

Central Canal
Runs through downtown's White River State Park
Paddleboat rental at Ohio and West Sts.
(317) 767-5072

The Children's Museum of Indianapolis
3000 N. Meridian St.
(317) 334-3322

Congressional Medal of Honor Memorial
North bank of the Central Canal, next to Military Park
650 Washington St. in White River State Pk.
(317) 233-2434 or (800) 665-9056

Conner Prairie
Living history museum
13400 Allisonville Rd., Fishers
(317) 776-6000 or (800) 966-1836

Crispus Attucks Museum
History museum honoring African Americans
1140 Dr. Martin Luther King Jr. St.
(317) 226-2430

Eiteljorg Museum of American Indians and Western Art
500 W. Washington St.
(317) 636-9378

Freetown Village
Living history museum about African American life in 19th-century Indiana
625 Indiana Ave.
(317) 631-1870

Indiana Basketball Hall of Fame
408 Trojan Ln., New Castle
(765) 529-1891

Indiana State Museum and IMAX Theater
650 W. Washington St.
(317) 232-1637

Indianapolis Motor Speedway and Hall of Fame Museum
4790 W. 16th St.
(317) 492-6784

Indianapolis Museum of Art
Includes historic estate and gardens
4000 Michigan Rd.
(317) 920-2660

Indianapolis Zoo and White River Gardens
1200 W. Washington St.
(317) 630-2001

NCAA Hall of Champions
700 W. Washington St.
(317) 916-4255 or (800) 735-6222

President Benjamin Harrison Home
1230 N. Delaware St.
(317) 631-1888

Riley Museum Home
Historic home of poet James Whitcomb Riley
528 Lockerbie St.
(317) 631-5885

State Soldiers' and Sailors' Monument
Meridian and Market Sts. on Monument Circle
(317) 232-7615

Victory Field
Home of Minor League Baseball's Indianapolis Indians
501 W. Maryland St.
(317) 269-3542

White River State Park
Urban state park with museums, canal, greenways, and bike/hiking paths
801 W. Washington St.
(317) 233-2434 or (800) 665-9056

▶ SHOPPING

Castleton Square Mall
Department and specialty stores
6020 E. 82nd St.
(317) 849-9993

Circle Centre Mall
Shopping, dining, and entertainment complex
49 W. Maryland St.
(317) 681-8000

The Fashion Mall at Keystone
Upscale department stores and specialty shops
8702 Keystone Crossing
(317) 574-4000

Fountain Square Merchants
Antique shops and specialty stores
Intersection of Virginia Ave., Shelby St., and Prospect St.
(317) 686-6010

Indianapolis City Market
Fresh foods and imported grocery items
222 E. Market St.
(317) 634-9266

▶ DON'T MISS DRIVE

Cruise Meridian Street between 38th and 86th Streets for a view of mansions built by the founders of Indianapolis. The Governor's Mansion is also on Meridian Street.

Lafayette Square Mall
38th St. and Lafayette Rd.
(317) 291-6390

▶ VISITOR INFORMATION

Indianapolis Convention and Visitors Association
1 RCA Dome, Ste. 100
Indianapolis, IN 46225
(317) 639-4282 or (800) 556-4639
www.indy.org

Indiana Convention Center Information Desk
100 S. Capitol Ave.
(317) 684-7574

Indianapolis Artsgarden Visitor Center
100 W. Washington St.
(317) 624-2563

White River State Park Visitor Center
801 W. Washington St.
(317) 233-2434

See next page for Indianapolis vicinity map

DIVERSION

The Wholesale District Tour and Monument Circle Tour provide a 90-minute walk through restored and historic areas. The Monument Circle Tour includes Christ Church Cathedral (1857), the oldest church in the city. The Wholesale District Tour includes Union Station, the first centralized train station in the country. Tours also focus on noteworthy architecture. Call (317) 639-4534 or (800) 450-4534 for both tours.

JACKSONVILLE, Florida

The most populous city in Florida, Jacksonville is a growing commercial and financial mecca. The city is home to the Cummer Museum of Art & Gardens, renowned for its collection of Meissen porcelain and the massive Cummer Oak that overspreads the grounds. The Jacksonville Zoo and Garden's rare and exotic fauna from around the world make it a favorite stop; take a walking safari through the African habitat or explore the Range of the Jaguar exhibit. Day or night, the Jacksonville Landing downtown on the riverbank offers a place to unwind with restaurants, shops, and live entertainment. *Tax: 13% hotel, 7% sales. For local weather, call (904) 741-4311.*

Lone Sailor *statue on* The Riverwalk

▶ SELECTED ATTRACTIONS

Adventure Landing
Water park, arcade, go-karts, and mini golf
1944 Beach Blvd.
(904) 246-4386

Baseball Grounds of Jacksonville
Home of Minor League Baseball's Jacksonville Suns
301 A. Philip Randolph Blvd.
(904) 358-2846

Budweiser Brewery Tours
111 Busch Dr.
(904) 696-8373

Cummer Museum of Art & Gardens
829 Riverside Ave.
(904) 356-6857

The Downtown Riverwalks
Boardwalks run along the St. Johns River through downtown Jacksonville

Fort Caroline National Memorial
12713 Fort Caroline Rd.
(904) 641-7155

Jacksonville Museum of Contemporary Art
333 N. Laura St.
(904) 366-6911

Jacksonville Veteran's Memorial Arena
300 A. Philip Randolph Blvd.
(904) 630-3900

Jacksonville Zoo and Gardens
370 Zoo Pkwy.
(904) 757-4463

Kathryn Abby Hanna Park
450-acre beachfront city park
500 Wonderwood Dr.
(904) 249-4700

Kingsley Plantation
Historic cotton and sugarcane plantation on Ft. George Island
11676 Palmetto Ave.
(904) 251-3537

Museum of Science and History (MOSH)
1025 Museum Circle
(904) 396-6674

Times Union Performing Arts Center
300 W. Water St.
(904) 633-6110

▶ SHOPPING

Avonlea Antique Mall
Antique dealers
8101 Phillips Hwy.
(904) 645-0806 or (904) 636-8785

The Avenues
Department stores and specialty shops
10300 Southside Blvd.
(904) 363-3060

Jacksonville Landing
A riverfront marketplace
2 Independent Dr.
(904) 353-1188

Orange Park Mall
Department stores and specialty shops
1910 Wells Rd., Orange Park
(904) 269-2422

Regency Square Mall
Department stores and specialty shops
9501 Arlington Expwy.
(904) 725-3830

San Marco District
Shopping and restaurants
San Marco and Atlantic Blvds.

▶ VISITOR INFORMATION

Jacksonville and the Beaches Convention and Visitors Bureau
550 Water St., Ste. 1000
Jacksonville, FL 32202
(904) 798-9111 or (800) 733-2668
www.visitjacksonville.com

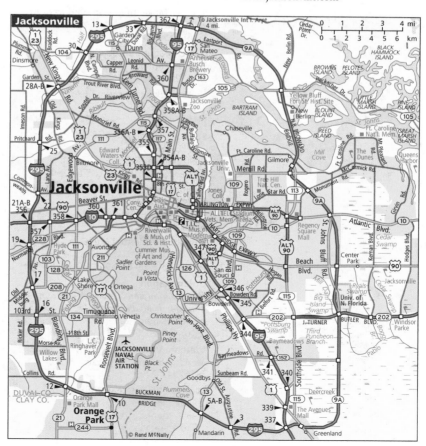

KANSAS CITY, Missouri

The Nelson-Atkins Museum of Art

The burghers of Kansas City, looking for a way to make their city stand out, came up with a winner: fountains, both large and small. They're now part of almost every developer's plans here—only Rome has more. With its rich musical past, the city makes a fitting home for the American Jazz Museum. It's part of the Museum Complex at 18th and Vine, which includes the Negro Leagues Baseball Museum, a memorial to the African American teams that played from the late 1800s until the 1960s. For great barbecue, everyone knows to head to Arthur Bryant's.
Tax 15.225% (15.725% downtown) hotel, 7.725% sales. For local weather, call (816) 540-6021.

DIVERSION

Drive over to Independence and visit the Harry S Truman National Historic Site, which includes his home and library as well as 15 other historic sites and museums. The National Frontier Trails Museum offers a history of wagon train journeys to the west. From Kansas City, take I-70 east to I-435 north to Winner Rd., US 24 east.
(816) 325-7111 or (800) 748-7323

SELECTED ATTRACTIONS

American Jazz Museum
1616 E. 18th St.
(816) 474-8463

Arabia Steamboat Museum
400 Grand Blvd.
(816) 471-1856

Children's Fountain
The fountain of and for youth
32nd St. and N. Oak Trafficway
(816) 842-2299

J.C. Nichols Memorial Fountain
47th and Main St. at the entrance to the Plaza District
(816) 842-2299

The Kansas City Zoo
6800 Zoo Dr. in Swope Park
(816) 513-5700

Kemper Museum of Contemporary Art
4420 Warwick Blvd.
(816) 753-5784

Negro Leagues Baseball Museum
1616 E. 18th St.
(816) 221-1920

Nelson-Atkins Museum of Art
4525 Oak St.
(816) 751-1278

Starlight Theater
Large outdoor theater
4600 Starlight Rd. in Swope Park
(816) 363-7827 or (800) 776-1730

Thomas Hart Benton Home and Studio State Historic Site
3616 Belleview Ave.
(816) 931-5722

Truman Presidential Museum and Library
500 W. US Hwy. 24, Independence
(816) 268-8200 or (800) 833-1225

Union Station
Restored train station, home to science museum, shops, theaters, and restaurants
30 W. Pershing Rd.
(816) 460-2020

Vietnam Veterans Fountain
W. 42nd St. and Broadway
(816) 842-2299

Worlds of Fun/Oceans of Fun
Theme and water parks
I-435, exit 54 (Parvin Rd.)
(816) 454-4545

SHOPPING

City Market
Shopping district with farmers' market
5th and Walnut Sts.
(816) 842-1271

Country Club Plaza
Upscale specialty shops and department stores
4745 Central St.
(816) 753-0100

Crown Center
Shopping, dining, entertainment, and hotels
2450 Grand Blvd.
(816) 274-8444

Independence Center
Department stores, specialty shops, and eateries
I-70 and M-291, Independence
(816) 795-8600

Oak Park Mall
Department stores and specialty shops
11461 W. 95th St., Overland Park, KS
(913) 888-4400

VISITOR INFORMATION

Kansas City Convention and Visitors Association
1100 Main St., Ste. 2200
Kansas City, MO 64105
(816) 221-5242 or (800) 767-7700
www.visitkc.com

Visitor Information Centers
Union Station
30 W. Pershing Rd.

County Club Plaza
4709 Central St.

City Center Square
1100 Main St., Ste. 2200

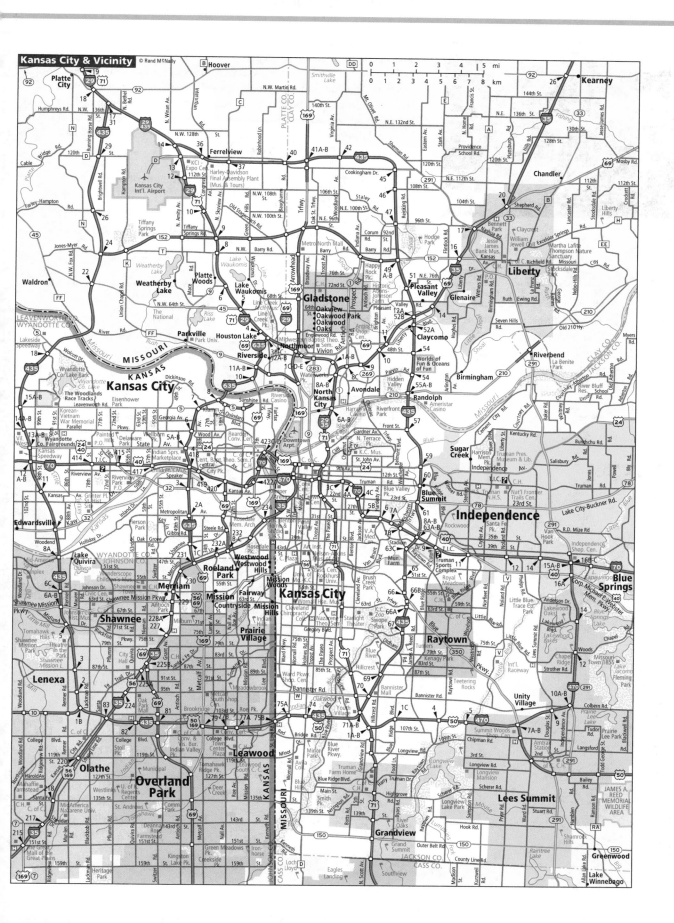

Kansas City & Vicinity

KEY WEST, Florida

Duval Street

In fun and funky Key West, the sunset is a big show in town. Street performers of all kinds gather at Mallory Square for an informal, raucous celebration at the end of each day. The city's many cottages and fine mansions are forever in some stage of restoration. Work on Audubon House in the 1950s started the trend toward preservation; James Audubon's original watercolor paintings are among its treasures. Ernest Hemingway's home now houses a museum and some sixty felines. The Shipwreck Historeum looks back to the wrecking industry. *Tax: 11.5% hotel, 7.5% sales. For local weather, call (305) 295-1324.*

DON'T MISS DRIVE

You haven't seen Key West until you've seen Duval Street, with its architectural and botanical treasures. Take Duval to Mallory Square for the best view of Key West's famed sunsets.

▶ SELECTED ATTRACTIONS

Audubon House & Tropical Gardens
205 Whitehead St.
(305) 294-2116 or (877) 294-2470

Dry Tortugas National Park
19th-century island fort
70 miles west in the Gulf of Mexico
(305) 242-7700

Ernest Hemingway Home and Museum
907 Whitehead St.
(305) 294-1136

Harry S Truman Little White House
Truman's winter White House
111 Front St. in Truman Annex
(305) 294-9911

Key West Aquarium
1 Whitehead St.
(305) 296-2051 or (800) 868-7482

Key West Butterfly and Nature Conservatory
1316 Duval St.
(305) 296-2988 or (800) 839-4647

Key West Lighthouse and Keeper's Quarters Museum
938 Whitehead St.
(305) 294-0012

Key West Museum of Art and History at the Custom House
281 Front St.
(305) 295-6616

Key West Shipwreck Historeum
1 Whitehead St.
(305) 292-8990

Mel Fisher Maritime Museum
200 Greene St.
(305) 294-2633

Southernmost House in the U.S.
1400 Duval St.
(305) 296-3141

Sunset Celebration
Daily festivities with crafts and food
Mallory Square at the foot of Duval St. on the Gulf of Mexico
(305) 292-7700

The Wrecker's Museum
Oldest house in Key West, maritime artifacts
322 Duval St.
(305) 294-9502

▶ SHOPPING

Clinton Square Market
Artisans, crafts, and specialty shops
291 Front St.

Duval Street
Galleries, antiques, and specialty shops
Duval St. between South and Front Sts. in Old Town

▶ VISITOR INFORMATION

Key West Chamber of Commerce
402 Wall St. at Mallory Square
Key West, FL 33040
(305) 294-2587 or (800) 352-5397
www.fla-keys.com

Key West Business Guild
513 Truman Ave.
P.O. Box 1208
Key West, FL 33040
(305) 294-4603 or (800) 535-7797

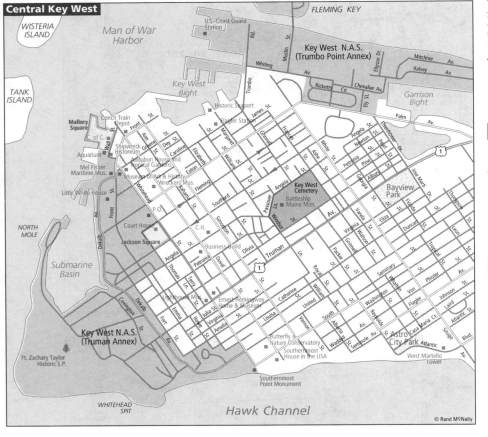

Central Key West

© Rand McNally

LAS VEGAS, Nevada

From one end to the other, the Strip in this legendary desert oasis throbs. Hotels and casinos compete for attention with dancing water displays, imitation cities, and exploding volcanoes. Downtown's Fremont Street, where the older gaming establishments are found, is topped with a multimedia canopy of high-tech effects. Thrill-seekers take the plunge from the top of the 900-foot Stratosphere Tower. At Star Trek: The Experience in the Las Vegas Hilton, visitors can meet a Klingon, check out the History of the Future exhibit, and have their picture taken in a captain's chair. *Tax: 11% hotel for downtown; 9% hotel for the Strip; 7.75% sales. For local weather, call (702) 263-9744 or 811.*

The Las Vegas Strip at night

SELECTED ATTRACTIONS

The Adventuredome at Circus Circus
Amusement park
2880 S. Las Vegas Blvd.
(702) 734-0410

The Auto Collections
3535 Las Vegas Blvd. S.
(702) 731-3311

Fountains of Bellagio
More than 1,000 fountains dance in sync to music
3600 Las Vegas Blvd. S.
(702) 693-7111

Fremont Street Experience
Canopy light show set to music
425 Fremont St.
(702) 678-5600

Guggenheim Hermitage in the Venetian Resort
3355 Las Vegas Blvd. S.
(702) 414-2440

Liberace Museum
1775 E. Tropicana Ave.
(702) 798-5595

Red Rock Canyon National Conservation Area
17 miles west on Charleston Blvd.
(NV 159)
(702) 515-5350

Star Trek: The Experience
Las Vegas Hilton
3000 Paradise Rd.
(702) 697-8700

Stratosphere Casino Hotel and Tower
2000 Las Vegas Blvd S.
(702) 380-7777 or (800) 998-6937

SHOPPING

Desert Passage at the Aladdin
Retails shops, restaurants, and entertainment
3663 Las Vegas Blvd. S.
(888) 800-8284

Fashion Outlets
32100 Las Vegas Blvd. S., I-15 south to exit 1, Primm
(702) 874-1400 or (888) 424-6898

Fashion Show Mall
High-end retailers and weekend fashion shows, on the runway and projected onto the "cloud" screen
3200 Las Vegas Blvd. S.
(702) 369-8382

The Forum Shops at Caesars Palace
Designer boutiques
3500 Las Vegas Blvd. S.
(702) 893-4800

Grand Canal Shoppes at the Venetian
Upscale specialty shops and restaurants
3377 Las Vegas Blvd. S.
(702) 414-4500

Las Vegas Outlet Center
Outlet stores
7400 Las Vegas Blvd. S.
(702) 896-5599

VISITOR INFORMATION

DIVERSION

Take a 31-mile drive east on Boulder Hwy. to see gorgeous Lake Mead, the largest man-made lake in the country. Go another four miles to Boulder City and tour the impressive Hoover Dam, which is 726 ft. high and 600 feet wide at the base.
(702) 293-8906 (Lake Mead),
(702) 494-2517 (Hoover Dam)

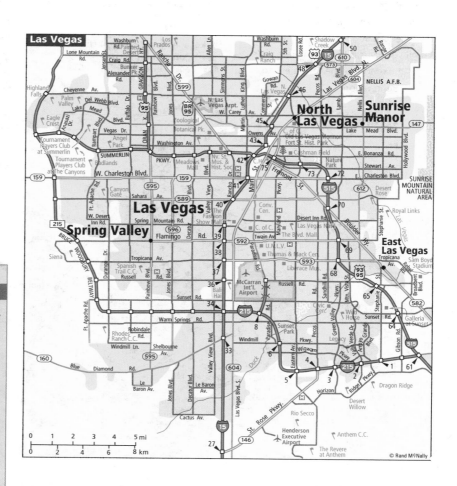

LEXINGTON, Kentucky

Bronze horse statues at Thoroughbred Park

The unofficial capital of the Bluegrass region, Lexington is horse country. The area's most familiar symbol: miles and miles of white plank fencing enclosing equestrian pastures on hundreds of ranches. More than 30 breeds are represented at the Kentucky Horse Park, where exhibits include the International Museum of the Horse and the American Saddlebred Museum. The countryside is also rich with elegant homes such as Ashland, where 19th-century politician and presidential hopeful Henry Clay resided, and the childhood home of Mary Todd Lincoln. *Tax: 13.4% hotel, 6% sales. For local weather, call (859) 253-4444 or (859) 281-8131.*

► SELECTED ATTRACTIONS

Applebee's Park
Minor League Baseball
1200 N. Broadway
(859) 422-7867

Ashland
19th-century home of Henry Clay
120 Sycamore Rd.
(859) 266-8581

► DON'T MISS DRIVE

Old Frankfort Pike, or KY 1681, is one of Kentucky's scenic byways. It has also been designated one of America's Scenic Byways. The rolling hills and vistas found on either side of the road provide testament to the designations.

Aviation Museum of Kentucky
4316 Hangar Dr., off US 60 at the Blue Grass Airport
(859) 231-1219

Headley-Whitney Museum
Art museum
4435 Old Frankfort Pike
(859) 255-6653

Keeneland Race Course
Horse racing
4201 Versailles Rd.
(859) 254-3412 or (800) 456-3412

Kentucky Horse Park and International Museum of the Horse
4089 Iron Works Pkwy.
(859) 233-4303 or (800) 678-8813

Lexington Cemetery
833 W. Main St.
(859) 255-5522

Mary Todd Lincoln House
Childhood home of former First Lady
578 W. Main St.
(859) 233-9999

Shaker Village of Pleasant Hill
3501 Lexington Rd., Harrodsburg
(859) 734-5411 or (800) 734-5611

The Thoroughbred Center
Horse training facility
3380 Paris Pike
(859) 293-1853

Thoroughbred Park
2.5-acre park with life-size bronze horses streaking toward the finish line
Main St. and Midland Ave.

Waveland State Historic Site
Plantation home and 10-acre park
225 Waveland Museum Ln.
off Nicholasville Rd.
(859) 272-3611

The Woodford Reserve Distillery
Bourbon distillery
7855 McCracken Pike, Versailles
(859) 879-1812

► SHOPPING

Clay Avenue Shops
Antiques and shops on historic street
Clay Ave. off E. Main St.

Fayette Mall
Department stores and specialty shops
3401 Nicholasville Rd.
(859) 272-3493 or (800) 972-9874

Heritage Antiques
Antiques and collectibles
380 E. Main St.
(859) 253-1035

Turfland Mall
Department and retail stores
2033 Harrodsburg Rd.
(859) 276-4411

Victorian Square
Specialty shops in renovated Victorian block
401 W. Main St.
(859) 252-7575

► VISITOR INFORMATION

Lexington Convention and Visitors Bureau
301 E. Vine St.
Lexington, KY 40507
(859) 233-7299 or (800) 845-3959
www.visitlex.com

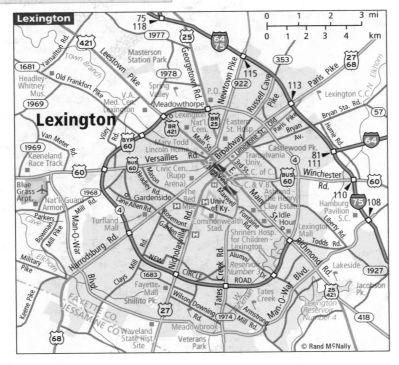

DIVERSION

Spend an afternoon touring the bluegrass countryside and passing horse farms. Self-drive tour directions are available. (800) 845-3959

LITTLE ROCK, Arkansas

Fueled by development of the William J. Clinton Presidential Center and Park, Arkansas's capital city is undergoing a downtown renaissance. The presidential library and museum houses millions of documents, photographs, and artifacts from the Clinton administration. The Center has spurred growth in the River Market district, now the city's hot spot for restaurants, shops, and entertainment. Elsewhere, history buffs can tour the Old State House Museum and the present state capitol. *Tax: 11.5% hotel, 7.5% sales, 2% prepared food. For local weather, call (501) 371-7777 or (501) 834-0308.*

River Market District

▶ SELECTED ATTRACTIONS

Aerospace Education Center and IMAX Theater
3301 E. Roosevelt Rd.
(501) 376-4232

Arkansas Arts Center
Home to the Arkansas Museum of Art, Children's Theatre, and Museum School
501 E. 9th St. in MacArthur Park
(501) 372-4000

Arkansas State Capitol
1 Capitol Mall
(501) 682-5080

Central High School National Historic Site
History of the 1957 desegregation crisis
2125 Daisy L. Gatson Bates Dr.
(501) 374-1957

Empress of Little Rock
Elaborate Gothic Queen Anne-style bed-and-breakfast with historic tours
2120 S. Louisiana
(501) 374-7966

Historic Arkansas Museum
200 E. 3rd St.
(501) 324-9351

Little Rock Zoo
1 Jonesboro Dr.
(501) 666-2406

MacArthur Museum of Arkansas Military History
503 E. 9th St. in MacArthur Park
(501) 376-4602

Museum of Discovery
Science, history, and anthropology
500 President Clinton Ave.
(501) 396-7050 or (800) 880-6475

Old State House Museum
Arkansas's first state capitol building
300 W. Markham St.
(501) 324-9685

Quapaw Quarter
Historic district
Bounded by Arkansas River, the old Rock Island Railroad tracks, Fourche Creek, and Central High School
(501) 371-0075

William Jefferson Clinton Presidential Center and Park
Library and school of public affairs
1200 E. President Clinton Ave., River Market District
(501) 374-4242

▶ SHOPPING

Bowman Curve/West Markham
Shops and restaurants
W. Markham St. and Bowman Rd.

Kavanaugh Boulevard–The Heights
Boutiques and gift shops in historic area
Between 3000 block of Markham St. and University Ave.

Lakewood Village
Specialty shops, restaurants, and theaters
2800 Lakewood Village Dr., McCain Blvd. and Justin Matthews Dr., North Little Rock
(501) 758-3080

McCain Mall
McCain Blvd. and US 67,
North Little Rock
(501) 758-6340

River Market District
Farmers' market and enclosed market hall
400 President Clinton Ave.
(501) 375-2552

▶ VISITOR INFORMATION

Little Rock Convention and Visitors Bureau
Robinson Center, 426 W. Markham St.
Little Rock, AR 72203
(501) 376-4781 or (800) 844-4781
www.littlerock.com

Little Rock Visitor Information Center
Curran Hall, 615 E. Capitol Ave.
(501) 370-3290 or (877) 220-2568

▶ DIVERSION

Experience the realities of global life in a variety of economically disadvantaged "villages" at Heifer Ranch and Global Village near Perryville. It's a learning center for sustainable solutions to global problems. AR 10 west to AR 9 north to Perryville. (800) 422-0474 or (501) 889-5124

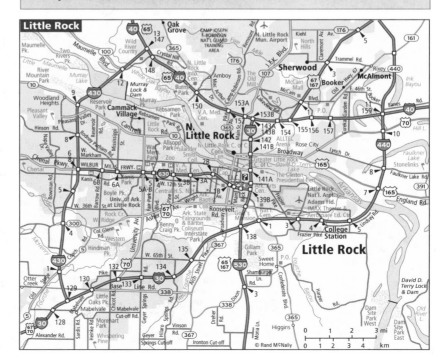

LOS ANGELES, California

Movie premiere in Hollywood

The city that sprawls from the ocean through valleys to mountain foothills is really a vast amalgamation of much smaller towns, including West Hollywood, Burbank, and Beverly Hills —home to the stars. Universal Studios and Warner Bros. offer tours of the sets and lots where feature films and television shows are made. High culture is on view at the imposing Getty Center. Kids old and young find all that hearts desire at the granddaddies of American theme parks—Disneyland and Knott's Berry Farm. *Tax: 14% hotel, 8.25% sales for L.A. County; 7.75% for Orange County. For local weather, call (805) 988-6610.*

▶ DON'T MISS DRIVE

Ride the crest of the Santa Monica Mountains along the curves of Mulholland Drive for spectacular views, day or night. On one side is the San Fernando Valley; on the other side lies Hollywood. On a clear day, you can see as far as the Pacific Ocean.

▶ SELECTED ATTRACTIONS

Aquarium of the Pacific
At the south end of I-710 at Shoreline Dr., Long Beach
(562) 590-3100

California Science Center
Science exhibits and IMAX theater in Exposition Park
700 State Dr.
(323) 724-3623

Disneyland Resort
Original Disneyland, California Adventure, and Downtown Disney
1313 S. Harbor Blvd., Anaheim
(714) 781-4565

El Pueblo de Los Angeles
Historic monument at Olvera St.
125 Paseo de la Plaza
(213) 485-8372

Getty Center
Art museum and architectural wonder
1200 Getty Center Dr. near I-405 and Sunset Blvd.
(310) 440-7300

Grauman's Chinese Theatre
Celebrity handprints and footprints
6925 Hollywood Blvd.
(323) 464-8111

Hollywood Walk of Fame
Sidewalk of entertainment legends' names
Hollywood Blvd. from Gower to La Brea, and Vine St. from Yucca to Sunset
(323) 469-8311

Hollywood Wax Museum
6767 Hollywood Blvd.
(323) 462-8860

Knott's Berry Farm
Theme park
8039 Beach Blvd., Buena Park
(714) 220-5200

continued on page 60

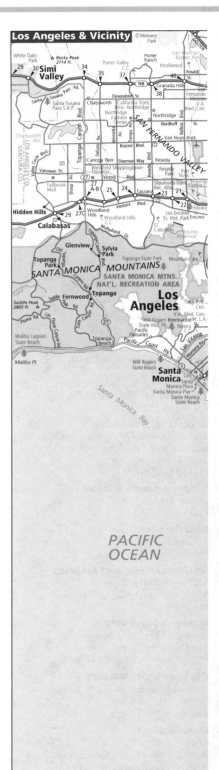

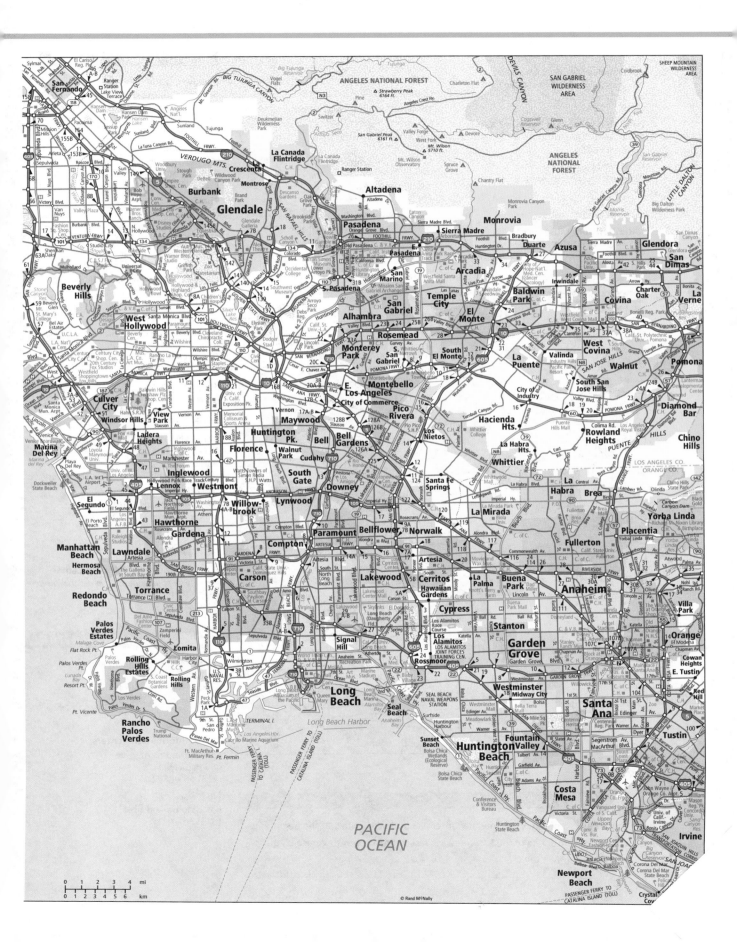

PACIFIC
OCEAN

Los Angeles attractions continued

Los Angeles Maritime Museum
6th St. and Harbor Blvd. on Berth 84,
San Pedro
(310) 548-7618

Los Angeles Zoo and Botanical Gardens
5333 Zoo Dr. in Griffith Park
(323) 644-4200

Museum of Tolerance
*Exhibits on racism, prejudice, and
the Holocaust*
9786 W. Pico Blvd.
(310) 553-8403

**Natural History Museum of
Los Angeles County**
900 Exposition Blvd. in Exposition Park
(213) 763-3466

Santa Monica Pier
Colorado Ave. at the Pacific Ocean,
Santa Monica
(310) 458-8900

Universal Studios Hollywood
Movie lot and theme park
Off US 101, Universal City
(800) 864-8377

Walt Disney Concert Hall
Home of the Los Angeles Philharmonic
111 S. Grand Ave.
(213) 972-7211

Warner Bros. Studio Tour
3400 W. Riverside Dr., Burbank
(818) 977-8687

SHOPPING

Beverly Center
Shops, department stores, and restaurants
8500 Beverly Blvd. between La Cienega and
San Vicente Blvds.
(310) 854-0071

Farmers Market
Restaurants, cafés, and produce
6333 W. 3rd St. at Fairfax Ave.
(323) 933-9211

The Grove
Stores, restaurants, theaters, and fountains
189 The Grove Dr.
(323) 900-8080 or (888) 315-8883

Hollywood & Highland Center
*Upscale shops, restaurants, entertainment, and
the Kodak Theatre (home of the Oscars)*
6801 Hollywood Blvd.
(323) 817-0220

Paseo Colorado
*Urban village of shops, restaurants, and
theaters along the Rose Parade route*
280 E. Colorado Blvd., Pasadena
(626) 795-8891

Rodeo Drive
Upscale boutiques
Wilshire Dr. to Santa Monica Blvd.,
Beverly Hills

Universal CityWalk
*Pedestrian promenade, shopping,
entertainment, and dining*
100 Universal City Plaza, Universal City
(818) 622-4455

Westfield Century City
*Department stores, specialty shops,
and restaurants*
10250 Santa Monica Blvd.
(310) 277-3898

Westside Pavillion Shopping Center
Specialty shops, restaurants, and department stores
10800 W. Pico Blvd.
(310) 474-6255

VISITOR INFORMATION

**LA INC. The Convention and
Visitors Bureau**
333 S. Hope St., 18th Floor
Los Angeles, CA 90071
(213) 624-7300 or (800) 228-2452
www.lacvb.com

Visitor Information Centers
Downtown Los Angeles
685 Figueroa St.
(213) 689-8822

Hollywood
6801 Hollywood Blvd.
(323) 467-6412

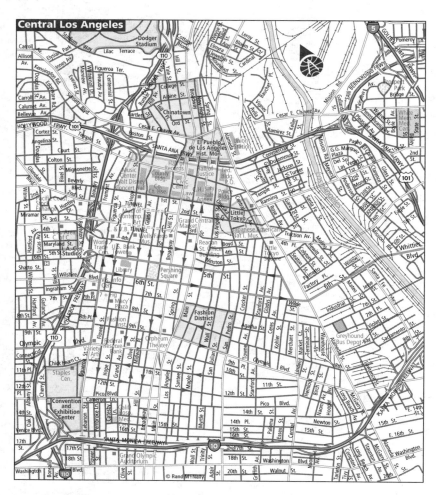

Central Los Angeles

DIVERSION

Visit Venice, a beach resort modeled after its namesake in Italy at the beginning of the last century. Take the I-10 freeway west to I-405 south to Venice Blvd., then turn south.

LOUISVILLE, Kentucky

Recognized worldwide for the annual Kentucky Derby at Churchill Downs, this Ohio River port is also a respected center for theater and the arts. The Actors Theatre is celebrated for its annual Humana Festival of new plays, while exhibits at the Speed Art Museum survey art history from Egyptian antiquities to the present. The Kentucky Derby Museum is the only one dedicated to a single sporting event. The city's latest addition, the Muhammad Ali Center, relates the story of boxing's greatest modern legend while promoting humanitarian ideals. *Tax: 15.01% hotel, 6% sales. For local weather, call (502) 968-6025.*

*Downtown
Louisville*

▶ SELECTED ATTRACTIONS

Actors Theatre of Louisville
Regional theater
316 W. Main St.
(502) 584-1205

American Printing House for the Blind
Plant tours and museum
1839 Frankfort Ave.
(502) 895-2405 or (800) 223-1839

Churchill Downs
Home of the Kentucky Derby
700 Central Ave.
(502) 636-4400 or (800) 283-3729

Farmington Historic House Museum
Early 19th-century home
3033 Bardstown Rd.
(502) 452-9920

Gheens Science Hall and Rauch Planetarium
North end of Belknap Campus, University of Louisville
(502) 852-6664

Glassworks
Galleries, glassblowing classes, and tours
815 W. Market St.
(502) 584-4510

The Kentucky Center
Theater and music
501 W. Main St.
(502) 562-0100

Kentucky Center for African-American Heritage
315 Guthrie Green
(502) 583-4100

Kentucky Derby Museum
704 Central Ave.
(502) 637-1111

Historic Locust Grove
1790 Georgian mansion on the Lewis and Clark National Historic Trail
561 Blankenbaker Ln.
(502) 897-9845

Louisville Slugger Museum
800 W. Main St.
(877) 775-8443 or (502) 588-7228

Louisville Zoo
1100 Trevilian Way
(502) 459-2181

Muhammad Ali Center
Immersive multimedia self-discovery exhibits
144 N. 6th St.
(502) 584-9254

Six Flags Kentucky Kingdom
937 Phillips Ln.
(800) 727-3267

The Speed Art Museum
2035 S. 3rd St.
(502) 634-2700

Stage One: The Louisville Children's Theatre
501 W. Main St.
(502) 584-7777

Waterfront Park
Family water park with events and concerts
129 E. River Rd.
(502) 574-3768

Whitehall
Antebellum home with Florentine garden
3110 Lexington Rd.
(502) 897-2944

▶ SHOPPING

Bardstown Road
Antique shops, boutiques, and restaurants
Bardstown Rd. east from downtown to Douglas Blvd. (Baxter Ave. in downtown)
(888) 568-4784

Mall St. Matthews
Department and specialty stores
5000 Shelbyville Rd.
(502) 893-0311

Summit Lifestyle Center
Shops and restaurants in Mediterranean setting
9401 Brownsboro Rd.
(502) 425-3441

▶ VISITOR INFORMATION

Greater Louisville Convention and Visitors Bureau
401 W. Main St., Ste. 2300
Louisville, KY 40202
(502) 584-2121 or (888) 568-4784
www.gotolouisville.com

Visitor Information Center
301 S. 4th Ave.
(502) 584-2121 or (888) 568-4784

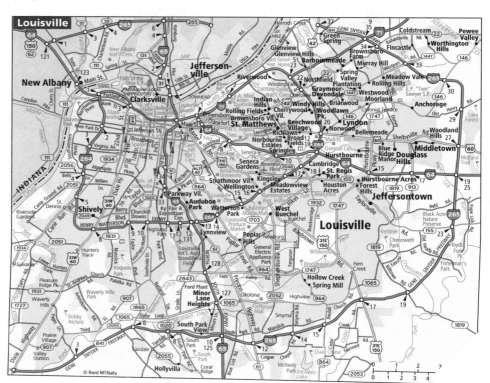

MEMPHIS, Tennessee

Graceland

Memphis means just two things in the popular mind: barbeque and roots music. The Memphis Rock 'n' Soul Museum traces the city's seminal influence on blues, country, gospel, rock and roll, and other musical genres. Historic recording studios, like the Stax Museum of American Soul Music, offer tours, as does Graceland, home of the oft-imitated, never-equaled king of rock and roll. More than 30 clubs and shops along Beale Street jump with the beat. Come springtime, the Memphis in May über-festival opens with the Beale Street Music Festival and closes with the World Championship Barbeque Cooking Contest. *Tax: 15.95% hotel, 9.25% sales. For local weather, call (901) 544-0399.*

▶ SELECTED ATTRACTIONS

Beale Street Entertainment District
Nightclubs, restaurants, and shopping
203 Beale St.
(901) 526-0110

The Children's Museum of Memphis
2525 Central Ave.
(901) 458-2678

Dixon Gallery and Gardens
Impressionist and post-Impressionist art and gardens
4339 Park Ave.
(901) 761-5250

Graceland
Home of Elvis Presley
3734 Elvis Presley Blvd.
(901) 332-3322 or (800) 238-2000

Libertyland
Theme park
940 Early Maxwell Blvd.
(901) 274-1776

Memphis Botanic Garden
750 Cherry Rd. in Audubon Park
(901) 576-4100

Memphis Brooks Museum of Art
1934 Poplar Ave. in Overton Park
(901) 544-6200

Memphis Pink Palace Museum
Regional history museum, Sharpe Planetarium, and IMAX theater
3050 Central Ave.
(901) 320-6320

Memphis Riverboats, Inc.
Riverboat cruise
Tickets and boat at 45 Riverside Dr.
(901) 527-2628 or (800) 221-6197

Memphis Rock 'n' Soul Museum
191 Beale St.
(901) 205-2533

Memphis Zoo
2000 Prentiss Pl.
(901) 276-9453

Mud Island River Park
125 N. Front St.
(901) 576-7241 or (800) 507-6507

National Civil Rights Museum
450 Mulberry St.
(901) 521-9699

The Peabody Ducks
Famous ducks that parade through the hotel lobby twice daily
Peabody Memphis Hotel, 149 Union Ave.
(901) 529-4000 or (800) 732-2639

Stax Museum of American Soul Music
926 E. McLemore Ave.
(901) 946-2535

▶ SHOPPING

Palladio International Antique Market
Unique antiques and collectibles
2169 Central Ave.
(901) 276-3808

Peabody Place
Retail shops, movie theaters, and restaurants
Peabody Pl. at 3rd St.
(901) 261-7529

South Main Arts District
Galleries and specialty shops
Bounded by Beale St., the Mississippi River, 4th St., and Crump Blvd.
(901) 578-7262

▶ VISITOR INFORMATION

Memphis Convention and Visitors Bureau
47 Union Ave., Memphis, TN 38103
(901) 543-5300 or (800) 873-6282
www.memphistravel.com

Memphis/Shelby County Visitors Center
12036 Arlington Trail (exits 24-25 on I-40)
(901) 543-5333

Tennessee State Welcome Center
119 N. Riverside Dr.

Memphis Visitor Center
3205 Elvis Presley Blvd.

▶ DON'T MISS DRIVE

The heart and soul of Memphis is Beale Street, where music fills the air. You'll find everything from blues, pop, and rock to fusion jazz and reggae. Note that Beale Street is closed to cars Thursday-Sunday between 2nd St. and 4th St.

MEXICO CITY, Distrito Federal, Mexico

As one of the world's largest cities, Mexico City is fast, loud, and in a continuous state of flux. Unlimited opportunities for exploration begin in the old city center, where the Palacio National is adorned with murals by Diego Rivera, and the Templo Mayor archaeological site reveals life in the time of the ancient Aztecs. Major museums dot the 1,600-acre green space known as Bosque de Chapultepec, including the exceptional Museo Nacional de Antropologia. The Zona Rosa area maintains its popularity for finer shops, galleries, restaurants and nightspots. And everyone goes to the Xochimilco neighborhood, home of many canals and gardens, to float amidst the flowers. *Tax: 17% hotel, 15% value-added sales tax is usually included in the retail price.*

Palace of Fine Arts

▶ SELECTED ATTRACTIONS

**Chapultepec Park
(Bosque de Chapultepec)**
World's largest city park
Av. Constituyentes 1a Sección,
San Miguel Chapultepec

**Frida Kahlo Museum
(Museo de Frida Kahlo)**
Londres 247 at Allende,
El Carmen Coyoacán
011-52-55-5554-5999*

**National Museum of Anthropology
(Museo Nacional de Antropología)**
Paseo de la Reforma at Gandhi
011-52-55-5553-6386*

National Palace (Palacio Nacional)
Murals by Diego Rivera
Plaza de la Constitución, Zocalo
011-52-55-9158-1252 or
011-52-55-9158-1256*

**Palace of Fine Arts
(Palacio de Bellas Artes)**
Home of the Folkloric Ballet of Mexico
Central Lázaro Cárdenas at Av. Juárez
011-52-55-5512-2593*

**Rufino Tamayo Museum
(Museo Rufino Tamayo)**
Tamayo's contemporary paintings
Av. Reforma and Gandhi, Chapultepec Park
011-52-55-5286-6519*

Templo Mayor
Ancient Aztec city's main ceremonial pyramid
Seminario 8 at the Zócalo
011-52-55-5542-4943*

Turibus
Double-decker tour bus that stops at selected attractions
Tickets available on board; check with your hotel front desk for pick-up locations

Xochimilco
Floating gardens and boat rides
Los Embarcaderos (The Piers)
011-52-55-5676-0810*

▶ SHOPPING

Bazaar Sabado
Weekly artisan market
Plaza San Jacinto, San Angel

Polanco
Upscale shopping and dining
Av. Presidente Masaryk at
Arquimedes, Polanco

Zócalo
UNESCO World Heritage site; shops and cafés
Centro Histórico

Zona Rosa
Boutiques and lively entertainment area
Calle Amberes at Paseo de la Reforma

▶ VISITOR INFORMATION

Mexico City Tourist Office
Nuevo León 56, 4th floor
Colonia Condesa 06100
Mexico City, D.F., Mexico
011-52-55-5212-0260 or (800) 482-9832
www.mexicocity.gob.mx

Mexico Tourism Board (U.S.)
(800) 446-3942
www.visitmexico.com

DON'T MISS DRIVE

Built by Emperor Maximilian of Hapsburg, the elegance of Paseo de la Reforma is often compared to Les Champs-Elysées in Paris. A series of parks with world-class sculptures complement the boulevard that passes through the center of the city.

*Number listed may or may not have an English-speaking person available.

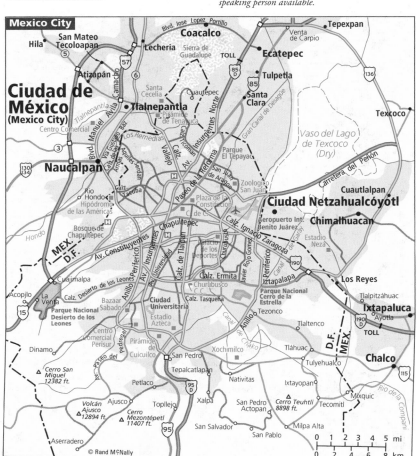

MIAMI, Florida

Miami skyline and marina

This busy seaport supports a huge fleet of cruise ships, but there's plenty to explore on land as well—like the Little Havana neighborhood's spicy foods, hot Latin music, and hand-embroidered guayabera shirts. Parrot Jungle Island hosts a one-ton crocodile dubbed "Crocosaurus" plus thousands of monkeys, reptiles, and birds. At its sparkling home, the Miami Children's Museum has 12 galleries of bilingual exhibits to stimulate young imaginations. *Tax: 13% hotel, 7% sales. For local weather, call (305) 229-4550.*

▶ SELECTED ATTRACTIONS

Art Deco District
1001 Ocean Dr. (Welcome Center)
(305) 672-2014

Bass Museum of Art
2121 Park Ave.
(305) 673-7530

Everglades National Park
40001 FL 9336, Homestead
(305) 242-7700

Fairchild Tropical Botanic Garden
10901 Old Cutler Rd., Coral Gables
(305) 667-1651

Little Havana District
8th St. from south of downtown to
SW 27th Ave.
(305) 644-8888

Miami Art Museum
101 W. Flagler St.
(305) 375-3000

Miami Children's Museum
980 MacArthur Causeway
(305) 373-5437

Miami Seaquarium
Exhibits, dolphin shows, and reef aquarium
4400 Rickenbacker Causeway
(305) 361-5705

Parrot Jungle Island
Gardens, exotic animals, shows, and exhibits
MacArthur Causeway (I-395) in downtown
Miami on Watson Island
(305) 400-7000

Vizcaya Museum and Gardens
Italian Renaissance-style villa
3251 S. Miami Ave.
(305) 250-9133

▶ SHOPPING

Bal Harbour Shops
Upscale shops in an open-air setting
9700 Collins Ave., Bal Harbour
(305) 866-0311

Bayside Marketplace
Shopping, open-air market, waterfront dining
401 Biscayne Blvd.
(305) 577-3344

Coco Walk
Retail shops and entertainment
3015 Grand Ave., Coconut Grove
(305) 444-0777

Downtown Miami Shopping District
*Department stores, specialty shops,
and restaurants*
Biscayne Blvd. to 2nd Ave. W., SE 1st St. to
NE 3rd St.
(305) 379-7070 or (305) 379-5445

▶ VISITOR INFORMATION

**Greater Miami Convention and
Visitors Bureau**
701 Brickell Ave., Ste. 2700
Miami, FL 33131
(305) 539-3000 or (800) 933-8448
www.gmcvb.com

MILWAUKEE, Wisconsin

Only one giant brewery and a handful of its micro-cousins remain, but Milwaukee will always be known for beer. The Miller Brewing Company offers daily tours of its huge facility, while a tour of the Pabst Mansion evokes the glory years of the city's most famous industry. Along the lakefront, the Henry Maier Festival Grounds host a series of annual ethnic festivals. An extraordinary wing-like moving sculpture above the Quaddracci Pavilion has brought worldwide cultural attention to the Milwaukee Art Museum. *Tax: 14.6% hotel, 5.6% sales. For local weather, call (414) 936-1212.*

Milwaukee Art Museum

SELECTED ATTRACTIONS

The Basilica of St. Josaphat
Historic church
2333 S. 6th St.
(414) 645-5623

Betty Brinn Children's Museum
929 E. Wisconsin Ave.
(414) 390-5437

Boerner Botanical Gardens
9400 Boerner Dr. in Whitnall Park,
Hales Corners
(414) 525-5600

The Captain Frederick Pabst Mansion
Flemish Renaissance Revival-style home
2000 W. Wisconsin Ave.
(414) 931-0808

Henry Maier Festival Grounds
200 N. Harbor Dr.
(414) 273-2680

Miller Brewing Company
Free tours
4251 W. State St.
(414) 931-2337

Milwaukee Art Museum
700 N. Art Museum Dr.
(414) 224-3200

Milwaukee County Historical Society
910 N. Old World 3rd St.
(414) 273-8288

Milwaukee Public Museum
800 W. Wells St.
(414) 278-2702

Mitchell Park Horticultural Conservatory
(The Domes)
524 S. Layton Blvd.
(414) 649-9800

RiverWalk
Eclectic shops, restaurants, nightlife, and art
Runs 13 blocks along the Milwaukee River
(800) 554-1448

SHOPPING

Brady Street
Unique specialty shops, bars, and restaurants
From Van Buren St. to N. Prospect Ave.
(414) 744-5156

Historic Third Ward
Entertainment district in 1890s neighborhood
Bounded by Milwaukee River, St. Paul Ave., and Jackson St.
(414) 273-1173

Old World Third Street
Shops and restaurants with Wisconsin favorites
From Wisconsin to Juneau Ave.
(800) 554-1448

VISITOR INFORMATION

Greater Milwaukee Convention and Visitors Bureau
648 N. Plankinton Ave.
Milwaukee, WI 53203
(414) 273-7222 or (800) 554-1448
www.visitmilwaukee.org

MINNEAPOLIS/SAINT PAUL, Minnesota

Minneapolis Sculpture Garden at Walker Art Center

The Twin Cities complement and complete each other with their individual personalities. In Minneapolis—all skyscrapers and modernity—the visually compelling Weisman Art Museum is noted for works by 20th-century American painters. After undertaking a major expansion, the Walker Art Center, ranked among the finest of its kind, reopened in 2005. On Hennepin Avenue, the latest Broadway productions attract theatergoers. *Tax: 13.5% hotel, 10.15% restaurant, 12.65% downtown liquor tax, 6.5% state sales tax (excluding clothing), 7% downtown state and city sales tax. For local weather, call (763) 512-1111.*

Saint Paul, more traditional in its outlook, is the seat of Minnesota state government. Tours of the impressive capitol building include a visit to the golden horses overlooking the main steps. The Science Museum of Minnesota has tons of hands-on activities and an extensive collection of artifacts and curiosities. Shoppers nationwide are drawn to the Twin Cities by the lure of the massive Mall of America in nearby Bloomington. *Tax: 13% hotel, 7% sales. For local weather, call (763) 512-1111.*

▶ SELECTED ATTRACTIONS

MINNEAPOLIS

American Swedish Institute
2600 Park Ave.
(612) 871-4907

The Bakken
Library and electrical science museum
3537 Zenith Ave. S.
(612) 926-3878

Bell Museum of Natural History
Corner of University and 17th Aves. SE at the University of Minnesota
(612) 624-7083

Frederick R. Weisman Art Museum
333 E. River Rd. at the University of Minnesota
(612) 625-9494

Mill City Museum
Hands-on exhibits about milling industry
704 S. 2nd St.
(612) 341-7555

Milwaukee Road Depot
Indoor water park and ice rink
5th and Washington Aves. S.
(612) 339-2253

Minneapolis Institute of Arts
2400 3rd Ave. S.
(612) 870-3131

Minneapolis Sculpture Garden
726 Vineland Pl.
(612) 375-7600

Theater District on Hennepin Ave.
Historic vaudeville theaters, currently home to Broadway productions and concerts
Orpheum Theatre: 910 Hennepin Ave.
Pantages Theater: 710 Hennepin Ave.
State Theater: 805 Hennepin Ave.
(651) 989-5151(Ticketmaster) or
(612) 339-7007 (box office)

Walker Art Center
1750 Hennepin Ave.
(612) 375-7600

▶ SHOPPING

MINNEAPOLIS

Gaviidae Common and City Center
Boutiques, restaurants, and trendy shops
651 Nicollet Mall
(612) 372-1222

Southdale Shopping Center
Retail stores, movie theaters, and restaurants
6601 France Ave., Edina
(952) 925-7885

▶ DON'T MISS DRIVE

No one should leave Saint Paul without taking a drive along Summit Avenue, the longest remaining stretch of residential Victorian architecture in the United States, which includes the Governor's Mansion.

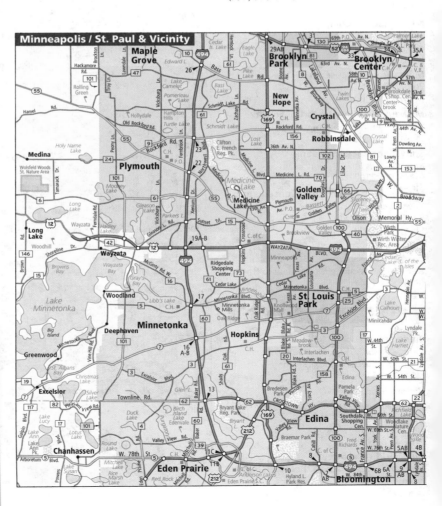

Minneapolis / St. Paul & Vicinity

SELECTED ATTRACTIONS

SAINT PAUL

Alexander Ramsey House
Restored Victorian home of first territorial governor
265 S. Exchange St.
(651) 296-0100

Como Zoo and Marjorie McNeely Conservatory
Lexington Pkwy. at Horton Ave.
(651) 487-8200

Landmark Center
Arts center in restored federal courthouse
75 W. 5th St.
(651) 292-3225

Minnesota History Center
Exhibits, collection, and library of Minnesota's history
345 W. Kellogg Blvd.
(651) 296-6126 or (800) 657-3773

Minnesota Museum of American Art
50 W. Kellogg Blvd. at Market St.
(651) 266-1030

Minnesota State Capitol
75 Constitution Ave.
(651) 296-2881

Ordway Center for the Performing Arts
345 Washington St.
(651) 224-4222

Padelford Packet Boat Co.
Sternwheel riverboat cruises
Dr. Justus Ohage Blvd. on Harriet Island
(651) 227-1100

Saint Paul Public Library
Restored Italian Renaissance building
90 W. 4th St.
(651) 266-7000

Science Museum of Minnesota
120 W. Kellogg Blvd.
(651) 221-9444

SHOPPING

SAINT PAUL

District del Sol
Specialty supermarkets, shops, and art
Saint Paul's west side
(651) 222-6347

Grand Avenue
26 blocks of restaurants and specialty boutiques
Parallels Summit Avenue from the Mississippi River to downtown area
(651) 699-0029

Mall of America
Nation's largest mall and entertainment complex with stores, restaurants, theme park
I-494 and MN 77, Bloomington
(952) 883-8800 or (800) 879-3555

DIVERSION

Take flight for a day to the Hiawatha Valley area in Red Wing. Scenic bluffs await. Located 50 miles southeast of Saint Paul on US 61.
(651) 385-5934 or (800) 498-3444

7th Avenue Antiques Mall
Antiques and collectibles
2563 7th Ave. E., North Saint Paul
(651) 773-7001

VISITOR INFORMATION

Greater Minneapolis Convention & Visitors Association
250 Marquette Ave. S., Ste. 1300
Minneapolis, MN 55401
(612) 767-8000 or (888) 676-6757
www.minneapolis.org

Saint Paul Convention and Visitors Bureau
175 W. Kellogg Blvd., Ste. 502
Saint Paul, MN 55102
(651) 265-4900 or (800) 627-6101
www.visitsaintpaul.com

Minneapolis Visitor Information Center
1301 2nd Ave. S. (in the Minneapolis Convention Center)
(612) 335-6000 or (888) 676-6757

Marjorie McNeely Conservatory, Saint Paul

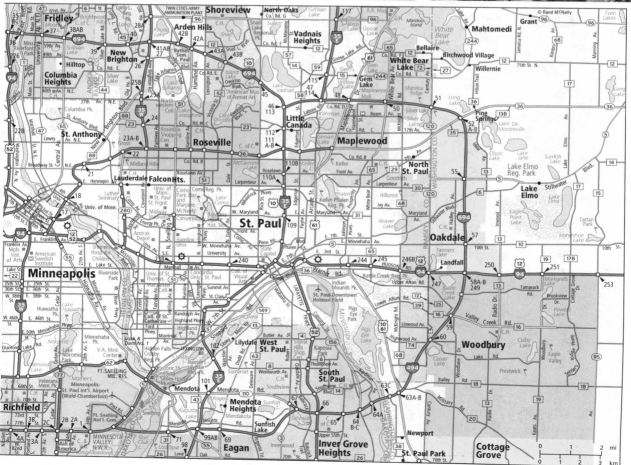

MOBILE, Alabama

*Bragg-
Mitchell
Mansion*

Brimming with historic homes and neighborhoods, Mobile has managed to preserve much of its storied past, even as it has developed into a major industrial seaport. Flowers bloom year-round at the Bellingrath Gardens and Home in nearby Theodore, where 65 acres of plantings and aquatic features surround a mansion filled with decorative arts. Grand antebellum Bragg-Mitchell Mansion is celebrated for its period furnishings and décor. The contributions of black Mobilians to local and national history are recalled at the National African-American Archives Museum. Visitors can tour two World War II-era ships at the USS *Alabama* Battleship Memorial Park. *Tax: 14% hotel, 9% restaurant sales, 9% retail sales. For local weather, call (251) 478-6666.*

DIVERSION

Explore the wonders of the nation's second-largest delta system at the Five Rivers Delta Resource Center off the Mobile Bay Causeway in Spanish Fort, Ala. Visit the museum and exhibits or take a ride in an airboat, canoe, or kayak. (251) 625-0814

▶ SELECTED ATTRACTIONS

Bellingrath Gardens and Home
Historic home and gardens
12401 Bellingrath Gardens Rd., Theodore
(251) 973-2217

Bragg-Mitchell Mansion
Antebellum mansion and museum
1906 Springhill Ave.
(251) 471-6364

Fort Condé Museum
Reconstructed fort and 18th-century living history museum
150 S. Royal St.
(251) 208-7569

Gulf Coast Explorium Science Center
Interactive exhibits and IMAX theater
65 Government St.
(251) 208-6873

Mobile Botanical Gardens
5151 Museum Dr., Langan Park
(251) 342-0555

Mobile Museum of Art
4850 Museum Dr., Langan Park
(251) 208-5200

National African-American Archives Museum
564 Dr. Martin Luther King Jr. Ave.
(251) 433-8511

Oakleigh Historic Complex
Antebellum mansion and two houses
300 Oakleigh Pl.
(251) 432-6161

Richards-DAR House Museum
19th-century Italianate home
256 N. Joachim St.
(251) 208-7320

USS *Alabama* Battleship Memorial Park and Pavilion
Vintage battleship, submarine, and aircraft
2703 Battleship Pkwy.
(251) 433-2703

▶ SHOPPING

Antiques at the Loop
Antiques and collectibles
2103 Airport Blvd.
(251) 476-0309

Cotton City Antique Mall
Antiques and collectibles
2012 Airport Blvd.
(251) 479-9747

Colonial Mall Bel Air
Department stores and specialty shops
Airport Blvd. at I-65
(251) 478-1893

▶ VISITOR INFORMATION

Mobile Bay Convention and Visitors Bureau
1 S. Water St., Mobile, AL 36602
(251) 208-2000 or (800) 566-2453
www.mobile.org

Fort Condé Welcome Center
150 S. Royal St.
(251) 208-7989

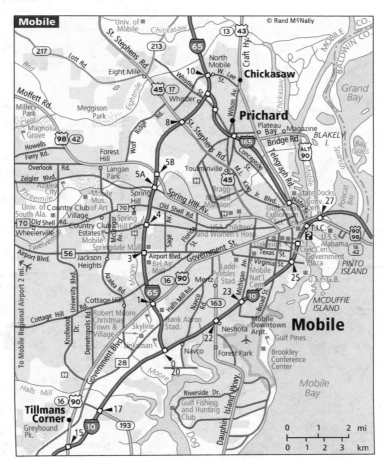

MONTRÉAL, Québec, Canada

This continent's most Continental city, Montréal boasts a deep connection with its French forebears. A state-of-the-art multimedia presentation enhances the already awe-inspiring interior of Notre Dame Basilica. In Old Montréal (Vieux Montréal), specialized street lighting adds charm to the narrow lanes of the city's historic center. *Tax: 3% room tax, 7% tax on federal goods and services, and 6% Québec sales tax applied on room rate and other tax. For local weather, call (514) 283-4006 or (514) 283-3010.*

Montréal skyline from Jean-Drapeau Park

▶ SELECTED ATTRACTIONS

Biodome
4777 av. Pierre-de-Coubertin
(514) 868-3000

Jean-Drapeau Park
Biosphere, casino games, and amusement park
Île Ste-Hélène
(514) 872-6120

Montréal Olympic Park
4141 av. Pierre-de-Coubertin
(514) 252-4737 or (877) 997-0919

Mount Royal Park and St. Joseph's Oratory
Designed by Frederick Law Olmsted
Mount Royal neighborhood
(514) 843-8240

Notre-Dame Basilica
110, rue Notre-Dame Ouest in
Old Montreal
(514) 842-2925

Old Montréal (Vieux Montréal)
Bounded approximately by rue McGill, rue Saint-Antoine, rue Berri, and the St. Lawrence River

Old Port of Montréal (Vieux-Port)
333 rue de la Commune Ouest between the St-Laurent River and Old Montreal
(514) 496-7678 or (800) 971-7678

Place Jacques-Cartier
Jugglers, artists, and restaurants
On Place Jacques-Cartier between rue Notre-Dame and rue Saint Paul
(877) 266-5687

▶ SHOPPING

Atwater Market
Farmers' market and specialty boutiques
138, av. Atwater
(514) 937-7754

Les Cours Mont-Royal
Upscale shops and boutiques
1455, rue Peel
(514) 842-7777

Les Promenades de la Cathedrale
Specialty shops
625 rue Ste-Catherine Ouest next to McGill Metro Station
(514) 849-9925

Sainte-Catherine and Crescent Street
Boutiques and upscale shopping
Between rue Guy and Berri

The Underground City
Interconnected downtown malls
Rue Ste-Catherine at McGill

▶ VISITOR INFORMATION

Tourisme Montréal
1001 Square-Dorchester St.
Montréal, QC H3B 1G2 Canada
(514) 873-2015 or (877) 266-5687
www.tourisme-montreal.org

Tourist Information Centre of Old Montreal
174 rue Notre-Dame Est
(514) 873-2015 or (877) 266-5687

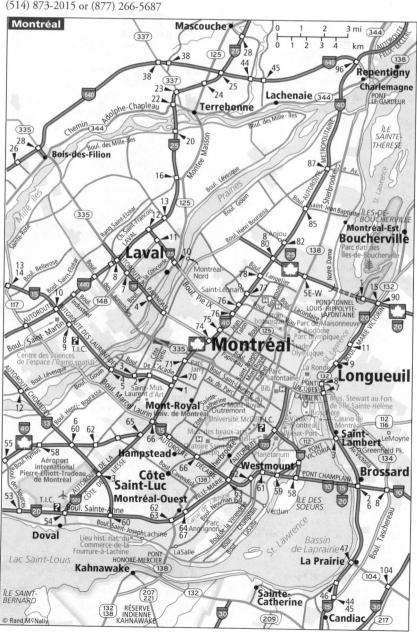

MYRTLE BEACH, South Carolina

Pier at Barefoot Landing

Myrtle Beach is one of the nation's most popular getaway locations. The area's plethora of attractions includes amusement parks such as Family Kingdom, which offers thrill rides and a water park, and the nightclubs, restaurants, and theaters at Broadway on the Beach. Nature lovers can retreat to the solitude of Brookgreen Gardens, a one-time rice plantation that boasts thousands of native and exotic species and some 550 works of sculpture. *Tax: 11% hotel, 5% sales. For local weather, call (843) 293-6600.*

SELECTED ATTRACTIONS

Alligator Adventure
4864 US 17 S. at Barefoot Landing
(843) 361-0789

Barefoot Landing
Dining, shopping, and entertainment
4898 US 17 S.
(800) 272-2320 or (843) 272-8349

Broadway at the Beach
Amusements, restaurants, and shops
US 17 Bypass between 21st and
29th Aves. N.
(843) 444-3200

Brookgreen Gardens
Sculpture gardens
15 miles south off US 17, Murrells Inlet
(843) 235-6000

The Carolina Opry
Live musical performances
8901-A US 17 N.
(843) 913-4000 or (800) 843-6779

Children's Museum of South Carolina
2501 N. Kings Hwy.
(843) 946-9469

Family Kingdom
Amusement and water parks
300 S. Ocean Blvd.
(843) 626-3447

Hobcaw Barony
Estate and wildlife refuge
35 miles south off US 17, Georgetown
(843) 546-4623

Myrtle Beach State Park
4401 S. Kings Hwy.
(843) 238-5325

Myrtle Waves Water Park
10th Ave. N. at US 17 Bypass
(843) 913-9260

The Palace Theater
Live music and dance performances
1420 Celebrity Cir. at Broadway at the Beach
(843) 448-9224

Waccatee Zoological Farm
8500 Enterprise Rd.
(843) 650-8500

SHOPPING

Coastal Grand Mall
Department stores, specialty shops, and restaurants
US 501 and US 17 Bypass
(843) 839-9100

Colonial Mall
Department stores, specialty shops, and restaurants
10177 N. Kings Hwy.
(843) 272-4040

Tanger Outlet Center
Factory outlet mall
US 501 at Waccamaw Pines Dr.
(843) 236-5100

VISITOR INFORMATION

Myrtle Beach Area Chamber of Commerce and Convention and Visitors Bureau
1200 N. Oak St.
Myrtle Beach, SC 29577
(843) 626-7444 or (800) 356-3016
www.myrtlebeachinfo.com

Myrtle Beach Welcome Center
1200 N. Oak St.
(843) 626-7444

Ashby Ward Official Myrtle Beach/Grand Strand Welcome Center
1800 US 501 W, Aynor
(843) 626-7444

South Strand Welcome Center
3401 US 17 Business S., Murrells Inlet
(843) 651-1010

Airport Welcome Center
1100 Jetport Rd.
(843) 626-7444

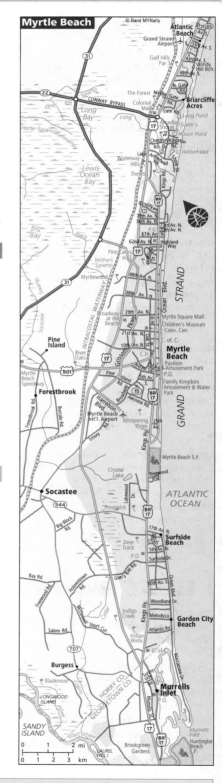

DON'T MISS DRIVE

A trip to Myrtle Beach should begin with a windows-rolled-down cruise along Ocean Boulevard. This street borders the waterfront, or as the locals say, the "Grand Strand."

NASHVILLE, Tennessee

Universally familiar as the capital of country music, Nashville is also noted for its keen appreciation for education and the arts. For music fans, the city offers a multitude of clubs in the downtown entertainment district, the live broadcast of the Grand Ole Opry from its 4,400-seat auditorium at Opryland, and the regalia, instruments, and mementos displayed at the Country Music Hall of Fame. Art and history buffs can visit Cheekwood, where contemporary and traditional art is on exhibit, and the Hermitage, the restored and accurately furnished home of President Andrew Jackson. *Tax: 14.25% hotel, 9.25% sales. For local weather, call (615) 259-2222 or (615) 754-4633.*

Country Music Hall of Fame and Museum at night

► SELECTED ATTRACTIONS

Adventure Science Center
800 Fort Negley Blvd.
(615) 862-5160

Belle Meade Plantation
19th-century house museum
5025 Harding Rd.
(615) 356-0501

Cheekwood Botanical Garden and Museum of Art
1200 Forrest Park Dr.
(615) 356-8000

Country Music Hall of Fame and Museum
222 5th Ave. S.
(615) 416-1000 or (800) 852-6437

Frist Center for the Visual Arts
919 Broadway
(615) 244-3340

General Jackson Showboat
2812 Opryland Dr.
(615) 458-3900

Grand Ole Opry and Museum
Live country music performances
2802 Opryland Dr.
(615) 871-6779 or (800) 733-6779

The Hermitage
Historic home of Andrew Jackson
4580 Rachel's Ln.
(615) 889-2941

Nashville Zoo at Grassmere
3777 Nolensville Rd.
(615) 833-1534

The Parthenon
Art museum and full-scale reproduction of the Greek temple
West End and 25th Aves. in Centennial Park
(615) 862-8431

Tennessee State Capitol
Between 6th and 7th Aves. on Charlotte Ave.
(615) 741-2692

Tennessee State Museum
505 Deaderick St.
(615) 741-2692 or (800) 407-4324

► SHOPPING

Green Hills Antique Mall
4108 Hillsboro Rd.
(615) 383-3893

Lower Broadway
Records and music collectibles
100-600 Broadway

The Mall at Green Hills
Upscale boutiques, department stores, and restaurants
2126 Abbott Martin Rd.
(615) 298-5478

Opry Mills
Factory outlets and specialty shops
433 Opry Mills Dr.
(615) 514-1100

► VISITOR INFORMATION

Nashville Convention and Visitors Bureau
150 4th Ave. N., Ste. G-250
Nashville, TN 37219
(615) 259-4700 or (800) 657-6910
www.nashvillecvb.com

Nashville Visitor Information Center
501 Broadway
(615) 259-4747

DON'T MISS DRIVE

One section of Nashville is called Midtown, but locals refer to it only by its street names, like Broadway. For a taste of the honky-tonks made famous by local musicians, a drive down Broadway is a must.

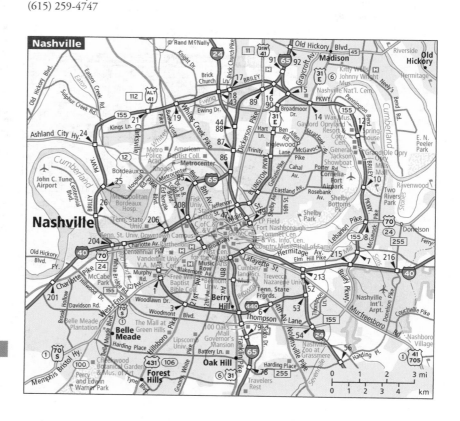

NEW ORLEANS, Louisiana

Mardi Gras festivities in the French Quarter

As it struggles to recover from the deadly effects of Hurricane Katrina, New Orleans is seeing a slow return to something approaching normalcy. Among the most encouraging signs: Mardi Gras and the Jazz and Heritage Festival continue undeterred, bringing music and party lovers from near and far to this much-loved city. Businesses in the famous French Quarter, one of the least affected areas, continue to reopen, although often with reduced staffs. And among the larger institutions, the Museum of Art, the Louisiana State Museum in The Cabildo, and the Audubon Zoo are again welcoming visitors in defiance of nature's wrath. *Tax: 13% hotel, with sliding scale of room-per-night charge: $1 (hotels with less than 300 rooms), $2 (hotels with less than 1000 rooms), or $3 (at hotels with 1000+ rooms). 9.75% sales. For local weather, call (504) 529-6259 or (504) 828-4000.*

▶ SELECTED ATTRACTIONS

Audubon Aquarium of the Americas
1 Canal St.
(800) 774-7394

Audubon Zoo
6500 Magazine St.
(800) 774-7394

Blaine Kern's Mardi Gras World
Tours of parade float studios
233 Newton St.
(504) 361-7821

Degas House
Historic home of artist Edgar Degas
2306 Esplanade Ave.
(504) 821-5009 or (800) 755-6730

French Quarter
Historic French and Spanish district
Canal St. to Esplanade Ave.
(Maps for self-guided walking tours available at the Visitors Bureau,
529 St. Ann St.)
(504) 566-5009

Harrah's New Orleans Casino
8 Canal St.
(504) 533-6000 or (800) 427-7247

Herman-Grima/Gallier Historic Houses
French Quarter landmark homes
820 St. Louis St.
(504) 525-5661

Lafayette Cemetery No. 1
Historic cemetery
1427 6th St.

Louisiana Children's Museum
420 Julia St.
(504) 523-1357

Louisiana State Museum
(504) 568-6968 or (800) 568-6968
• The Cabildo
Site of the Louisiana Purchase transfer
701 Chartres St. in Jackson Square

National WWII Museum
945 Magazine St.
(504) 527-6012

New Orleans Museum of Art
1 Collins C. Diboll Cir. in City Park
(504) 488-2631

New Orleans Pharmacy Museum
514 Chartres St.
(504) 565-8027

Ogden Museum of Southern Art
945 Camp St.
(504) 539-9600

Old Ursuline Convent
Oldest building in the Mississippi Valley
1100 Chartres St.
(504) 529-3040 or (877) 529-2242

St. Louis Cathedral
720 Chartres St. in Jackson Square
(504) 525-9585

▶ DON'T MISS DRIVE

St. Charles Avenue is really a boulevard with a 150-year-old streetcar system winding down the middle. Other sights include huge oaks, period architecture, and the idyllic campuses of Tulane and Loyola Universities.

▶ SHOPPING

The Esplanade Mall
140 specialty shops and restaurants
1401 W. Esplanade Ave., Kenner
(504) 465-2161

French Market
Arts and crafts, farmers' market, and souvenir stalls
1008 N. Peters St. between Barracks St. and Jackson Square
(504) 522-2621

French Quarter
Souvenir shops and specialty boutiques
84-block area bounded by Esplanade Ave., Rampart St., Canal St., and the Mississippi River
(800) 672-6124

Jackson Brewery
Mall with shops and restaurants
600 Decatur St.
(504) 566-7245

Magazine Street
Six miles of antique shops, art galleries, restaurants, and specialty shops
2616 Hessmer Ave.
(504) 455-1224

Riverwalk Marketplace
Specialty stores, boutiques, and restaurants
Bounded by Poydras, Canal, and Julia Sts. and the Mississippi River
(504) 522-1555

Royal Street
Antique stores and upscale galleries
Royal St. in the French Quarter

The Shops at Canal Place
Designer boutiques and department stores
333 Canal St.
(504) 522-9200

▶ VISITOR INFORMATION

New Orleans Metropolitan Convention and Visitors Bureau
2020 St. Charles Ave.
New Orleans, LA 70130
(504) 566-5011 or (800) 672-6124
www.neworleanscvb.com

Louisiana Tourism Office
529 St. Ann St.
New Orleans, LA 70116
(504) 568-5661

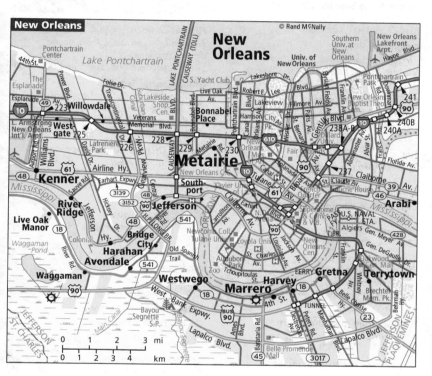

▶ DIVERSION

Drive out to Crawford Landing in Slidell for Dr. Wagner's Honey Island Swamp Tour. The two-hour boat tour explores the beauty of a cypress swamp. Only 30 minutes north of New Orleans, off I-10. (985) 641-1769

Mardi Gras—Let the good times roll!

One of the signatures of Mardi Gras in New Orleans is a series of spectacular parades beginning 12 days before Mardi Gras. During that time, some 60 parades are held in the four-parish area of Orleans, Jefferson, St. Bernard, and St. Tammany.

Mardi Gras parades follow a standard carnival format with a King and Queen in the lead. The royalty are followed by a procession of floats, krewes (organized parade groups), dancing groups, marching bands, clowns, sometimes motorcycle units . . . you name it. It is not uncommon for parade participants to total in the thousands.

Want to see an official New Orleans Mardi Gras parade? Parade routings are printed in advance, so it is easy to find out which street will be used as a route. Curbside seats are free of charge. Grandstand seats for the first week are free from City Hall at (504) 658-4055, and seats for the second week are available for advance purchase from Ticketmaster at (504) 522-4900. Upcoming Mardi Gras dates include February 5, 2008 and February 24, 2009.

NEW YORK, New York

New York's five distinctive boroughs come together to form one magnificent city. Many visitors stick to Manhattan to gawk in Times Square, shop on Fifth Avenue, gallery-hop in Soho, drop by the museums bordering Central Park, or take in Broadway's latest hit show. But when time allows, cross the Brooklyn Bridge to the Brooklyn Academy of Music. Take the subway to the Bronx Zoo or the Museum of the Moving Image in Queens. And don't forget chugging past the Statue of Liberty on the Staten Island Ferry; at $0 a ticket, it's by far the city's best sightseeing value. *Tax: 13.375% hotel tax plus a $3.50 per-room-per-night surcharge, 4.375% sales. For local weather, call (631) 924-0517.*

Central Park

SELECTED ATTRACTIONS

American Museum of Natural History
W. 79th and Central Park W.
(212) 769-5100

Broadway
Theater district
Roughly E. 42nd to W. 50th Sts.,
5th to 8th Aves.

Bronx Zoo/Wildlife Conservation Society
2300 Southern Blvd., Bronx
(718) 367-1010

Brooklyn Academy of Music
30 Lafayette Avenue, Brooklyn
(718) 636-4100

Carnegie Hall
Concert and recital hall
881 7th Ave.
(212) 247-7800

Cathedral of St. John the Divine
World's largest Gothic cathedral
1047 Amsterdam Ave.
(212) 932-7347

Central Park Zoo
830 5th Ave.
(212) 439-6500

Coney Island
Amusement park rides, famous boardwalk
1015 Surf Ave., Brooklyn
(718) 266-1234

Ed Sullivan Theater
"Late Show with David Letterman" tapings
1697 Broadway
(212) 247-6497

Ellis Island Immigration Museum
Ferry departs from Battery Park
(866) 782-8834

DIVERSION

Visit the historic and breathtaking Hudson Valley. This is one of the oldest settled regions in the United States. Take in the mighty Hudson River, pass historic mansions on the Palisades, even tour a vineyard. 50 miles north of New York City on I-87.

Empire State Building Observatory
350 5th Ave.
(212) 736-3100

Greenwich Village
Trendy shops, boutiques, and galleries
W. 14th St. to Houston St., and West St. to Ave. C

Guggenheim Museum
Art museum designed by Frank Lloyd Wright
1071 5th Ave. at 89th St.
(212) 423-3500

Harlem
Historic African American neighborhood
163 W. 125th St. (Harlem visitor information center)

Intrepid Sea, Air and Space Museum
Historic aircraft carrier
W. 46th St. at 12th Ave.
(212) 245-0072

Little Italy and NoLIta (North of Little Italy)
Boutiques, ethnic shops, and great eats
Houston St. to Canal St., and Cleveland to Bowery

Metropolitan Museum of Art
1000 Fifth Ave. at 82nd St.
(212) 535-7710

Museum of the Moving Image
35th Ave. at 36th St., Astoria
(718) 784-4520 or (718) 784-0077

NBC Tours
30 Rockefeller Plaza at 49th St.
(212) 664-7174

South Street Seaport Museum
12-square block district of galleries, historic ships, printing shop; harbor sails
12 Fulton St. (Tickets at Pier 16)
(212) 748-8600

Staten Island Ferry
Whitehall Terminal, Whitehall St. and South St., Lower Manhattan
St. George Ferry Terminal, Richmond Terrace, Staten Island

Times Square
Broadway from 42nd to 47th Sts.

SHOPPING

Fifth Avenue
High-end designer stores, jewelers, and department stores
5th Ave. between 50th and 59th Sts.

Grand Central Terminal
Renovated Beaux-Arts landmark with boutiques, restaurants, and gift stalls
42nd St. and Park Ave.
(212) 340-2347

Historic Orchard Street Shopping District
Discount specialty shops
261 Broome St., Orchard, Grand, and Delancey Sts.
(212) 226-9010

Macy's Herald Square
Famous department store
151 W. 34th St.
(212) 695-4400

Madison Avenue
High-end designer stores
Madison Ave. between 59th and 96th Sts.

SoHo (South of Houston)
Art galleries and boutiques
Between Houston and Canal Sts.

VISITOR INFORMATION

NYC & Company
810 7th Ave., New York City, NY 10019
(212) 484-1200 or (800) 692-8474
www.nycvisit.com

NYC Heritage Tourism Center
City Hall Park
Broadway at Park Row

Chinatown Visitor Information Kiosk
Triangle where Canal, Walken, and Baxter Sts. meet

Harlem Visitor Information Center at the Apollo Theater
253 W. 125th St.

continued on page 77

Viewing the World Trade Center Site

There is a viewing area at Liberty St. and Church St., near Broadway. NYC & Company operates an Official Visitors Information kiosk in City Hall Park at Broadway and Park Row, only a five-minute walk from the viewing area. For walking tours, call (866) 737-1184, ext. 138.

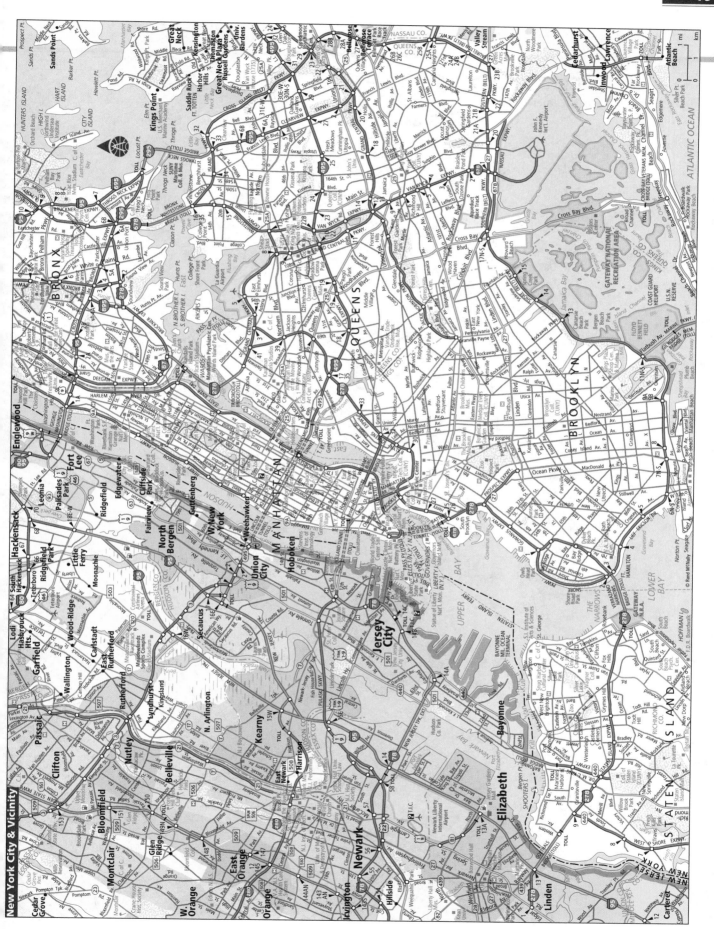

New York City & Vicinity

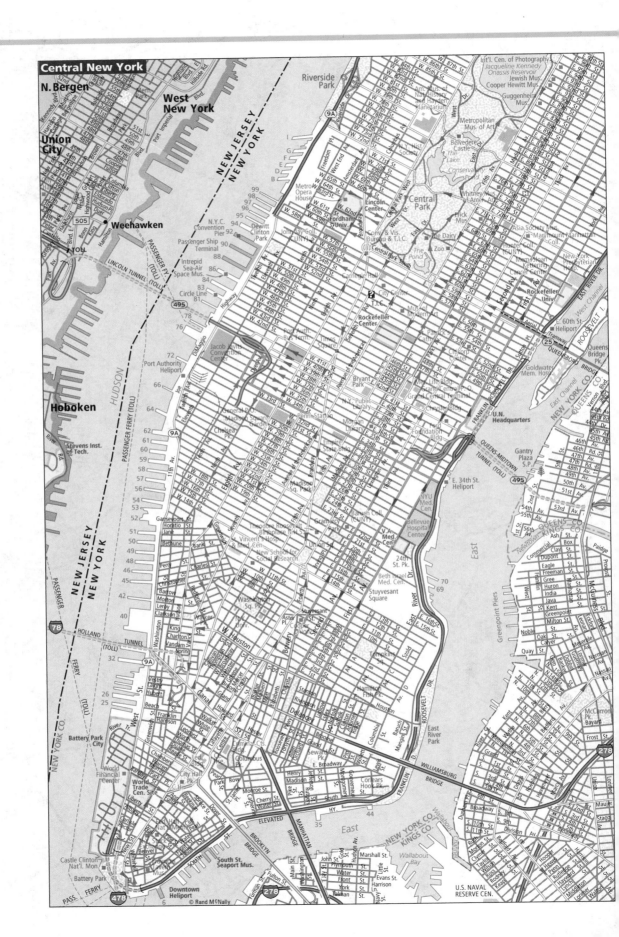

Central New York

© Rand McNally

"The play's the thing." — *Hamlet/Act II, Scene II*

When in New York, do as tourists and residents do: Take in a play! The New York stage is legendary. It razzles and dazzles like no other.

Box Offices

Al Hirschfeld Theater
302 W. 45th St., between 8th & 9th Aves.

Ambassador Theater
219 W. 49th St.,
between Broadway & 8th Aves.

American Airlines Theater
227 W. 42nd St., between 7th & 8th Aves.

Apollo Theatre
253 W. 125th St. at 8th Ave.
(212) 531-5301

August Wilson Theater
245 W. 52nd St.,
between Broadway & 8th Ave.

Avery Fisher Hall
10 Lincoln Center Plaza,
Columbus Ave. & W. 65th St.
(212) 875-5030

Belasco Theater
111 W. 44th St., between 6th & 7th Aves.

Bernard B. Jacobs Theatre
242 W. 45th St.,
between Broadway & 8th Ave.

Biltmore Theater
261 W. 47th St.
between Broadway & 8th Ave.

Booth Theater
222 W. 45th St.,
between Broadway & 8th Ave.

Broadhurst Theater
235 W. 44th St.,
between Broadway & 8th Ave.

Broadway Theater
1681 Broadway, between 52nd & 53rd Sts.

Brooks Atkinson Theater
256 W. 47th St.,
between Broadway & 8th Ave.

Cadillac Winter Garden Theater
1634 Broadway, between 50th & 51st Sts.

Carnegie Hall
57th St. and 7th Ave.
(212) 247-7800

Circle in the Square
235 W. 50th at Broadway

Cort Theater
138 W. 48th St., between 6th & 7th Aves.

Ethel Barrymore Theater
243 W. 47th St.,
between Broadway & 8th Ave.

Eugene O'Neill Theater
2309 W. 49th St.,
between Broadway & 8th Ave.

Gerald Schoenfeld Theater
236 W. 45th St.,
between Broadway & 8th Ave.

Gershwin Theater
222 W. 51st St.,
between Broadway & 8th Ave.

Helen Hayes Theater
240 W. 44th St.,
between Broadway & 8th Ave.

Hilton Theatre
213 W. 42nd St.,
between 7th & 8th Aves.

Imperial Theater
249 W. 45th St.,
between Broadway & 8th Ave.

John Golden Theater
252 W. 45th St.,
between Broadway & 8th Ave.

Julliard School
60 Lincoln Center Plaza, Broadway &
W. 65th St.
(212) 799-5000

Longacre Theatre
220 W. 48th St.,
between Broadway & 8th Ave.

Lunt-Fontanne Theater
205 W. 46th St.,
between Broadway & 8th Ave.

Lyceum Theatre
149 W. 45th St.
between 6th & 7th Aves.

Majestic Theater
247 W. 44th St.,
between Broadway & 8th Ave.

Marquis Theatre
1535 Broadway, between 45th & 46th Sts.

Metropolitan Opera House
Lincoln Center Plaza, Columbus Ave.
between 62nd & 65th Sts.
(212) 362-6000

Minskoff Theater
200 W. 45th St. at Broadway

Music Box Theater
239 W. 45th St.,
between Broadway & 8th Ave.

Nederlander Theater
208 W. 41st St., between 7th & 8th Aves.

Neil Simon Theater
250 W. 52nd St.,
between Broadway & 8th Ave.

New Amsterdam Theater
214 W. 42nd St., between 7th & 8th Aves.

Palace Theater
1564 Broadway at 47th St.

Radio City Music Hall
1260 Avenue of the Americas at 50th St.

Richard Rodgers Theater
226 W. 46th St.,
between Broadway & 8th Ave.

New York City's theater district

Sam S. Shubert Theater
225 W. 44th St.,
between Broadway & 8th Ave.

St. James Theater
246 W. 44th St.,
between Broadway & 8th Ave.

Studio 54
254 W. 54th St., between 7th & 8th Aves.

Vivian Beaumont Theater
150 W. 65th St., Lincoln Center

Walter Kerr Theater
219 W. 48th St.,
between Broadway & 8th Ave.

Line up at a TKTS Ticket Booth for last-minute seats at great prices*:

Times Square Theatre Center at W. 46th St. (Broadway & 8th Ave.)

Lower Manhattan Theatre Center at South Street Seaport, 199 Water St. (Corner of Front & John Sts. or the rear of the Resnick/Prudential Building)

*TKTS accepts only cash and travelers' checks

Tickets by telephone:

Telecharge: (212) 239-6200 or
(800) 545-2559

Ticketmaster: (212) 307-4747

Ticket Central: (212) 279-4200

NORFOLK/VIRGINIA BEACH, Virginia

Tall ships in Norfolk Harbor

Home port of the Atlantic Fleet, Norfolk has transformed itself into more than a Navy town. The *American Rover*, a three-masted schooner, offers narrated harbor cruises. The Chrysler Museum of Art houses 30,000 pieces ranging from antiquities of Africa, Asia, and the Middle East to a renowned Tiffany glass collection. Interactive exhibits at the Nauticus National Maritime Center give visitors a chance to explore life on and under the waves. *Tax: 13% hotel (plus $1 per room occupancy tax per night), 5% sales tax.*

Neighboring Virginia Beach has long been a place to find an oceanfront resort, breathe the salt air, and relax. When not lolling about on the beach, visitors can explore the depths of Chesapeake Bay at the Virginia Aquarium and Marine Science Center. High-speed slides, a wave pool, and river floats make for freshwater fun at Ocean Breeze Waterpark. Daring ocean rescues of yore are recounted at the Old Coast Guard Station. *Tax: 13% hotel (plus $1 per-room occupancy tax per night), 5% sales. For local weather, call (757) 899-4200.*

DON'T MISS DRIVE

Feel suspended over water during the 17.6-mile drive on the Chesapeake Bay Bridge Tunnel, the world's largest bridge-tunnel complex, which connects Norfolk/Virginia Beach to Virginia's Eastern Shore. (757) 331-2960

SELECTED ATTRACTIONS

NORFOLK

American Rover Tall Ship Cruises
Waterside Dr. at Waterside
Festival Marketplace
(757) 627-7245

Busch Gardens Williamsburg
I-64, exit 243A, Williamsburg
(800) 343-7946

Cannonball Trail
Self-guided walking tour of downtown Norfolk's historic sites
Begins at Freemason Street Reception Center, 401 E. Freemason St.
(757) 664-6620

Carrie B. Harbor Tours
Mississippi-style paddle wheeler cruises
Waterside Dr. at Waterside Festival Marketplace
(757) 393-4735

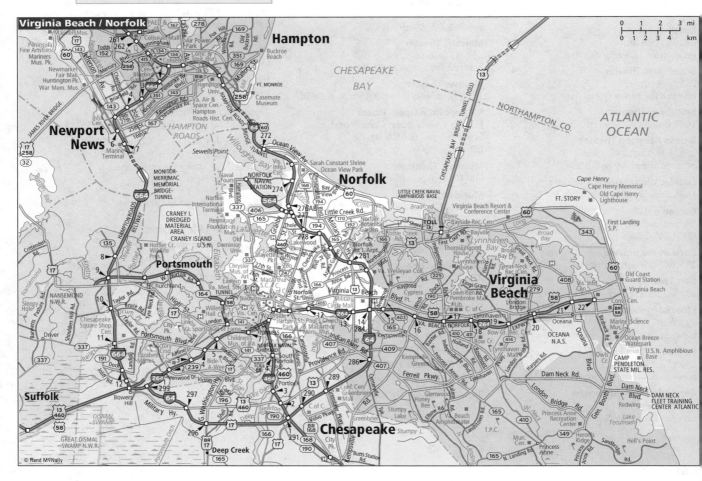

Children's Museum of Virginia
221 High St., Portsmouth
(757) 393-5258

Chrysler Museum of Art
245 W. Olney Rd. at Mowbray Arch
(757) 664-6200

Crispus Attucks Theatre
Historic African American theater
1010 Church St.
(757) 622-4763

Douglas MacArthur Memorial
Bounded by Bank St., Plume St., Court St.,
and City Hall Ave. in MacArthur Square
(757) 441-2965

Hampton Roads Naval Museum
1 Waterside Dr. inside Nauticus
(757) 322-2987

Hermitage Foundation Museum
Art museum in Tudor home
7637 N. Shore Rd.
(757) 423-2052

**Nauticus: The National Maritime Center
& Battleship** *Wisconsin*
1 Waterside Dr.
(757) 664-1000 or (800) 664-1080

Norfolk Botanical Garden
6700 Azalea Garden Rd.
(757) 441-5830

Norfolk Naval Station
9079 Hampton Blvd., adjacent to Gate 5
(757) 444-7955

Virginia Zoo
3500 Granby St.
(757) 441-2374

SHOPPING

NORFOLK

Historic Ghent District
Specialty shops, galleries, and antiques
Bounded by Monticello Ave., 22nd St.,
Brambleton Ave., and Hampton Blvd.

MacArthur Center
Department stores and specialty shops
300 Monticello Ave.
(757) 627-6000

Waterside Festival Marketplace
Specialty boutiques
333 Waterside Dr.
(757) 627-3300

SELECTED ATTRACTIONS

VIRGINIA BEACH

Adam Thoroughgood House
17th-century hall and parlor house
1636 Parish Rd.
(757) 431-4000

Atlantic Wildfowl Heritage Museum
Wildfowl art and decoys
1113 Atlantic Ave. in de Witt Cottage
(757) 437-8432

Cape Henry Lighthouse
Off US 60 at Fort Story
(757) 422-9421

**Chesapeake Bay Center/First Landing
State Park**
*Interactive information center, touch tank,
historic displays, and kayak rental*
2500 Shore Dr.
(757) 412-2300 or (800) 933-7275

Contemporary Art Center of Virginia
2200 Parks Ave.
(757) 425-0000

Francis Land House Historic Site
*200-year-old plantation home, gardens, and
wooded wetlands trail*
3131 Virginia Beach Blvd.
(757) 431-4000

Lynnhaven House
Early colonial planter's home
4405 Wishart Rd.
(757) 460-7109

Ocean Breeze Waterpark
849 General Booth Blvd.
(757) 422-4444 or (800) 678-9453

Old Coast Guard Station
Museum in former lifesaving station
24th St. and Atlantic Ave.
(757) 422-1587

Virginia Legends Walk
Self-guided tour honoring famous Virginians
13th Street Park, 1300 Atlantic Ave.
(757) 463-4500

**Virginia Aquarium & Marine
Science Center**
Exhibits, aquarium, and IMAX theater
717 General Booth Blvd.
(757) 425-3474

Virginia Aquarium and Marine Science Center

SHOPPING

VIRGINIA BEACH

Farmers Market
Local produce and food items, gift stores
3640 Dam Neck Rd.
(757) 427-4395

Lynnhaven Mall
Department stores and specialty shops
701 Lynnhaven Pkwy.
(757) 340-9340

Pembroke Mall
*Department stores, specialty shops, and
movie theater*
Virginia Beach and Independence Blvds.
(757) 497-6255

VISITOR INFORMATION

Norfolk Convention and Visitors Bureau
232 E. Main St.
Norfolk, VA 23510
(757) 664-6620 or (800) 368-3097
www.norfolkcvb.com

**Virginia Beach Convention and
Visitor Bureau**
2101 Parks Ave., Ste. 500
Virginia Beach, VA 23451
(757) 437-4700 or (800) 700-7702
www.vbfun.com

Norfolk Visitor Information Center
9401 4th View St.
(757) 441-1852

Virginia Beach Visitors Center
2100 Parks Ave.
(800) 822-3224

DIVERSION

Experience life before the American Revolution at Colonial Williamsburg, a
301-acre living-history village about 50 miles northwest of Norfolk. Shop at
authentic 18th-century stores and eat in colonial taverns. I-64 west to exit 238,
VA 143. (800) 447-8679

OKLAHOMA CITY, Oklahoma

Bricktown Canal

Born of the 1889 land rush, Oklahoma's state capital thrived with the discovery of oil. Range riders still herd cattle on the surrounding plains; their legendary way of life is celebrated at the National Cowboy & Western Heritage Museum. At the center of the modern downtown of glass and steel, the Myriad Botanical Gardens offer 17 acres of landscaped grounds with the stunning Crystal Bridge Tropical Conservatory at its heart. The Oklahoma City National Memorial, a quiet and powerful tribute to those who lost their lives in the bombing of the Murrah Federal Building, lies a short distance away. *Tax: 13.88% hotel, 8.375% sales. For local weather, call (405) 478-3377.*

DON'T MISS DRIVE

Spend a few hours exploring the Heritage Hills Historic District, just north of downtown between NW 13th St. and NW 23rd St. In this part of Oklahoma City, mansions from the turn of the last century grace tree-lined streets.

▶ SELECTED ATTRACTIONS

Bricktown
Entertainment, shopping, and dining district
Bordered by E. Main St. and Gaylord, Reno, and Byers Aves.
(405) 236-8666

Myriad Botanical Gardens & Crystal Bridge
301 W. Reno Ave.
(405) 297-3995

National Cowboy & Western Heritage Museum
1700 NE 63rd St.
(405) 478-2250

Oklahoma City Museum of Art
415 Couch Dr.
(405) 236-3100

Oklahoma State Capitol
NE 23rd St. and Lincoln Blvd.
(405) 521-3356

Oklahoma City National Memorial and Museum
620 N. Harvey Ave.
(405) 235-3313 or (888) 542-4673

Oklahoma City Zoo and Botanical Garden
2101 NE 50th St.
(405) 424-3344

SBC Bricktown Ballpark
Home of the Oklahoma Redhawks
2 S. Mickey Mantle Dr.
(405) 218-1000

Stockyards City
Livestock auction, shops, and restaurants
Agnew exit off I-40 to Exchange Ave.
(405) 235-7267

▶ SHOPPING

Crossroads Mall
Family shopping destination
7000 Crossroads Blvd.
(405) 631-4422

Paseo Arts District
Galleries, shops, and restaurants
NW 30th St. and Dewey Ave.
(405) 525-2688

50 Penn Place
Upscale retail shops, restaurants
1900 NW Expwy.
(405) 848-7588

Penn Square Mall
Department stores and specialty shops
NW Expwy. and Pennsylvania Ave.
(405) 842-4424

Quail Springs Mall
Department stores and retro food court
2501 W. Memorial Rd.
(405) 755-6530

Western Avenue
Boutiques, clubs, and restaurants
NW 36th St. to Wilshire Blvd.
(405) 412-5990

▶ VISITOR INFORMATION

Oklahoma City Convention and Visitors Bureau
189 W. Sheridan Ave.
Oklahoma City, OK 73102
(405) 297-8912 or (800) 225-5652
www.visitokc.com

OMAHA, Nebraska

A center for agriculture, insurance, and telecommunications, Omaha got its first big boost when the transcontinental railroad began its western journey here. The Durham Western Heritage Museum in the restored Union Station displays exhibits on the city's railroading past, early settlers, and first inhabitants. The Old Market district offers restaurants, galleries, and shops in a former warehouse area. The latest additions to the outstanding Henry Doorly Zoo include the Hubbard Gorilla Valley, a free-range exhibit where only the spectators are in captivity, and Orangutan Forest, which opened in 2005. *Tax: 16.48% hotel, 7% sales. For local weather, call (402) 392-1111.*

Gene Leahy Pedestrian Mall

SELECTED ATTRACTIONS

Boys Town
Historic home for at-risk youth
137th and W. Dodge Rd.
(402) 498-1140 or (800) 625-1400

Durham Western Heritage Museum
801 S. 10th St.
(402) 444-5071

El Museo Latino
Art and history museum and cultural center
4701 S. 25th St.
(402) 731-1137

Eugene T. Mahoney State Park
28500 W. Park Hwy., Ashland
(402) 944-2523

Gerald R. Ford Birth Site and Gardens
3202 Woolworth Ave.
(402) 444-5955

Henry Doorly Zoo
3701 S. 10th St.
(402) 733-8401

Joslyn Art Museum
2200 Dodge St.
(402) 342-3300

Joslyn Castle
1908 historic home
3902 Davenport St.
(402) 595-2199

Lauritzen Gardens
Botanical garden and center
100 Bancroft St.
(402) 346-4002

Lewis and Clark Landing
6th St. on the Missouri River
(402) 444-5900

Mormon Trail Center
Covered wagon, cabin, and pioneer artifacts
3215 State St.
(402) 453-9372

Neale Woods Nature Center
14323 Edith Marie Ave.
(402) 453-5615

Omaha Children's Museum
500 S. 20th St.
(402) 342-6164

Strategic Air & Space Museum
28210 W. Park Hwy., off I-80, exit 426, Ashland
(402) 944-3100 or (800) 358-5029

Wildlife Safari Park
16406 N. 292nd St., off I-80, exit 426, Ashland
(402) 944-9453

SHOPPING

Nebraska Crossing Outlet Center
Off I-80, exit 432 (NE 31 west), Gretna
(402) 332-4940

Old Market
Boutiques, specialty shops, and restaurants
10th to 13th Sts. and Farnam to Jones Sts.
(402) 341-7151

Regency Court
Unique designer shops and boutiques
120 Regency Pkwy.
(402) 393-8474

Westroads Mall
Department stores and specialty shops
10000 California St.
(402) 397-2398

VISITOR INFORMATION

Greater Omaha Convention and Visitors Bureau
1001 Farnam-on-the-Mall, Ste. 200
Omaha, NE 68102
(402) 444-4660 or (866) 937-6624
www.visitomaha.com

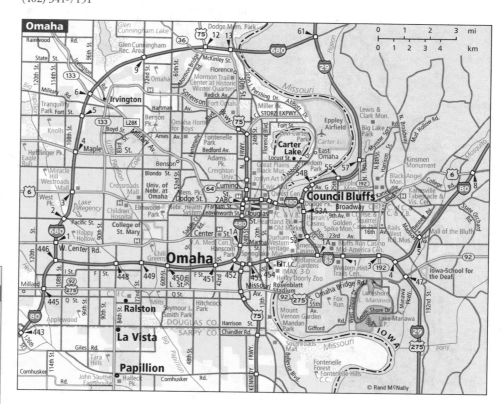

DIVERSION

Check out 1,400 acres of forest and 26 miles of trails at the Fontenelle Forest Nature Center. Located on the Missouri River south of Omaha on US 75 to Bellevue. (402) 731-3140

ORLANDO, Florida

At one time little more than a peaceful orange grove, Orlando began its ascendance to theme-park supremacy with the arrival of Walt Disney's Magic Kingdom 35 years ago. Since then, Disney World has developed into an empire of resorts and multiple amusement parks, and others such as Universal Orlando Resort have brought along their own brand of thrills. For a true immersion experience, Discovery Cove offers lagoons where visitors can swim with playful dolphins and watch sharks and barracuda from a close (but safe) distance. *Tax: 12.5% hotel, 6.5% sales. For local weather, call (321) 255-0212.*

Epcot Center, Walt Disney World

▶ SELECTED ATTRACTIONS

Discovery Cove Orlando
Snorkel and swim with dolphins
6000 Discovery Cove Way, adjacent to
SeaWorld off I-4 at FL 528
(407) 370-1280 or (877) 434-7268

Kennedy Space Center Visitor Complex
35 miles east of Orlando off
FL 405, Titusville
(321) 449-4444

Orlando Museum of Art
American and African collections
2416 N. Mills Ave.
(407) 896-4231

**Ripley's Believe It or Not!
Orlando Odditorium**
8201 International Dr.
(407) 345-0501 or (800) 998-4418, ext. 3

SeaWorld Orlando
7007 SeaWorld Dr. off I-4 at FL 528
(407) 351-3600 or (800) 327-2424

Universal Orlando Resort
Theme park and entertainment complex
1000 Universal Studios Plaza, off I-4
(407) 363-8000

Walt Disney World Resort
25 miles southwest of Orlando off I-4,
Lake Buena Vista
(407) 824-4321 or (407) 824-2222

Wet 'n Wild Orlando
Water park
6200 International Dr.
(407) 351-1800 or (800) 992-9453

▶ SHOPPING

The Florida Mall
8001 S. Orange Blossom Trail
(407) 851-6255

Lake Buena Vista Factory Stores
Outlet stores
15591 Apopka-Vineland Rd. (SR 535)
(407) 238-9301

The Mall at Millenia
Upscale stores and specialty shops
4200 Conroy Rd.
(407) 363-3555

Pointe Orlando
Specialty shops, entertainment, restaurants
9101 International Dr.
(407) 248-2838

Prime Outlets Orlando
Upscale and designer outlet stores
5401 Oakridge Rd.
(407) 352-9600

▶ VISITOR INFORMATION

**Orlando/Orange County Convention
& Visitors Bureau**
6700 Forum Dr., Ste. 100
Orlando, FL 32821
(407) 363-5872 or (800) 972-3304
www.orlandoinfo.com

The Official Visitor Center
8723 International Dr., Ste. 101
(407) 363-5872 or (800) 643-9492

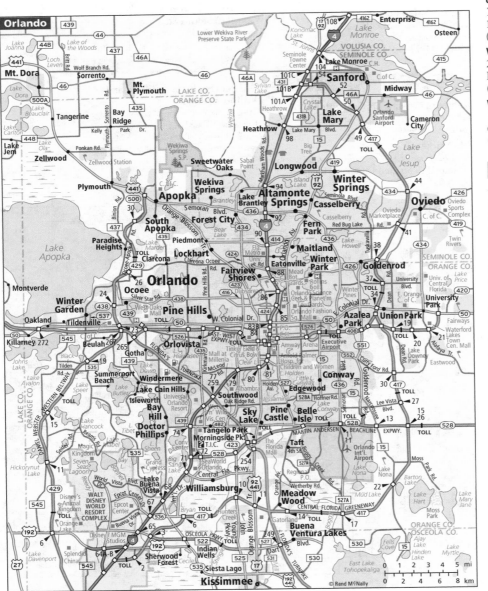

OTTAWA, Ontario, Canada

With its blend of English and French cultures, New World and Old, Canada's capital city displays cosmopolitan flair while retaining a small-town feel. For a taste of British tradition, tour Rideau Hall, official home of the Queen's representative, and the Parliament buildings, where colorful changing of the guard ceremonies are performed during summer months. One of Ottawa's many museums, the Bytown, traces the city's early history. At the river's edge, the architecturally splendid National Gallery houses a collection of modern, traditional, and aboriginal art.
Tax: 15% hotel, 7% goods and services, 8% provincial sales tax.

Changing of the guard at Parliament Hill

▶ SELECTED ATTRACTIONS

Bytown Museum and Ottawa Locks
History museum and Rideau Canal locks
1 Canal Ln., along the Rideau Canal
(613) 234-4570

Canada Aviation Museum
11 Aviation Pkwy. at Rockcliffe Pkwy.
(613) 993-2010

Canadian Museum of Civilization
100 Laurier St., Gatineau, QC
(819) 776-7000 or (800) 555-5621

Canadian Museum of Contemporary Photography
1 Rideau Canal (entrance on Wellington St.)
(613) 990-8257

Canadian Museum of Nature
240 McLeod St.
(613) 566-4700 or (800) 263-4433

Canadian War Museum
1 Vimy Pl.
(819) 776-8600 or (800) 555-5621

Casino du Lac-Leamy
1 Casino Blvd., Gatineau, QC
(819) 772-2100 or (800) 665-2274

Currency Museum of the Bank of Canada
245 Sparks St.
(613) 782-8914

Gatineau Park
33 Scott Rd. across the Macdonald-Cartier Bridge
(819) 827-2020 or (800) 465-1867

Laurier House
19th-century home and former residence of two Canadian prime ministers
335 Laurier Ave. E. at Chapel St.
(613) 992-8142

National Gallery of Canada
380 Sussex Dr.
(613) 990-1985 or (800) 319-2787

Parliament Hill
Headquarters of the Canadian government
90 Sparks St.
(613) 996-0896

Rideau Hall
Historic residence and workplace of Canada's Governor General
1 Sussex Dr.
(613) 993-8200 or (800) 465-6890

Royal Canadian Mint
320 Sussex Dr.
(800) 267-7000 (Canada) or
(800) 242-9071 (U.S.)

▶ SHOPPING

ByWard Market
Fashion boutiques and unique shops
Between Sussex and Cumberland Sts. and Rideau and Cathcart Sts.
(613) 562-3325

Rideau Centre
Department stores and specialty shops
50 Rideau St.
(613) 236-6565

Sparks Street Mall
Department stores and specialty shops
Sparks St. from Elgin to Lyon Sts.
(613) 230-0984

Westboro Village
Antiques and studios
Richmond Rd. at Churchill Ave.

▶ VISITOR INFORMATION

Ottawa Tourism and Convention Authority
130 Albert St., Ste. 1800
Ottawa, ON K1P 5G4, Canada
(613) 237-5150 or (800) 363-4465
www.ottawatourism.org

▶ DIVERSION

View the world-famous Thousand Islands from a small cruise ship departing from Brockville, 100 kilometers (about 60 miles) from Ottawa, passing spectacular scenery, even castles. Take ON 416 south to ON 401 west. (613) 345-7333

PHILADELPHIA, Pennsylvania

Philadelphia Museum of Art with the city's skyline

Philadelphia, the "Cradle of Liberty," successfully integrates modern growth with its colonial past. The city's centerpiece, Independence National Historical Park, preserves the Liberty Bell, the hall in which the Declaration of Independence was adopted, and other significant sites large and small. Benjamin Franklin's personal effects are at the Franklin Institute Science Museum. The popular Manayunk neighborhood and posh Rittenhouse Square offer boutiques and galleries for a leisurely afternoon (or two) of shopping. For a personal Philly cheese steak taste-off, visitors head to the legendary Geno's Steaks, then across the street to the equally legendary Pat's King of Steaks. *Tax: 14% hotel, 7% sales. For local weather, call (215) 936-1212 or (609) 261-6600.*

▶ SELECTED ATTRACTIONS

Academy of Natural Sciences
1900 Benjamin Franklin Pkwy.
(215) 299-1000

Adventure Aquarium
4 miles from downtown across the Benjamin Franklin Bridge
1 Riverside Dr., Camden, NJ
(856) 365-3300

African American Museum in Philadelphia
701 Arch St.
(215) 574-0380

Atwater Kent Museum of Philadelphia
Museum of Philadelphia history
15 S. 7th St.
(215) 685-4830

Betsy Ross House
18th-century home of American flag designer
239 Arch St.
(215) 686-1252

Christ Church
First U.S. Protestant Episcopal Church and Benjamin Franklin's grave site
2nd St. above Market St.
(215) 922-1695

Franklin Institute Science Museum
222 N. 20th St. at Benjamin Franklin Pkwy.
(215) 448-1200

Franklin Court Underground Museum
Site where Benjamin Franklin's home once stood
Market St. between 3rd and 4th Sts.
(215) 965-2305

Historic Bartram's Garden
Botanic garden, 18th-century coachhouse, and wildflower meadow
54th St. and Lindbergh Blvd.
(215) 729-5281

Independence National Historical Park
Includes the Liberty Bell, Independence Hall, and Benjamin Franklin National Memorial
143 S. 3rd St.
(215) 965-2305

▶ DON'T MISS DRIVE

A drive down Benjamin Franklin Parkway between City Hall and the Philadelphia Art Museum captures the stately and historic aura of Philadelphia. It is replete with cathedrals, fountains, parks, and monuments.

Philadelphia & Vicinity
© Rand McNally

John Heinz National Wildlife Refuge at Tinicum
8601 Lindbergh Blvd.
(215) 365-3118

National Constitution Center
Museum dedicated to the U.S. Constitution
525 Arch St. in Independence Mall
(215) 409-6600

Philadelphia Museum of Art
2600 Benjamin Franklin Pkwy.
(215) 763-8100

Philadelphia Zoo
3400 W. Girard Ave. in Fairmount Park
(215) 243-1100

Please Touch Museum
Children's museum
210 N. 21st St.
(215) 963-0667

Valley Forge National Historical Park
Revolutionary War site
18 miles northwest off I-76, exit 326,
Valley Forge
(610) 783-1077

▶ SHOPPING

Chestnut Hill Shopping District
Boutiques, galleries, antique shops, cafes, and restaurants
Along Germantown Ave.
(215) 247-6696

Franklin Mills Mall
Outlet stores
1455 Franklin Mills Cir., I-95 and Woodhaven Rd.
(215) 632-1500

Jewelers Row
8th St. between Chestnut and Walnut Sts. and Sansom St. between 7th and 8th Sts.
(215) 627-1834

Manayunk National Historic District
Boutiques, galleries, and restaurants
7 miles west of Center City off I-76, exit 338
(215) 482-9565

Rittenhouse Row
Upscale boutiques and galleries
Bounded by the Avenue of the Arts (Broad St.) and 21st, Pine, and Market Sts.

Shops at Liberty Place
Upscale boutiques and specialty shops
Liberty Place at 1625 Chestnut St. between 16th and 17th Sts.
(215) 851-9055

South Street/Headhouse District
Eclectic shops and restaurants
Bounded by Front, 11th, Pine, and Christian Sts.
(215) 413-3713

▶ VISITOR INFORMATION

Philadelphia Convention and Visitors Bureau
1700 Market St., Ste. 3000
Philadelphia, PA 19103
(215) 636-3300 or (800) 225-5745
www.pcvb.org

Independence Visitor Center
1 N. Independence Mall W.,
6th and Market Sts.
(215) 965-7676 or (800) 537-7676

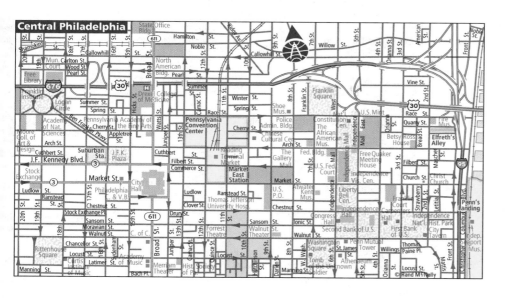

▶ DIVERSION

In nearby Merion, view 4,000 objects of art on display, including a stunning collection of French early Modern and Post-Impressionist paintings, Native American pottery, and Greek, Roman, and Egyptian artifacts at the Barnes Foundation Gallery and Arboretum. Stroll the 13 acres of gardens. Advance reservations are required. Call (610) 667-0290, option 5, or go to www.barnesfoundation.org for reservation forms. Take I-76 west to exit 339 to US 1 south. Turn right onto 54th St. (Old Lancaster Rd.), taking a left onto N. Latch's Lane, then follow signs.

PHOENIX, Arizona

Hot-air balloon race over Phoenix

Baking in the dry Southwestern sun, Phoenix is a busy, growing metropolis surrounded by mountain resorts and fertile, well-irrigated fields. In the heart of the city, Cooper Square is filled with restaurants, stores, theaters, and big-time sports venues, plus the Arizona Science Center, a family-oriented exploration arena with more than 350 hands-on activities, a planetarium, and a large-screen theater. The Heard Museum also offers interactive exhibits among its ten galleries devoted to the art and culture of the Southwest's Native Americans. At the Desert Botanical Garden in Papago Park, visitors can stroll through 145 acres of cacti and other dry-region plants. *Tax: 12.07% hotel, 8.1% sales. For local weather, call (602) 275-0073.*

▶ SELECTED ATTRACTIONS

Arizona Capitol Museum
1700 W. Washington St.
(602) 542-4675

Arizona Mining and Mineral Museum
1502 W. Washington St.
(602) 255-3795

Arizona Science Center
600 E. Washington St.
(602) 716-2000

Deer Valley Rock Art Center
Ancient petroglyphs in a desert preserve
3711 W. Deer Valley Rd.
(623) 582-8007

Desert Botanical Garden
1201 N. Galvin Pkwy.
(480) 941-1225

Dolly Steamboat Excursion
Canyon Lake tours
45 miles east off AZ 88 (via US 60),
Canyon Lake
(480) 827-9144

Gila River Indian Arts & Crafts Center & Heritage Museum
20 miles south off I-10, Sacaton
(520) 315-3411

Hall of Flame Museum of Firefighting
6101 E. Van Buren St.
(602) 275-3473

Heard Museum
Native American art
2301 N. Central Ave.
(602) 252-8848

Hot Air Expeditions
Hot-air balloon flights
2243 E. Rose Garden Loop
(480) 502-6999 or (800) 831-7610

Museo Chicano
Museum of Latino arts, history, and culture
147 E. Adams St.
(602) 257-5536

Oasis Water Park
Pointe South Mountain Resort
7777 S. Pointe Pkwy.
(602) 438-9000

Phoenix Art Museum
1625 N. Central Ave.
(602) 257-1880

Phoenix Zoo
455 N. Galvin Pkwy.
(602) 273-1341

Pioneer Arizona Living History Village
95 acres of historic buildings and Fort Brent Wood
3901 W. Pioneer Rd., exit 225 off I-17
(625) 465-1052

Pueblo Grande Museum and Archaeological Park
Prehistoric Hohokam Indian ruins
4619 E. Washington St.
(602) 495-0901 or (877) 706-4408

Taliesin West
Frank Lloyd Wright's winter home and studio
Cactus Rd. and Frank Lloyd Wright Blvd.,
Scottsdale
(480) 860-8810 or (480) 860-2700

▶ SHOPPING

Arizona Center
Restaurants, specialty shops, and nightclubs
3rd and Van Buren Sts.
(602) 271-4000

Arizona Mills
Factory outlet stores
US 60 and I-10, Tempe
(480) 491-7300

Arrowhead Towne Center
Specialty retailers, eateries, and cinema
7700 W. Arrowhead Towne Center Dr.,
Glendale
(623) 979-9764

Biltmore Fashion Park
Upscale boutiques
2502 E. Camelback Rd.
(602) 955-8400

The Borgata of Scottsdale
Unique stores and eateries in an open-air setting
6166 N. Scottsdale Rd., Scottsdale
(602) 953-6311

Chandler Fashion Center
Shops, restaurants, and movie theaters
3111 W. Chandler Blvd., Chandler
(480) 812-8488

Scottsdale Fashion Square
7014 E. Camelback Rd.
(480) 949-0202

Tlaquepaque
Spanish colonial village with specialty galleries and shops
336 AZ 179, Sedona
(928) 282-4838

▶ VISITOR INFORMATION

Greater Phoenix Convention and Visitors Bureau
400 E. Van Buren St., Ste. 600
Phoenix, AZ 85004
(602) 254-6500 or (877) 225-5749
www.visitphoenix.com

▶ DON'T MISS DRIVE

Cruise downtown Phoenix, especially Copper Square to see the murals, copper-painted fixtures, and newer architectural icons like the BOB, home of the city's Major League Baseball team, the Arizona Diamondbacks.

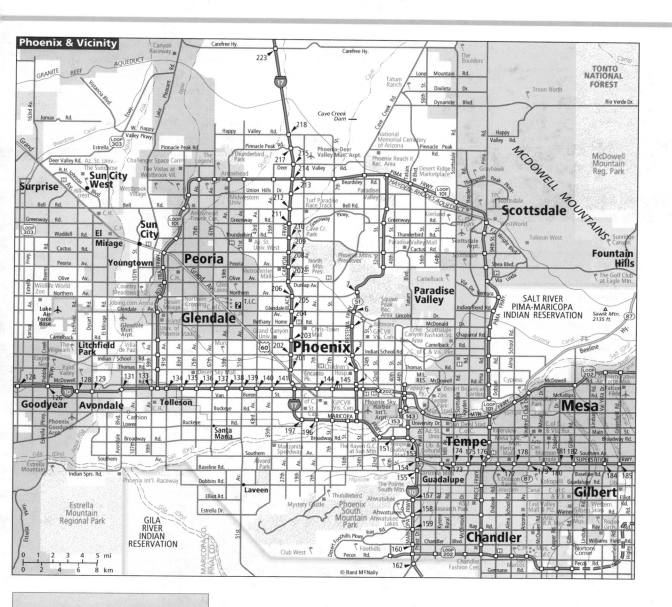

Phoenix & Vicinity

DIVERSION

See the majesty of purple mountains on a day trip to Sedona and Oak Creek Canyon. It's about a 90-minute drive. Take I-17 north to AZ 179 and look for the Sedona exit.

PITTSBURGH, Pennsylvania

Point State Park

Tucked into the steep hills of the Allegheny Plateau, this once-grimy town now sparkles with steel and glass. Barges ply the waters of the Ohio, Alleghany, and Monongahela rivers past Point State Park, where the Fort Pitt Museum interprets Pittsburgh's early history. North of the rivers, the Carnegie Science Center invites visitors to try hundreds of hands-on experiments, and the Andy Warhol Museum displays some 500 works by the most well-known American artist of the late 20th century. For a taste of commuting Pittsburgh-style, ride the century-old Duquesne Incline cable cars. *Tax: 14% hotel, 7% sales. For local weather, call (412) 936-1212 or (412) 262-2170.*

▶ SELECTED ATTRACTIONS

Andy Warhol Museum
117 Sandusky St.
(412) 237-8300

Carnegie Museums of Art and Natural History
4400 Forbes Ave.
(412) 622-3131

Carnegie Science Center
Includes planetarium and Omnimax theater
1 Allegheny Ave.
(412) 237-3400

Duquesne Incline
Cable car incline up Mt. Washington
1220 Grandview Ave.
(412) 381-1665

Frick Art & Historical Center
7227 Reynolds St.
(412) 371-0600

Hartwood Mansion and Estate
Tudor mansion in 629-acre park
215 Saxonburg Blvd.
(412) 767-9200

Kennywood
Amusement park
4800 Kennywood Blvd., West Mifflin
(412) 461-0500

National Aviary
Allegheny Commons West at Ridge and Arch Sts.
(412) 323-7235

Phipps Conservatory and Botanical Gardens
1 Schenley Park
(412) 622-6914

Point State Park
Fort Pitt Blockhouse and Museum
101 Commonwealth Pl., Golden Triangle
(888) 727-2757

▶ SHOPPING

Downtown
Department stores and specialty shops
Bounded by Wood St., Sixth St., Smithfield St., and Forbes Ave.

The Mall at Robinson
Department stores and specialty shops
100 Robinson Centre Dr.
(412) 788-0816

Shadyside
Upscale specialty shops and boutiques
Walnut St. between Aiken and Negley Aves.
(412) 682-1298

The Waterfront
Shops and entertainment
285 E. Waterfront Dr., Homestead
(412) 476-8889

▶ VISITOR INFORMATION

Greater Pittsburgh Convention and Visitors Bureau
425 6th Ave., 30th Fl.
Pittsburgh, PA 15219
(412) 281-7711 or (800) 359-0758
www.visitpittsburgh.com

Downtown Visitor Center
On Liberty Ave. at Stanwix St., adjacent to Gateway Center

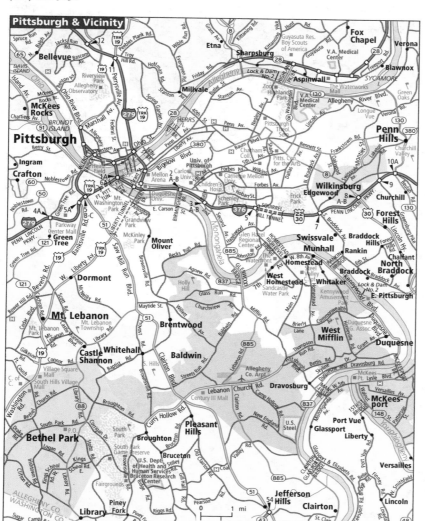

PORTLAND, Oregon

Under the gaze of Mount Hood, Portland takes pride in citywide environmental consciousness. The transportation system, much of it free, connects neighborhoods, suburbs, and attractions. The International Rose Test Gardens in Washington Park help the city earn its title as the "City of Roses." Anchoring the Culture District, the Oregon Historical Society brings the story of the Northwest alive through artifacts and multimedia presentations. The reinvented Pearl District finds shoppers looking through boutiques and tasting daring cuisines in what was once an area of heavy industry. *Tax: 12.5% hotel, no sales tax. For local weather, call (503) 275-9792 or (503) 261-9246.*

Portland skyline with Mount Hood

▶ SELECTED ATTRACTIONS

The Grotto: National Sanctuary of Our Sorrowful Mother
Catholic shrine and botanical garden
NE 85th Ave. and Sandy Blvd.
(503) 254-7371

Hoyt Arboretum
4000 SW Fairview Blvd. in Washington Park
(503) 865-8733

International Rose Test Gardens
400 SW Kingston Ave. in Washington Park
(503) 823-3636

Oregon Historical Society Museum
1200 SW Park Ave.
(503) 222-1741

Oregon Museum of Science and Industry
1945 SE Water Ave.
(503) 797-4000

Oregon Zoo
4001 SW Canyon Rd. in Washington Park
(503) 226-1561

Pittock Mansion
1914 mansion of the founder of The Oregonian *newspaper*
3229 NW Pittock Dr.
(503) 823-3624

Portland Art Museum
1219 SW Park Ave.
(503) 226-2811

Portland Children's Museum
4015 SW Canyon Rd. in Washington Park
(503) 223-6500

Portland Classical Chinese Garden
NW 3rd Ave. at Everett St.
(503) 228-8131

World Forestry Center
4033 SW Canyon Rd. in Washington Park
(503) 228-1367

▶ SHOPPING

Lloyd Center Mall
Department stores and specialty shops
NE Multnomah St. and 9th Ave.
(503) 282-2511

Nob Hill/Northwest Portland
Trendy shops, restaurants, and cafés
Along NW 23rd and 21st Aves.
(503) 706-6532

Pearl District
Industrial-chic architecture, shops, and cafés
Bounded by NW Broadway Ave., I-405, NW Naito-Parkway, and Burnside Ave.
(503) 227-8519

Pioneer Place
Department stores and specialty shops
888 SW 5th Ave.
(503) 228-5800

▶ VISITOR INFORMATION

Portland Oregon Visitors Association
1000 SW Broadway, Ste. 2300
Portland, OR 97205
(503) 275-9750 or (800) 962-3700
www.travelportland.com

Portland Oregon Information Center
701 SW 6th Ave.
Pioneer Square
(503) 275-8355 or (877) 678-5263

PROVIDENCE, Rhode Island

Morning in Providence

Founded on principles of religious freedom by Roger Williams, Providence is still regarded as a bastion of liberal idealism. Home to Brown University, the city displays its Colonial-era roots along Benefit Street. The collections at the RISD Museum touch upon all eras of human endeavor. Five thousand years of cooking and hospitality are the focus of the Culinary Archives and Museum. Bargain hunters head to The Arcade, reputedly the nation's first enclosed shopping area. *Tax: 13% hotel, 7% sales. For local weather, call (508) 822-0634.*

► SELECTED ATTRACTIONS

Culinary Archives & Museum at Johnson & Wales University
315 Harborside Blvd.
(401) 598-2805

DePasquale Square/Federal Hill
Historic Italian neighborhood
Atwells Ave.

John Brown House
Historic home of 18th-century merchant
52 Power St.
(401) 273-7507

The Meeting House
America's first Baptist church
75 N. Main St.
(401) 454-3418

Providence Children's Museum
100 South St.
(401) 273-5437

The RISD Museum
Fine and decorative arts
224 Benefit St.
(401) 454-6500

Roger Williams National Memorial
Tribute to Rhode Island's founder
282 N. Main St.
(401) 521-7266

► SHOPPING

The Arcade
Specialty shops
65 Weybosset St.
(401) 598-1199

Providence Place Mall
1 Providence Pl.
(401) 270-1000

Thayer Street Shops
Galleries and boutiques
Between Lloyd Ave. and George St.

Wickenden Street
Antiques, galleries, and coffeehouses
Between Benefit and Hope Sts.

► VISITOR INFORMATION

The Providence Warwick Convention and Visitors Bureau
1 W. Exchange St.
Providence, RI 02903
(401) 456-0200 or (800) 233-1636
www.pwcvb.com

Providence Visitors Center
1 Sabin St. (in the Rhode Island Convention Center)
(401) 751-1177 or (800) 233-1636

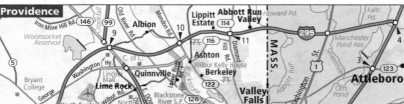

► DIVERSION

Relive Gilded Age glamour on a tour of Newport, where historic, opulent mansions were built as summer homes by some of America's wealthiest families at the turn of the 20th century. Take I-195 east to RI 24 south, then RI 114 south into downtown Newport and to Bellevue Ave. (401) 847-1000

RALEIGH/DURHAM/CHAPEL HILL, North Carolina

The three cities that make up the Research Triangle region are unusually well endowed with institutions of higher learning. Raleigh is home to North Carolina State University as well as many fine museums. The Museum of History features displays on the Civil War, health and healing, and a sports hall of fame, while the Exploris Museum encourages visitors to connect with other cultures of the world. *Tax: 13% hotel, 6% sales, 1% food and beverage. For local weather, call (919) 515-8209.*

Durham first came to prominence thanks to bright leaf tobacco. Duke University was founded through the largess of tobacco's wealthiest families. The rough existence of the first tobacco farmers is retold by costumed interpreters at the Duke Homestead historic site. Downtown, former tobacco warehouses now house galleries, restaurants, and shops in the redeveloped Brightleaf Square. *Tax: 12.75% hotel, 6.75% sales (retail and restaurants), 2% sales (groceries), car rental: 16% in Durham, 25.61% at RDU International Airport. For local weather, call (919) 515-8225.*

The original University of North Carolina was chartered at Chapel Hill in 1789. Budding stargazers can travel to the edge of the universe through the Star Theatre at the campus's Morehead Planetarium. The Collection Gallery displays diverse artifacts, including items from the Sir Walter Raleigh collection. Lovers of flowers and trees can stop at the Coker Arboretum on campus or head to the 600-acre North Carolina Botanical Garden. *Tax: 5% hotel, 6.75% sales.*

Raleigh skyline

▶ SELECTED ATTRACTIONS

RALEIGH

African-American Cultural Complex
Exhibits, performances, and outdoor drama
119 Sunnybrook Rd.
(919) 250-9336

Artspace
Art gallery
201 E. Davie St. in City Market
(919) 821-2787

Exploris
Interactive world cultures museum
201 E. Hargett St.
(919) 834-4040

North Carolina Museum of History
5 E. Edenton St.
(919) 807-7900

North Carolina State Capitol
1 E. Edenton St. in Capitol Square
(919) 733-4994

Playspace
Children's museum
410 Glenwood Ave.
(919) 832-1212

continued on the next page

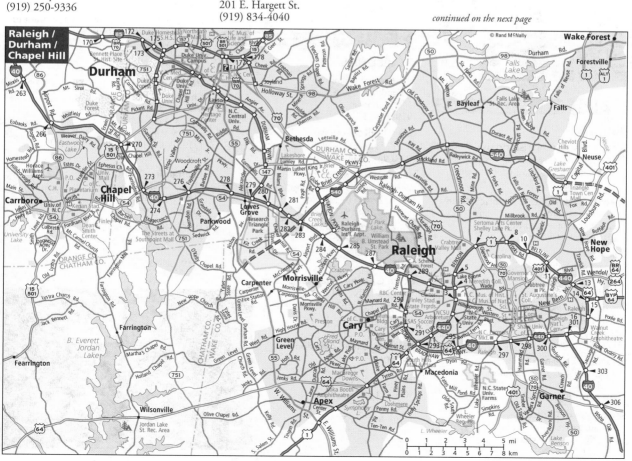

Raleigh attractions continued

▶ **SHOPPING**

RALEIGH

Cameron Village Shopping Center
Upscale boutiques, salons, and antiques
1900 Cameron St.
(919) 821-1350

City Market
Art galleries, specialty shops, and restaurants
Blake St. at Martin and Blount Sts.
(919) 832-9300

Crabtree Valley Mall
Department stores and specialty shops
4325 Glenwood Ave.
(919) 787-8993 or (800) 963-7467

Triangle Town Center
Department stores and specialty shops
5959 Triangle Town Blvd. at Capital Blvd.
and Old Wake Forest Rd.
(919) 792-2222

Butterfly house at the North Carolina Museum of Life and Science in Durham

▶ **SELECTED ATTRACTIONS**

DURHAM

Bennett Place State Historic Site
Site of Confederate surrender
4409 Bennett Memorial Rd.
(919) 383-4345

Duke Homestead State Historic Site and Tobacco Museum
2828 Duke Homestead Rd.
(919) 477-5498

Duke University Chapel
Chapel Dr. on the Duke University
West campus
(919) 684-2572

Hayti Heritage Center
African American artifacts and performances
804 Old Fayetteville St.
(919) 683-1709

Museum of Life and Science
Butterfly house and insectarium
433 Murray Ave.
(919) 220-5429

Sarah P. Duke Gardens
426 Anderson St. on the Duke
University West campus
(919) 684-3698

DON'T MISS DRIVE

Visit Raleigh's Historic Oakwood District, a Victorian neighborhood listed on the National Register of Historic Places. The restored homes in this 20-block enclave, bordered by Franklin, Watauga, Linden, Jones and Person Sts., date from 1870 to 1912. The Oakwood Cemetery (701 Oakwood Ave.) is the burial site of 2,800 Confederate soldiers and five Civil War generals.

▶ **SHOPPING**

DURHAM

Brightleaf Square
Art galleries and specialty shops
905 W. Main St.
(919) 682-9229

Ninth Street Shopping District
Shops, boutiques, and restaurants
Between Main St. and Club Blvd., near
Duke University's East campus

Northgate Mall
Department stores and specialty shops
1058 W. Club Blvd. off I-85, exit 176-A
(919) 286-4400

The Streets at Southpoint
Department stores and specialty shops
6910 Fayetteville Rd.
(919) 572-8808

▶ **SELECTED ATTRACTIONS**

CHAPEL HILL

Ackland Art Museum
E. Franklin St. at S. Columbia St. on the
UNC campus
(919) 966-5736

Chapel Hill Museum
523 E. Franklin St.
(919) 967-1400

Horace Williams House
19th-century home and art gallery
610 E. Rosemary St.
(919) 942-7818

Morehead Planetarium and Science Center
250 E. Franklin St. on the UNC campus
(919) 962-1236

North Carolina Botanical Garden
US 15-501/NC 54 Bypass
(Fordham Blvd.) to Old Mason
Farm Rd.
(919) 962-0522

North Carolina Collection Gallery
Sir Walter Raleigh rooms and North Carolina history
Wilson Library on the
UNC campus
(919) 962-1172

▶ **SHOPPING**

CHAPEL HILL

Downtown Shopping District
Boutiques and specialty shops
Franklin and Rosemary Sts. at Columbia St.

University Mall
Department stores and specialty shops
201 S. Estes Dr.
(919) 967-6934

▶ **VISITOR INFORMATION**

Greater Raleigh Convention and Visitors Bureau
421 Fayetteville Street Mall, Ste. 1505
Raleigh, NC 27602
(919) 834-5900 or (800) 849-8499
www.visitraleigh.com

Durham Convention and Visitors Bureau and Information Center
101 E. Morgan St.
Durham, NC 27701
(919) 687-0288 or (800) 446-8604
www.durham-nc.com

Chapel Hill/Orange County Visitors Bureau
501 W. Franklin St.
Chapel Hill, NC 27516
(919) 968-2060 or (888) 968-2060
www.chocvb.org

Capital Area Visitor Center
Lobby of Museum of History
5 E. Edenton St., Raleigh
(919) 807-7950

UNC Visitors Center at Morehead Planetarium
250 E. Franklin St., Chapel Hill
(919) 962-1630

North Carolina Botanical Garden in Chapel Hill

RENO, Nevada

Self-tagged "The Biggest Little City in the World," Reno is expanding beyond its image as a glittery gambler's oasis. While casinos and top-name musical acts are still the main draw, the city's newer attractions stress the arts and outdoors activities. The Nevada Museum of Art collection focuses on land and the environment. Another recent addition, the Truckee River Whitewater Park, runs straight through downtown, offering class II and III rapids over a half-mile course. *Tax: 12.5% hotel, 7.375% sales. For local weather, call (775) 673-8100 or (775) 673-8130.*

Nightlife in Reno

▶ SELECTED ATTRACTIONS

Brüka Theater
Live theater
99 N. Virginia St.
(775) 323-3221

Eldorado Hotel and Casino
345 N. Virginia St.
(775) 786-5700 or (800) 648-5966

Fleischmann Planetarium and Science Center
Off N. Virginia St., north of
Lawor Events Center
(775) 784-4812

Mackay Mansion
Comstock King's Victorian mansion
129 S. D St., Virginia City
(775) 847-0336

National Automobile Museum
Vintage, classic, and special-interest vehicles
10 S. Lake St.
(775) 333-9300

Nevada Museum of Art
160 W. Liberty St.
(775) 329-3333

Sierra Safari Zoo
Seasonal wildlife park
10200 N. Virginia St.
(775) 677-1101

Truckee River Whitewater Park
Wingfield Park, First St. and Arlington Ave.
(775) 334-2262

Wilbur D. May Center/Great Basin Adventure
Museum, arboretum, and seasonal children's park
Rancho San Rafael Park, 1595 N. Sierra
(775) 785-5961

Wild Island Family Adventure Park
Water park
250 Wild Island Ct.
I-80 and Sparks Blvd., Sparks
(775) 359-2927

W.M. Keck Museum
Nevada mining exhibits
Center and 9th Sts. in the Mackay School of Mines, University of Nevada
(775) 784-4528

▶ SHOPPING

Arlington Gardens
Specialty shops
606 W. Plumb Ln.
(775) 828-3664

Meadowood Mall
Department and specialty stores
5000 Meadowood Mall Cir.,
S. Virginia St., and McCarran Blvd.
(775) 827-8451

The River Walk
Art galleries and upscale boutiques
1st St. at Sierra St.
(775) 348-8858

▶ VISITOR INFORMATION

Reno-Sparks Convention and Visitors Authority
4001 S. Virginia
Reno, NV 89501
(775) 827-7600 or (800) 367-7366
www.visitrenotahoe.com

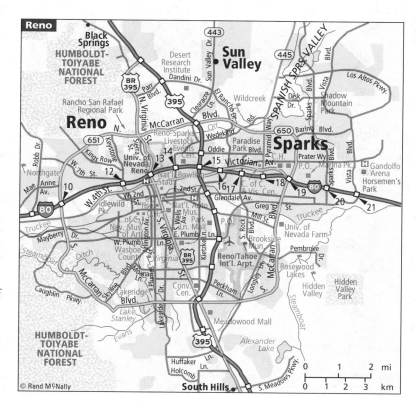

RICHMOND, Virginia

Sunken Garden at Agecroft Hall

Bristling with history, the capital of Virginia has witnessed much modern development even as it has successfully preserved its past. The Canal Walk offers an attractive stroll along the historic banks of the James River. Hipsters head to Shockoe Slip and Shockoe Bottom—areas once ravaged by floods and now reborn as headquarters for nightclubs, restaurants, and artists' lofts. A tour of the state capitol offers a view of its surprising hidden dome. *Tax: 13% hotel, 5% sales, 10% meal. For local weather, call (757) 899-4200.*

▶ SELECTED ATTRACTIONS

Agecroft Hall and Gardens
15th-century mansion moved from England
4305 Sulgrave Rd.
(804) 353-4241

Edgar Allen Poe Museum
1914 E. Main St.
(804) 648-5523

Lewis Ginter Botanical Garden
1800 Lakeside Ave.
(804) 262-9887

Maymont
House museum, children's farm, and nature/visitor center
2201 Shields Lake Dr.
(804) 358-7166

Museum and White House of the Confederacy
1201 E. Clay St.
(804) 649-1861

Paramount's Kings Dominion
Theme park
20 miles north off I-95, Doswell
(804) 876-5000

St. John's Church
Site of Patrick Henry speech
2401 E. Broad St.
(804) 648-5015

State Capitol
Capitol Square
(804) 698-1788

Three Lakes Nature Center and Aquarium
400 Sausiluta Dr.
(804) 652-3474

Virginia Historical Society Museum
428 North Blvd.
(804) 358-4901

Virginia Museum of Fine Arts
200 N. Boulevard
(804) 340-1400

▶ SHOPPING

Carytown
Unique shops and boutiques
Cary St. from Thompson St. to the Boulevard

Chesterfield Towne Center
Department stores and specialty shops
11500 Midlothian Tpk.
(804) 794-4662

Regency Square Mall
Department stores and specialty shops
1420 Parham Rd.
(804) 740-7467

Short Pump Town Center
Open-air market with high-end stores
11800 W. Broad St.
(804) 364-9500

▶ VISITOR INFORMATION

Richmond Metropolitan Convention and Visitors Bureau
401 N. 3rd St., Richmond, VA 23219
(804) 782-2777, (800) 370-9004, or
(888) 742-4666
www.richmondva.org

Richmond Region Visitor Center
405 N. 3rd St.
(804) 783-7450

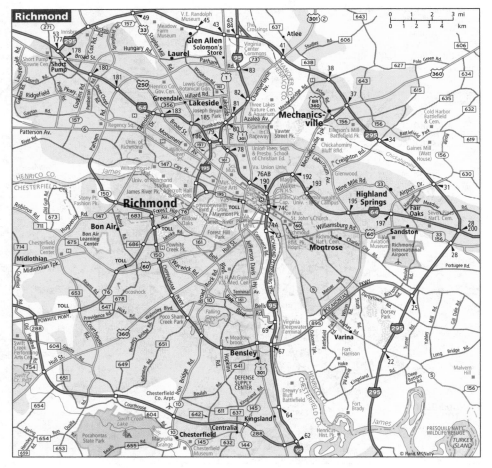

▶ DON'T MISS DRIVE

Tree-lined Monument Avenue commemorates Richmondites in statues of figures such as Confederate General Robert E. Lee, Confederate President Jefferson Davis, scientist/oceanographer Matthew Fontaine Maury, and tennis legend Arthur Ashe.

SACRAMENTO, California

California's state capital, where the gold rush began in 1849, is a major commercial center and inland port thanks to a deep water channel to San Francisco Bay. The city enjoys a wealth of historic sites including Sutter's Fort, the area's first European outpost, and the Governor's Mansion, which includes period furnishings of the 19th century. The clapboard buildings and cobblestone streets of Old Sacramento give visitors a taste of pioneer days. The many museums found here include the State Railroad Museum and its collection of painstakingly restored engines, coaches, dining, and work cars. *Tax: 12% hotel, 7.75% sales, 7.75% food and beverage. For local weather, call (916) 646-2000.*

Paddlewheelers on the Sacramento River

▶ SELECTED ATTRACTIONS

California Museum for History, Women and the Arts
1020 O St.
(916) 653-7524

California State Capitol Museum
10th and L Sts.
(916) 324-0333

California State Indian Museum
2618 K St.
(916) 324-0971

California State Railroad Museum
111 I St., Old Sacramento
(916) 445-6645

Crocker Art Museum
216 O St.
(916) 264-5423

Discovery Museum History Center
History exhibits
101 I St., Old Sacramento
(916) 264-7057

Discovery Museum Science and Space Center
Science and technology museum
3615 Auburn Blvd.
(916) 575-3941

Governor's Mansion State Historic Park
16th and H Sts.
(916) 323-3047

Old Sacramento Historic District
Museums and entertainment district
1004 2nd St.
(916) 442-7644

Sutter's Fort State Historic Park
2701 L St.
(916) 445-4422

Towe Auto Museum
2200 Front St.
(916) 442-6802

Wells Fargo History Museum
Commercial history exhibits
400 Capitol Mall
(916) 440-4161

Wells Fargo Pavilion
Home to Music Circus
1419 H St.
(916) 557-1999

▶ SHOPPING

Arden Fair
Department stores and specialty shops
Capital City Frwy. at Arden Way
(916) 920-1167

Pavilions
Upscale fashion boutiques and specialty shops
563 Pavilions Ln.
(916) 925-4463

Downtown Plaza
Department stores and specialty shops
K St. between 4th and 7th Sts.
(916) 442-4000

▶ VISITOR INFORMATION

Sacramento Convention and Visitors Bureau
1608 I St.
Sacramento, CA 95814
(916) 808-7777 or (800) 292-2334
www.sacramentocvb.org

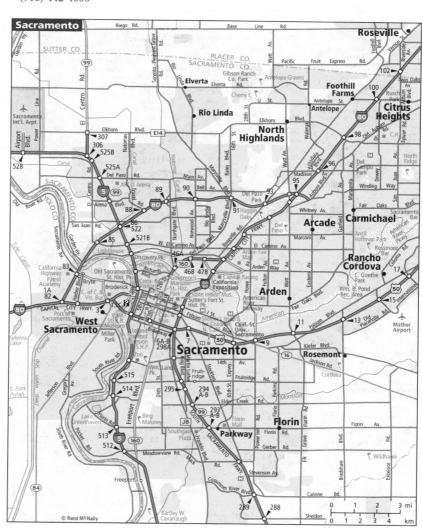

ST. LOUIS, Missouri

Downtown St. Louis and the Gateway Arch

Rolling westward from the banks of the Mississippi River, St. Louis offers a vision of national expansion symbolized in the city's most prominent landmark, the Gateway Arch. A ride to the top of this engineering marvel yields far-flung views of city, rivers, and plains. The green expanse of Forest Park is home to the top-rated St. Louis Zoo and the wide-ranging collections of the St. Louis Art Museum. Fine dining establishments line the quiet streets of the Central West End.

Tax: 7.25% hotel, 3.516% city sales, 4.225% state sales. For local weather, call (314) 321-2222 or (636) 441-8467.

► SELECTED ATTRACTIONS

Anheuser-Busch Brewery Tour
Clydesdale horse paddock/stable, historic brew house, and hospitality center
12th and Lynch Sts.
(314) 577-2626

Gateway Arch-Jefferson National Expansion Memorial
St. Louis Riverfront
(314) 655-1700

Laumeier Sculpture Park
Monumental contemporary sculpture
12580 Rott Rd., Sunset Hills
(314) 821-1209

Magic House/St. Louis Children's Museum
516 S. Kirkwood Rd.
(314) 822-8900

Missouri Botanical Garden
4344 Shaw Blvd.
(314) 577-9400

St. Louis Art Museum
1 Fine Arts Dr.
(314) 721-0072

St. Louis Zoo
1 Government Dr. in Forest Park
(314) 781-0900

► SHOPPING

Cherokee Antique Row
Fine antiques to funky collectibles
Cherokee St. from Indiana to Lempe Sts.
(314) 772-9177

St. Louis Union Station
Specialty shops, entertainment, and restaurants
1820 Market St.
(314) 421-6655

St. Louis Galleria
Upscale boutiques and department stores
1155 St. Louis Galleria
(314) 863-5500

► VISITOR INFORMATION

St. Louis Convention and Visitors Commission
701 Convention Plaza, Ste. 300
St. Louis, MO 63101
(314) 421-1023 or (800) 888-3861
www.explorestlouis.com

► DON'T MISS DRIVE

Relive the glory days of Route 66. Markers along Chippewa and Manchester Roads will guide you. Follow it west through St. Louis County to see roadside motels and diners scattered among busy modern areas.

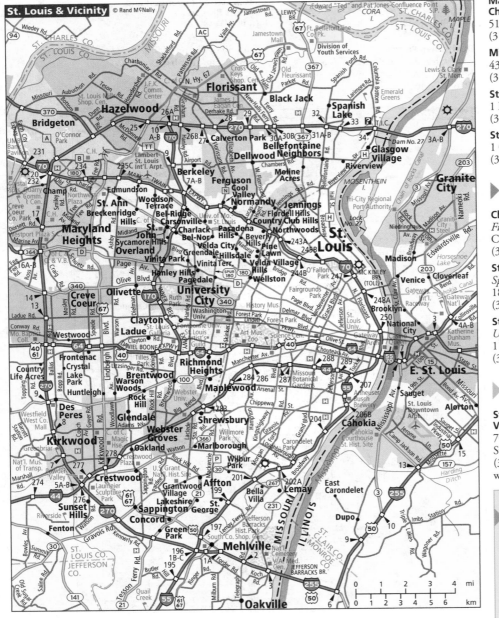

St. Louis & Vicinity © Rand McNally

SALT LAKE CITY, Utah

Founded as a haven for the Mormon church in 1847, Salt Lake City has become a magnet for outdoor enthusiasts who find plenty of mountain resort areas within a few miles of downtown. Temple Square and the Beehive House once occupied by early Mormon leader Brigham Young are two of the historic sites related to the Latter-day Saints. Of more recent vintage, Olympic Park, where the 2002 Winter Games were held, is now a training site for the U.S. Olympic team; tours are available. *Tax: 12.45% hotel, 6.6% goods and services, 7.6% restaurants. For local weather, call (801) 524-5133.*

Beehive House

▶ SELECTED ATTRACTIONS

Beehive House
Restored residence of Brigham Young
67 E. South Temple St.
(801) 240-2671

Clark Planetarium at the Gateway
Star shows, science exhibits, and theater
110 S. 400 West St.
(801) 456-7827

Family History Library
World's largest genealogical research library
35 N. West Temple St.
(801) 240-2584 or (800) 346-6044

Historic Temple Square
Mormon Tabernacle, museums, and choir
Bounded by N., S., and W. Temple Sts. and Main St.
(801) 240-4872 or (800) 537-9703

Utah's Hogle Zoo
2600 Sunnyside Ave.
(801) 582-1631

▶ SHOPPING

Fashion Place Mall
Department stores and specialty shops
6191 S. State St., Murray
(801) 262-9447

Gardner Village
Specialty shops in historic area
1100 W. 7800 S.
(801) 566-8903

Historic Trolley Square
Shops, dining, and entertainment marketplace
367 Trolley Square
(801) 521-9877

The ZCMI Center
Department stores and specialty shops
365 State St.
(801) 321-5945

▶ VISITOR INFORMATION

Salt Lake City Convention and Visitors Bureau
90 S. West Temple St.
Salt Lake City, UT 84101
(801) 521-2822 or (800) 541-4955
www.visitsaltlake.com

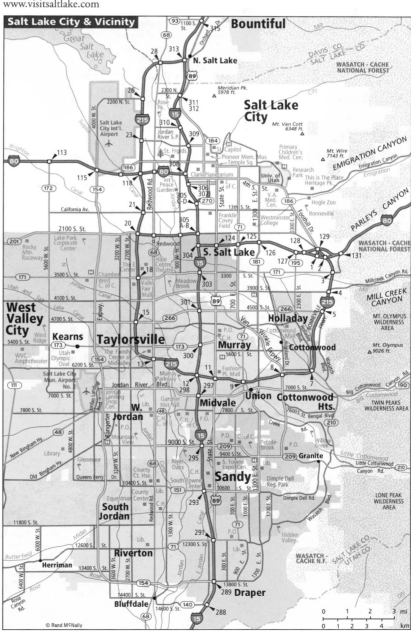

▶ DIVERSION

Swoosh! Site of the 2002 Olympic Winter Games, Utah Olympic Park is located 28 miles east of Salt Lake City on I-80, off exit 145. Tours include competition sites plus an opportunity to see future Olympians in training. You can even ride a bobsled at 70 mph. (435) 658-4200

SAN ANTONIO, Texas

Although it has earned a place among the top 10 largest cities in the country, San Antonio retains a laidback atmosphere amid the singular charms of its Spanish colonial past. A nine-mile walking and biking path connects the mission churches preserved along the Mission National Historic District. Shops, hotels, and restaurants line three miles of riverwalk along the San Antonio River. Tour boats ply the water here, too. First and foremost, the city will always be known for the Alamo, the most enduring symbol of Texas's independent frame of mind. *Tax: 16.75% hotel, 8.125% sales. For local weather, call (830) 606-3617 or (830) 609-2029.*

Entrance to the Spanish Governor's Palace

DON'T MISS DRIVE

Relive history along the Mission Trail. Pick up a map and start at the headquarters for the San Antonio Missions National Historic Park, 2202 Roosevelt Ave. (210) 932-1001

The Alamo
Site of Texan holdout in 1836
300 Alamo Plaza
(210) 225-1391

Buckhorn Saloon and Museum
Texas history artifacts
318 E. Houston St.
(210) 247-4000

Casa Navarro State Historical Park
Texas history preserved in a circa-1800 house
228 S. Laredo St.
(210) 226-4801

IMAX Theatre at Rivercenter
849 E. Commerce, Rivercenter Mall
(800) 354-4629

Japanese Tea Garden
3800 N. St. Mary's St.
(210) 207-7275

King William Historic District
Shopping and entertainment district
King William St. and surrounding area
(210) 227-8786

Majestic Theater
Historic vaudeville movie palace and home of the San Antonio Symphony
224 E. Houston
(210) 226-3333

McNay Art Museum
6000 N. New Braunfels St.
(210) 824-5368

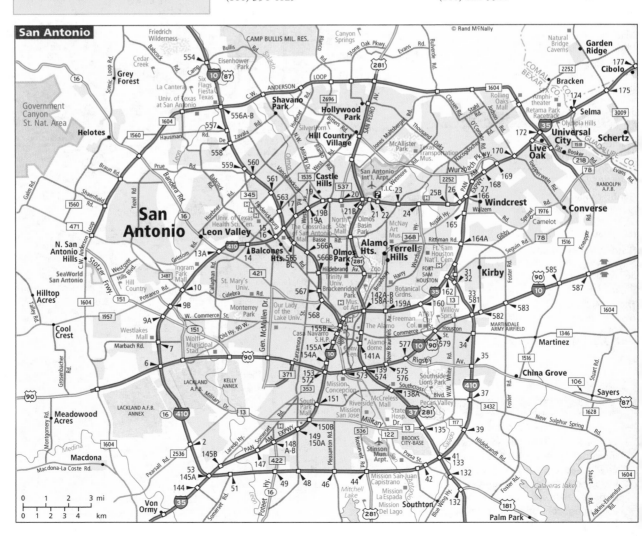

Natural Bridge Wildlife Park
26515 Natural Bridge Caverns Rd.
(830) 438-7400

San Antonio Botanical Gardens
555 Funston Pl.
(210) 207-3250

San Antonio Missions National Historic Park
2202 Roosevelt Ave.
(210) 534-8833

San Antonio Museum of Art
200 W. Jones Ave.
(210) 978-8100

San Antonio Zoological Gardens and Aquarium
3903 N. St. Mary's St.
(210) 734-7184

SeaWorld San Antonio
10500 SeaWorld Dr.
(800) 700-7786

Six Flags Fiesta Texas
15 miles west off I-10
(210) 697-5050

Spanish Governor's Palace
105 Plaza de Armas, behind City Hall
(210) 224-0601

Tower of the Americas
Panoramic views and restaurant
600 HemisFair Park
(210) 223-3101

University of Texas Institute of Texan Cultures
Texas history and culture
801 S. Bowie St. at HemisFair Park
(210) 458-2300

Witte Museum
Museum of history, science, and culture
3801 Broadway St. in Brackenridge Park
(210) 357-1900

▶ SHOPPING

Artisan's Alley
Handcrafted pottery and folk art
555 West Bitters Rd.
(210) 494-3226

El Mercado—Market Square
Farmers' market and specialty shops
514 W. Commerce St.
(210) 207-8600

La Villita
Arts and crafts shops
418 Villita St.
(210) 207-8610

North Star Mall
Fine shops and the world's largest cowboy boots
7400 San Pedro
(210) 342-2325

River Walk
Specialty shops, restaurants, and nightlife
Downtown along the San Antonio River
(210) 227-4262

▶ VISITOR INFORMATION

San Antonio Convention and Visitors Bureau
203 S. St. Mary's St., 2nd Floor
San Antonio, TX 78205
(210) 207-6700 or (800) 447-3372
www.sanantoniocvb.com

The Alamo

▶ DIVERSION

Mission San Juan Capistrano, established along the banks of the San Antonio River in 1731, has a bell tower still in operation and self-guided nature trails. 9101 Graf Rd. (210) 534-0749

The Ursuline Campus of the Southwest School of Art & Craft is located within walking distance of the Riverwalk. The convent was established in 1851 and the complex expanded throughout the 1800s under the architectural direction of Francois Giraud. In 1971, it came into the hands of the Southwest School of Art & Craft, which continues to restore the buildings and grounds. The facility is now on the National Register of Historic Places. Visitors are taken aback by the elegant architecture, the serenity of the chapel with some original stained glass windows, and the gardens. Parking, tours, a restaurant, museum, and retail shop are located at 300 Augusta in San Antonio. (210) 224-1848

SAN DIEGO, California

Gaslamp Quarter National Historic District

With sunshine and mild temperatures year-round, San Diego enjoys an ideal climate few cities can match. Balboa Park—part urban wilderness, part cultural domain—houses a dozen museums and the world-famous San Diego Zoo. The city's original settlement is preserved at Old Town Park, now filled with specialty shops and restaurants. Trendy nightspots are found downtown in the Gaslamp Quarter. Animals and people cavort at Mission Bay Park on the north side, where SeaWorld's manatees, dolphins, and other sea creatures reside. *Tax: 10.5% hotel, 7.75% sales. For local weather, call (858) 289-1212 or (858) 297-2107.*

▶ SELECTED ATTRACTIONS

Balboa Park
Zoo, museums, theaters, and gardens
1549 El Prado
(619) 239-0512

DON'T MISS DRIVE

Prospect Street in San Diego's La Jolla neighborhood is lined with boutiques and art galleries and offers some of the finest seaside dining around.

Birch Aquarium at Scripps Institute
2300 Expedition Way, La Jolla
(858) 534-3474

Cabrillo National Monument
Museum, historic lighthouse, and trails
At the end of Cabrillo Memorial Dr.
(619) 557-5450

Hotel del Coronado
Historic lodging featuring Victorian architecture and design
1500 Orange Ave., Coronado
(619) 435-6611

LEGOLAND California
Amusement park, rides, and games
1 Legoland Dr., Carlsbad
(760) 918-5346

Mission San Luis Rey de Francia
California's largest mission
4050 Mission Ave., Oceanside
(760) 757-3651

Museum of Contemporary Art San Diego
1001 Kettner Blvd.
(619) 234-1001
700 Prospect St., La Jolla
(858) 454-3541

Old Town San Diego State Historic Park
San Diego Ave. and Twiggs St.
(619) 220-5422

Reuben H. Fleet Science Center
1875 El Prado in Balboa Park
(619) 238-1233

San Diego Air & Space Museum
2001 Pan American Plaza in Balboa Park
(619) 234-8291

San Diego Museum of Man
1350 El Prado in Balboa Park
(619) 239-2001

San Diego Zoo's Wild Animal Park
15500 San Pasqual Valley Rd., Escondido
(760) 747-8702

San Diego Zoo
2920 Zoo Dr. in Balboa Park
(619) 231-1515

SeaWorld San Diego
500 SeaWorld Dr. in Mission Bay Park
(619) 226-3900 or (800) 257-4268

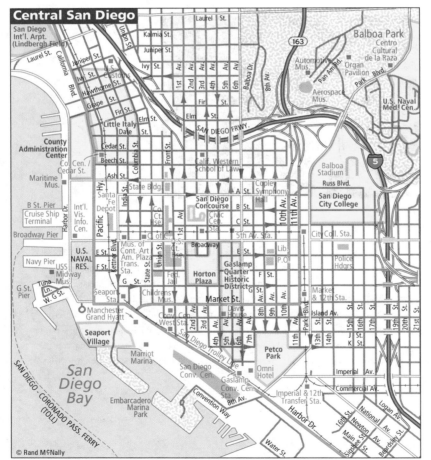

Central San Diego

© Rand McNally

▶ SHOPPING

Gaslamp Quarter National Historic District
Shops, restaurants, clubs, and theaters
Between Broadway and W. Harbor Dr. and 4th and 6th Aves.
(619) 233-5227

Seaport Village
Waterfront shops, dining, and entertainment
Kettner Blvd. and W. Harbor Dr.
(619) 235-4014

Horton Plaza
Shops, dining, and entertainment
Between Broadway and G St. and 1st and
4th Aves.
(619) 239-8180

▶ VISITOR INFORMATION

**San Diego Convention and
Visitors Bureau**
2215 India St.
San Diego, CA 92101
(619) 232-3101
www.sandiego.org

International Visitor Information Center
1040 1/3 W. Broadway
(619) 236-1212

La Jolla Visitor Information Center
7966 Herschel Ave.
(619) 236-1212

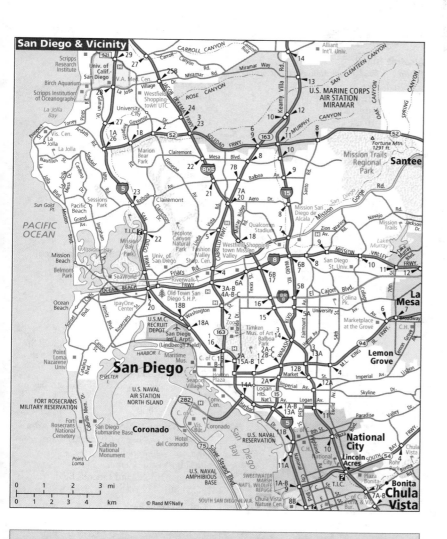

DIVERSION

Only 17 miles south of San Diego in Baja California, Mexico, Tijuana offers duty-free shopping, great food, and authentic Mexican folk art. Take I-5 or I-805 south to the border. For more on Tijuana, see page 111. For tips on border crossing, see page 177.

SAN FRANCISCO, California

Alcatraz Island, part of Golden Gate National Recreation Area

Cable cars, Chinatown, and the Golden Gate Bridge are just a few of the symbols by which the world recognizes this, the most romantic of American cities. Restaurants and souvenir shops swarm the waterfront at places like The Cannery and Fisherman's Wharf. Tours of Alcatraz Island show visitors life at the former prison, which lies within earshot of the city. For a bit of quiet time, sit and sip at the Japanese Tea Garden, one of many pleasures found within enormous Golden Gate Park. Silver dollar pancakes at the famous 65-year-old Sears Fine Foods restaurant satisfy hungry breakfast patrons. *Tax: 14% hotel, 8.5% sales. For local weather, call (831) 656-1725.*

▶ SELECTED ATTRACTIONS

Alcatraz Island
Historic federal prison, now part of a national recreation area
Ferry leaves from Pier 33 on
The Embarcadero
(415) 705-1042

Aquarium of the Bay
Embarcadero at Beach St. on Pier 39
(415) 623-5300 or (888) 732-3483

Asian Art Museum of San Francisco
200 Larkin St.
(415) 581-3500

Chinatown
Largest Chinatown in the U.S.
Bounded by Bush, Stockton, Jackson, and Kearney Sts.
(415) 982-3000

Coit Tower on Telegraph Hill
Said to be a memorial to San Francisco's firefighters
Lombard St. and Grant Ave.
(415) 362-0808

Exploratorium
Hands-on science and art museum
3601 Lyon St.
(415) 561-0360

Ferry Building, Port of San Francisco
Culinary-themed shops and eateries
On the Embarcadero
(415) 693-0996

Fisherman's Wharf
Waterfront marketplace and entertainment district
Jefferson St. between Hyde and Powell Sts.
(415) 956-3493

Golden Gate Bridge
Spans the entrance to San Francisco Bay on US 101
(415) 923-2000

Golden Gate National Recreation Area
Recreation and nearly 60 miles of coastline in and near San Francisco
Presidio Visitor Center
Montgomery St. and Lincoln Blvd.
(415) 561-4323

Golden Gate Park
Museums, arboretum, and Japanese garden
Bounded by the Great Highway, Lincoln Way, and Stanyan and Fulton Sts.
(415) 831-2700

Grace Cathedral
Third-largest Episcopal cathedral in the country and a re-creation of Notre Dame
1100 California St.
(415) 749-6300

Legion of Honor
European fine art museum
34th Ave. and Clement St. in Lincoln Park
(415) 863-3330

Central San Francisco

PACIFIC OCEAN

San Francisco Bay

© Rand McNally

▶ DON'T MISS DRIVE

Drive the "crookedest street in the world" in San Francisco: Lombard Street between Hyde and Leavenworth Streets. It zigzags down steep Russian Hill, passing beautiful homes and affording views of Coit Tower and North Beach.

continued on page 104

San Francisco & Vicinity

© Rand McNally

San Francisco attractions continued

North Beach/Little Italy
Italian neighborhood and nightlife area
Along Columbus Ave.

Pacific Heights
Stately Victorian mansions
Jackson Street near the northwest corner of
Alta Plaza Park

San Francisco Art Institute Galleries
800 Chestnut St.
(415) 771-7020

San Francisco Cable Car Museum
1201 Mason St.
(415) 474-1887

San Francisco Maritime National Historical Park
Historical ships and maritime museum
Visitors Center at Hyde and Jefferson Sts.
(415) 447-5000

San Francisco Museum of Modern Art
151 3rd St.
(415) 357-4000

San Francisco Zoo
Sloat Blvd. and 47th Ave.
(415) 753-7080

Wax Museum at Fisherman's Wharf
145 Jefferson St.
(415) 202-0400 or (800) 439-4305

Yerba Buena Center for the Arts
Visual and performing arts complex
701 Mission St.
(415) 978-2787

SHOPPING

Anchorage Square
Specialty shops, dining, and entertainment
2800 Leavenworth St. at Fisherman's Wharf
(415) 775-6000

The Cannery
Waterfront marketplace
2801 Leavenworth St.
(415) 771-3112

Crocker Galleria
Restaurants, shops, and services
50 Post St.
(415) 393-1505

Embarcadero Center
Specialty stores, shops, restaurants, and movie theater
Bounded by Clay, Sacramento, Drumm, and Battery Sts.
(415) 772-0700

Ghirardelli Square
Specialty stores, restaurants, landscaped gardens, and great views of the bay
N. Point St. just west of Fisherman's Wharf
(415) 775-5500

Pier 39
Shops, restaurants, cinema, aquarium, bay cruises, and other attractions
Two blocks east of Fisherman's Wharf
(415) 705-5500

DIVERSION

Visit Sonoma County's coastal and historic towns, heirloom produce farms, and state parks as well as its many vineyards and wineries. Only 35 miles north of the Golden Gate Bridge on US 101. (800) 380-5392

San Francisco Centre
Large nine-story mall with the only spiral escalators in the U.S.
865 Market St.
(415) 512-6776

Stonestown Galleria
Stores and a theater
3251 20th Ave.
(415) 564-8848

VISITOR INFORMATION

San Francisco Convention and Visitors Bureau
Convention Plaza
201 3rd St., Ste. 900
San Francisco, CA 94103
(415) 974-6900
www.sfvisitor.org

Visitor Information Center
900 Market St., lower level,
Hallidie Plaza
(415) 391-2000

Golden Gate Bridge

SAN JOSE, California

San Jose boomed when the computer revolution changed a thriving agricultural center into the heart of Silicon Valley. Through interactive exhibits, the Tech Museum of Innovation demonstrates how everyday lives are affected by advances in communications and information sharing. Area theme parks range from the high-tech thrills of Paramount's Great America to the horticultural wonders and old-fashioned rides found at Bonfante Gardens in nearby Gilroy. Another older attraction still well worth a look is the Winchester Mystery House; its nonsensical design was meant to keep evil spirits at bay. *Tax: 10% hotel, 8.25% sales. For local weather, call (831) 656-1725.*

Downtown San Jose

▶ SELECTED ATTRACTIONS

Bonfante Gardens Family Theme Park
3050 Hecker Pass Hwy., Gilroy
(408) 840-7100

Children's Discovery Museum of San Jose
180 Woz Way
(408) 298-5437

Guadalupe River Park and Gardens
438 Coleman Ave.
(408) 298-7657

Happy Hollow Park and Zoo
Children's rides and amusements
1300 Senter Rd.
(408) 277-3000

History Park at Kelley Park
Original and replica buildings c.1890
1650 Senter Rd.
(408) 287-2290

Monopoly in the Park
Discovery Meadow, Guadalupe Park
(408) 995-6487

Paramount's Great America
Theme park
3 miles north off US 101, Santa Clara
(408) 988-1776

Peralta Adobe and Fallon House
Historic Spanish and Victorian homes
175 W. St. John St.
(408) 993-8300

Raging Waters
Water park
2333 S. White Rd.
(408) 238-9900

Roaring Camp Railroads
Off Graham Hill Rd., Felton
(831) 335-4484

Rosicrucian Egyptian Museum & Planetarium
1342 Naglee Ave.
(408) 947-3636

San Jose Museum of Art
110 S. Market St.
(408) 271-6840

San Jose Museum of Quilts and Textiles
520 S. 1st St.
(408) 971-0323

Tech Museum of Innovation
Technology museum and IMAX theater
201 S. Market St.
(408) 294-8324

Winchester Mystery House
525 S. Winchester Blvd.
(408) 247-2101

▶ SHOPPING

Great Mall
Department stores and specialty shops
447 Great Mall Dr., Milpitas
(408) 945-4022

Santana Row
Unique stores and specialty shops
368 Santana Row
(408) 551-4611

Westfield Oakridge Mall
Department stores and specialty shops
925 Blossom Hill Rd. at CA 85 and CA 87
(408) 578-2912

Valley Fair
Department stores and specialty shops
2855 Stevens Creek Blvd., Santa Clara
(408) 248-4451

▶ VISITOR INFORMATION

San Jose Convention and Visitors Bureau
408 Almaden Blvd.
San Jose, CA 95110
(408) 295-9600 or (800) 726-5673
www.sanjose.org

▶ DON'T MISS DRIVE

Proceed west on Heading St. to see the full diversity of the city. Take in varied architecture, from industrial nouveau to traditional estate-style homes. The drive also passes elaborate rose gardens and is a good way to enjoy fall foliage.

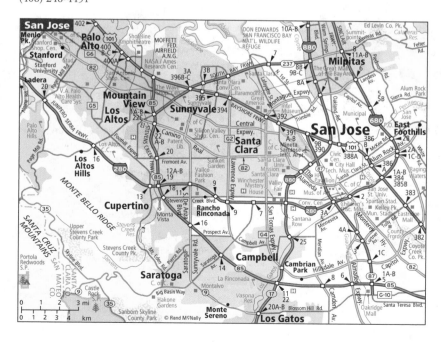

SANTA FE, New Mexico

El Rancho de las Golondrinas

Artists' colony, state capital, and repository of Spanish and Native American culture, Santa Fe attracts both art and history buffs. Adobe architecture abounds; it's the signature style of public buildings including the state capitol. The four facilities of the Museum of New Mexico include the Palace of the Governors, which dates from 1610, and the Museum of Fine Arts, where works by American painters and sculptors are displayed. More art can be found at the Georgia O'Keeffe Museum and at the many galleries and studios of the working artists living along Canyon Road. *Tax: 14.625% hotel, 7.625% sales. For local weather, call (505) 988-5151.*

DIVERSION

Steep, narrow canyons and acres of backcountry form a dramatic backdrop at Bandelier National Monument. Just 40 miles north of Santa Fe, via US 84 to NM 502 and then NM 4, Bandelier provides spectacular views, especially of the ancestral dwellings of the Anasazi people. (505) 672-3861

SELECTED ATTRACTIONS

Canyon Road
Gallery district
Canyon Rd. between Paseo de Peralta and Camino Cabra

Cathedral Church of St. Francis of Assisi
131 Cathedral Pl.
(505) 982-5619

Chapel of Our Lady of Guadalupe
Oldest U.S. shrine to patron saint of Mexico
100 S. Guadalupe St.
(505) 988-2027

Chapel of San Miguel
Oldest active U.S. church
401 Old Santa Fe Trail
(505) 983-3974

El Rancho de las Golondrinas
Spanish Colonial living history museum
334 Los Pinos Rd.
(505) 471-2261

Georgia O'Keeffe Museum
217 Johnson St.
(505) 946-1000

Institute of American Indian Arts Museum
Contemporary Native American art
108 Cathedral Pl.
(505) 983-1777

Loretto Chapel/Miraculous Staircase
207 Old Santa Fe Trail
(505) 982-0092

Museum Hill
Includes the Museum of International Folk Art, Museum of Indian Arts and Culture, Museum of Spanish Colonial Art, and Wheelwright Museum of the American Indian
Camino Lejo off Old Santa Fe Trail
(505) 476-1203

Museum of Fine Arts
107 W. Palace Ave.
(505) 476-5072

Palace of the Governors
Regional history museum
105 W. Palace Ave.
(505) 476-5100

Santa Fe Children's Museum
1050 Old Pecos Trail
(505) 989-8359

Santa Fe Opera
7 miles north on US 84/285
(505) 986-5955

SITE Santa Fe
Modern art museum
1606 Paseo de Peralta
(505) 989-1199

SHOPPING

Guadalupe Street/Historic Railyard District
Boutiques, galleries, and specialty shops
Guadalupe St. and Cerrillos Rd.
(505) 982-3373

Santa Fe Outlets
Designer factory outlet shops
8380 Cerrillos Rd.
(505) 474-4000

Santa Fe Place
Department stores, upscale shops, and restaurants
4250 Cerrillos Rd.
(505) 473-4253

Santa Fe Plaza
Boutiques, galleries, and specialty shops
Bounded by Palace Ave., Old Santa Fe Trail, San Francisco St., and Lincoln Ave. in the downtown area

VISITOR INFORMATION

Santa Fe Convention and Visitors Bureau
125 Lincoln St.
Santa Fe, NM 87501
(505) 955-6200 or (800) 777-2489
www.santafe.org

New Mexico Visitors Center
491 Old Santa Fe Trail
(505) 827-7400 or (800) 545-2070

SEATTLE, Washington

Bounded by Puget Sound and Lake Washington, Seattle is surrounded by four national parks and a wealth of outdoor adventures. Above the harbor, Pike Place Market entertains with its vendors of fish, flowers, and vegetables. Head to Chittenden Locks for a close-up look at salmon climbing from the ocean to the lakes above. A four-hour tour across Puget Sound to Tillicum Village includes a salmon dinner and lively stage show celebrating Native American life. High-tech wizardry gives the unique Experience Music Project—a museum where visitors can explore their inner rock stars—an energy all its own. *Tax: 15.6% hotel, 8.8% sales, 0.5% food and beverage. For local weather, call (206) 526-6087.*

Pike Place Market and Puget Sound

▶ SELECTED ATTRACTIONS

The Children's Museum
305 Harrison St. at Seattle Center
(206) 441-1768

Experience Music Project (EMP)
Interactive music museum
325 5th Ave. N. at Seattle Center
(206) 367-5483

Hiram M. Chittenden Locks
Canal locks, botanical garden, and fish ladder
3015 NW 54th St.
(206) 783-7059

Museum of Flight
9404 E. Marginal Way S.
(206) 764-5720

Pacific Science Center
200 2nd Ave. N.
(206) 443-2001

Seattle Aquarium
1483 Alaskan Way on Pier 59
(206) 386-4300

Seattle Art Museum
100 University St.
(206) 654-3100

Seattle Monorail
Runs between downtown and Seattle Center
370 Thomas St., Ste. 200
(206) 905-2600

Seattle Underground Tours
19th-century Seattle storefronts now ten feet below city streets
608 1st Ave.
(206) 682-4646

Space Needle
400 Broad St. in Seattle Center
(206) 905-2100

Tillicum Village
Native American village tour
Tour leaves from Pier 55
(206) 933-8600 or (800) 426-1205

Washington State Ferries
20 Terminals
(206) 464-6400

Woodland Park Zoo
750 N. 50th St.
(206) 684-4800

▶ SHOPPING

Fremont Neighborhood
Artsy, one-of-a-kind shops
N. 34th St. and Fremont Ave.
(206) 632-1500

Pacific Place
Department stores and upscale boutiques
600 Pine St.
(206) 405-2655

Pike Place Market
Fresh produce and unique shops
1st Ave. and Pike St.
(206) 682-7453

continued on the next page

DON'T MISS DRIVE

Take Highland Drive up steep Queen Ann Hill to see Seattle with spectacular Mount Rainier in the background. Continue west on Highland to Parsons Gardens for super views of Puget Sound and the Olympic Mountains, too.

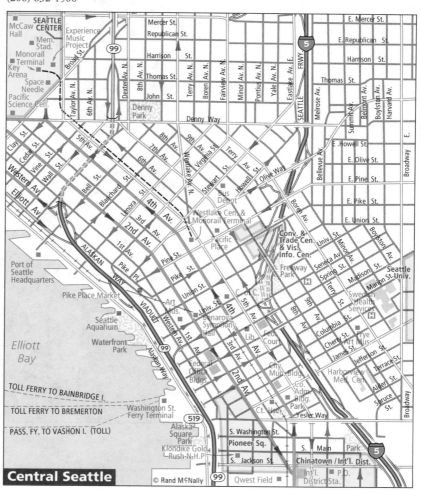

Central Seattle

© Rand McNally

Seattle shopping continued

Rainier Square
Upscale boutiques and specialty shops
5th Ave. between Union and University Sts.

Westlake Center
Specialty stores
400 Pine St.
(206) 467-1600

VISITOR INFORMATION

Seattle Convention and Visitors Bureau
701 Pike St., Ste. 800
Seattle, WA 98101
(206) 461-5800
www.seeseattle.org

Seattle Visitor Center
Washington State Convention and
Trade Center
7th and Pike, Main Floor
(206) 461-5888 or (866) 732-2695

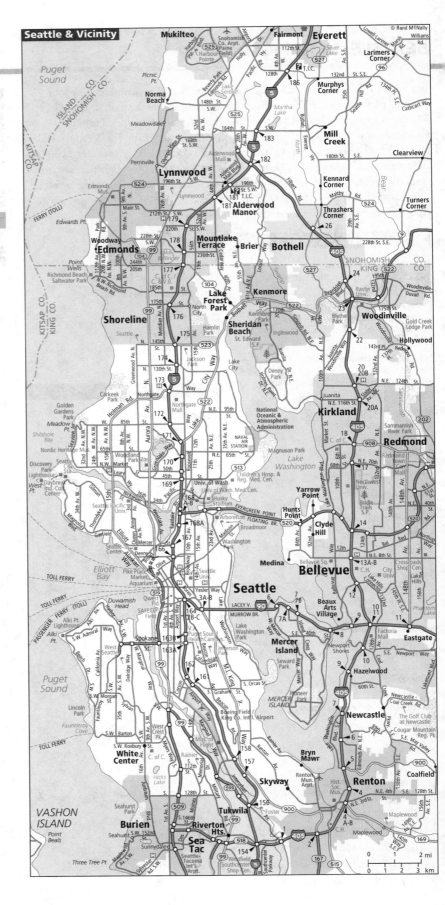

TAMPA/ST. PETERSBURG, Florida

The business, technology, and shipping center for southwest Florida, Tampa also claims its share of attractions with family appeal. Waterparks such as Buccaneer Bay and Adventure Island help cool kids down. And at Busch Gardens, thrill rides overlook African jungles patrolled by elephants, lions, and tropical predators. *Tax: 12% hotel, 7% sales tax. For local weather, call (813) 645-2507.*

St. Petersburg—all sunshine and sparkling blue waters—has outgrown its image as an icon of retirement living. Miles of white-sand beaches and waterfront parks attract sunseekers and kayakers. Families enjoy attractions such as Great Explorations, a museum with hands-on science exhibits, and the Children's Art Museum, where exhibits are designed to stimulate young creativity. Works by the 20th-century surrealist Salvador Dali are on display at the eponymous museum. *Tax: 12% hotel, 7% sales. For local weather, call (813) 645-2506.*

The Florida Aquarium

▶ SELECTED ATTRACTIONS

TAMPA

Adventure Island
Amusement and water park
10001 McKinley Dr.
(813) 987-5600

Busch Gardens Tampa Bay
Busch Blvd. and 40th St.
(888) 800-5447

The Florida Aquarium
701 Channelside Dr.
(813) 273-4000

Kid City: Children's Museum of Tampa
7550 North Blvd.
(813) 935-8441

Museum of Science and Industry
4801 E. Fowler Ave.
(813) 987-6100

Tampa Bay History Center
Regional history museum
225 S. Franklin St.
(813) 228-0097

Tampa Museum of Art
Greek and Roman antiquities to contemporary art
600 N. Ashley Dr.
(813) 274-8130

Tampa's Lowry Park Zoo
Natural habitats, children's zoo, shows, rides
1101 W. Sligh Ave.
(813) 935-8552

University of South Florida Botanical Gardens
Pine and Alumni Dr. on USF campus
(813) 974-2329

Weeki Wachee Springs/Buccaneer Bay
Mermaid shows and water park
6131 Commercial Way, Weeki Wachee
(352) 596-2062

Ybor City Museum State Park
History of cigar-making and local culture
1818 E. 9th Ave.
(813) 247-6323

continued on the next page

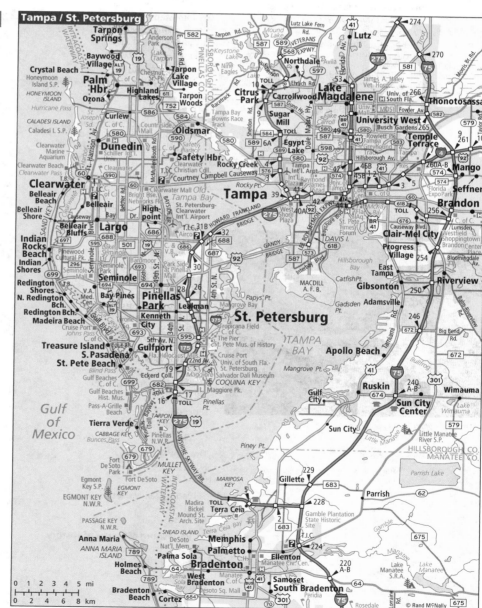

Tampa continued

▶ SHOPPING

TAMPA

Centro Ybor
Shopping and nightlife
1600 E. 8th Ave.
(813) 242-4660

Citrus Park
Department stores, upscale shops, and restaurants
8021 Citrus Park Town Center
(813) 962-4644

International Plaza and Bay Street
Department stores, boutiques, and outdoor restaurants
2223 N. Westshore Blvd.
(813) 342-3790

Old Hyde Park Village
Old-world setting of upscale shops, dining, and theaters
Swann and Dakota Aves.
(813) 251-3500

Westfield Citrus Park
Department stores, specialty shops, theaters, and dining
250 WestShore Pl.
(813) 286-0790

The Pier shopping area in St. Petersburg

▶ DON'T MISS DRIVE

In St. Petersburg, cruise down Coffee Pot Blvd. in the Granada Terrace Historic District among beautiful plazas and parkways. The drive parallels the waterfront, and the southern portion takes drivers through Granada Park.

▶ SELECTED ATTRACTIONS

ST. PETERSBURG

Boyd Hill Nature Center
1101 Country Club Way S.
(727) 893-7326

Captain Memo's Pirate Cruise
Family-friendly scenic cruise
25 Causeway Blvd., Dock 3
(727) 446-2587

Celebration Station
Go-karts, bumper boats, mini-golf, and shows
24546 US 19 North, Clearwater
(727) 791-1799

Dunedin Fine Art Center and David L. Mason Children's Art Museum
1143 Michigan Blvd., Dunedin
(727) 298-3322

Florida International Museum
Smithsonian affiliate with changing cultural exhibits
244 2nd Ave. N.
(727) 341-7900

Fort DeSoto Park
Five connected islands with beaches, camping, trails, and boat docks
3500 Pinellas Bayway S., Tierra Verde
(727) 582-2267

Great Explorations: The Children's Museum
1925 4th St. N.
(727) 821-8992

Heritage Village
Restored homes, pioneer museum
11909 125th St. N., Largo
(727) 582-2123

Museum of Fine Arts
255 Beach Dr. NE
(727) 896-2667

The Pier Aquarium
800 2nd Ave. NE
(727) 895-7437

Salvador Dali Museum
1000 3rd St. S.
(727) 823-3767

St. Petersburg Museum of History
335 2nd Ave. NE
(727) 894-1052

▶ SHOPPING

ST. PETERSBURG

BayWalk
Open-air plaza with shopping, restaurants, and nightlife
153 2nd Ave. N.
(727) 895-9277

Beach Drive
Specialty shops, art galleries, and museums
Downtown waterfront

John's Pass Village & Boardwalk
Shops along the waterfront
150 John's Pass Boardwalk, Madeira Beach
(727) 397-1667

The Pier
Shops, dining, and entertainment
800 2nd Ave. NE
(727) 821-6443

Tyrone Square Mall
Department stores and specialty shops
6901 22nd Ave. N.
(727) 347-3889

▶ VISITOR INFORMATION

Tampa Bay Convention and Visitors Bureau
401 E. Jackson St., Ste. 2100
Tampa, FL 33602
(813) 223-1111 or (800) 448-2672
www.visittampabay.com

St. Petersburg/Clearwater Area Convention and Visitors Bureau
13805 58th St. N., Ste. 2-200
Clearwater, FL 33760
(727) 464-7200 or (877) 352-3224
www.floridasbeach.com

TIJUANA, Baja California, Mexico

Bumping against the border, Tijuana draws thousands of immigrant hopefuls from the south and hordes of American citizens from the north. Southern Californians have long enjoyed making quick excursions for shopping, dining, and partying all night at the clubs and discotheques along Avenida Revolucion. For a more in-depth take, the Centro Cultural Tijuana offers outstanding performances, an Omnimax theater, and a museum devoted to Mexican identities. Exhibits on the area's cultural and natural history are featured at the Museo de las Californias. *Tax: 10% hotel, 10% value-added sales tax is usually included in the retail price.*

Tijuana Cultural Center

▶ SELECTED ATTRACTIONS

Bronzart
Tours of bronze sculptures
Blvd. Água Azul 7004, Fracc. Industrial
Agua Azul
011-52-664-684-6533*

**Bullfighting Ring of Tijuana
(El Toreo de Tijuana)**
Ave. Santa Maria 22, Col. Gabilondo
011-52-664-686-1219 or
011-52-664-686-1510*

Caliente Racetrack
Greyhound races and bingo saloon
Blvd. Agua Caliente and Tapachula 12027,
Col. Hipódromo
011-52-664-633-7300*

Fun World (Mundo Divertido La Mesa)
Amusement park and children's games
Via Rapida, Poniente 15035 Fracc. San Jose
011-52-664-701-7133*

L.A. Cetto Winery
Ave. Cañón Johnson 2108, Col. Hidalgo
011-52-664-685-3031 or
011-52-664-685-1644*

**Museum of the Californias
(Museo de las Californias)**
Missions, petroglyphs, historical exhibits
Paseo de los Heroes at Javier Mina Zona Rio
in the Tijuana Cultural Center
011-52-664-687-9600 or
011-52-664-687-9635*

Tijuana Brewery (Cerveceria Tijuana)
Blvd. Fundadores 2951 Colonia Juarez
011-52-664-638-8662 or
011-52-664-638-8663*

**Tijuana Cultural Center
(Centro Cultural Tijuana)**
*Museum, Omnimax theater, and
performing arts theater*
Paseo de los Heroes at Javier Mina
Zona Rio
011-52-664-687-9600*

Wax Museum (Museo de Cera)
Calle 1a 8281, Zona Centro
011-52-664-688-2478*

▶ SHOPPING

Av. Revolución
Jewelry, clothing, pottery, arts and crafts
Between 1st and 10th Sts.

Mercado de Artesanías
Handmade crafts and leather goods
Calle 1 between Ave. Negrete and Ave.
Ocampo

Mercado Hidalgo
Authentic Mexican market
Av. Independencia at Av. Sánchez Taboada

Plaza Río Tijuana
Shops, movie theaters, and restaurants
Paseo de los Héroes #96 and 98, Zona Rio
011-52-664-684-0402*

Pueblo Amigo
Restaurants, shops, and nightlife
Via Oriente # 9211, Zona Rio
011-52-664-684-2711*

Shopping is also found at these local markets:
- Centro Comercial Viva Tijuana
  Via de la Juventud Norte #8800
- Plaza Carrusel
  Blvd. Diaz Ordaz #15602, Las Brisas
- Plaza Mundo Divertido La Mesa
  Via Rapida, La Mesa

▶ VISITOR INFORMATION

Tijuana Convention and Visitors Bureau
Paseo de los Héroes No. 9365-201
Tijuana, BC, Mexico
011-52-664-684-0537 or
011-52-664-684-0538
www.tijuanaonline.org

Tijuana Tourism Board
Blvd. Agua Caliente 4558, 11th Floor
Tijuana, BC, Mexico
011-52-664-686-1103,
011-52-664-686-1345, or
(888) 775-2417 (U.S. only)
www.seetijuana.com

Mexico Tourism Board (U.S.)
(800) 446-3942
www.visitmexico.com

▶ DIVERSION

Rosarito is 30 kilometers (about 18 miles) south of Tijuana on Federal Highway 10. It has one of Baja California's largest beaches and decent waves for surfing, and has been featured in many Hollywood films. Don't pass up the lobster Puerto Nuevo—the town is famous for it.

San Diego Convention and Visitors Bureau
2215 India St.
San Diego, CA 92101
(619) 232-3101
www.sandiego.org

Pedestrian Border Crossing International Visitor Information Center
Across the pedestrian border crossing ramp
011-52-664-607-3097 (Spanish and English spoken)

Puerta Mexico International Visitor Information Center
90 feet from the San Ysidro border crossing
011-52-664-683-1405 (Spanish and English spoken)

Number listed may or may not have an English-speaking person available.

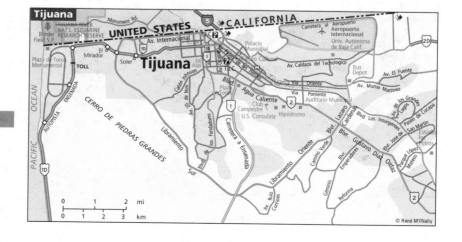

TORONTO, Ontario, Canada

Ontario Place theme park

Lying at the western edge of Lake Ontario, Canada's most international city fairly bursts with ethnic diversity. This is a city with no fewer than three Chinatowns as well as a Greektown, Little Italy, and other cultural enclaves. Many popular attractions line the lakeside. Ontario Place offers rides, attractions and live entertainment for each member of the family. For shopping, recreation, and a year-round lineup of events with a cultural flair, visitors head to Harbourfront Centre. Overlooking all is the impressive view from the observation deck of the CN Tower, the city's most familiar landmark. Its glass floor gives visitors a 1,122-foot view straight down. *Tax: 14% hotel, 6% GST, 8% PST.*

▶ SELECTED ATTRACTIONS

Art Gallery of Ontario
317 Dundas St. W.
(416) 979-6648

The Bata Shoe Museum
377 Bloor St. W.
(416) 979-7799

Casa Loma
Historic castle
1 Austin Terr.
(416) 923-1171

CN Tower
World's tallest free-standing structure
301 Front St. W.
(416) 868-6937

The Distillery Historic District
Arts, culture, food, and entertainment
55 Mill St.
(416) 364-1177

Harbourfront Centre
Theaters, galleries, marina, ice skating
235 Queen's Quay W.
(416) 973-4000

Hockey Hall of Fame
30 Yonge St. in BCE Place
(416) 360-7735

Ontario Place
Theme park
955 Lakeshore Blvd. W.
(416) 314-9900

Paramount's Canada's Wonderland
Theme park
ON 400 at Rutherford Rd. exit
(905) 832-7000

Royal Botanical Gardens
680 Plains Road W., Burlington
(905) 527-1158

Royal Ontario Museum
Nature and history museum
100 Queen's Park
(416) 586-8000

Rogers Centre (SkyDome)
Tours of the home of Blue Jays baseball
1 Blue Jays Way
(416) 341-1707

Toronto Zoo
Meadowvale Rd. off ON 401, Scarborough
(416) 392-5900

▶ DON'T MISS DRIVE

Bloor Street W. at the southern edge of Yorkville is known as the "Mink Mile" because it is home to designer boutiques such as Tiffany, Chanel, Hermes, and Giorgio Armani.

▶ SHOPPING

Toronto Antiques on King
Antiques and collectibles
276 King St. W.
(416) 345-9941

Queen's Quay Terminal
Specialty shops on the waterfront
207 Queen's Quay W.
(416) 203-0510

St. Lawrence Market
Fresh produce and specialty foods
Front and Jarvis Sts.
(416) 392-7210

Toronto Eaton Centre
Department stores and specialty shops
220 Yonge St.
(416) 598-8560

▶ VISITOR INFORMATION

Tourism Toronto
207 Queen's Quay W., Ste. 590
Toronto, ON M5J 1A7 Canada
(416) 203-2600 or (800) 499-2514
www.torontotourism.com

TUCSON, Arizona

Surrounded by five mountain ranges and the cactus-speckled expanse of the upper Sonoran Desert, Arizona's second-largest metropolis combines resort community living with college-town amenities. The Flandrau Science Center has interactive exhibits and a large collection of gems and minerals. For a first-hand look at the wonders of the surrounding landscape, the Arizona-Sonora Desert Museum combines features of a zoo, natural history museum, and botanical garden. South of the city, Mission San Xavier del Bac is partially encased in scaffolding, but the interior is still quite beautiful. *Tax: 11.5% hotel, 5.6% state sales, 2% city sales. For local weather, call (520) 670-6526.*

Mural in historic downtown Tucson

▶ SELECTED ATTRACTIONS

Arizona-Sonora Desert Museum
Zoo, natural history museum, and botanical garden
2021 N. Kinney Rd.
(520) 883-2702

Center for Creative Photography at the University of Arizona
1030 N. Olive Rd.
(520) 621-7968

Colossal Cave Mountain Park
Cave, ranch, and museum
20 miles east off I-10 on Old Spanish Trail, Vail
(520) 647-7275

Flandrau Science Center and Planetarium
Cherry Ave. and University Blvd., University of Arizona
(520) 621-7827

International Wildlife Museum
Taxidermy exhibits
4800 W. Gates Pass Rd.
(520) 629-0100

Kartchner Caverns State Park
9 miles south of I-10 off State Hwy. 90, exit 302, Benson
(520) 586-4100 or (520) 586-2283

Mission San Xavier del Bac
"White Dove of the Desert"
1950 W. San Xavier Rd.
(520) 294-2624

Old Tucson Studios
Movie studio and Old West replica town
201 S. Kinney Rd.
(520) 883-0100

Pima Air and Space Museum
6000 E. Valencia Rd.
(520) 574-0462

Sabino Canyon Tours
5900 N. Sabino Canyon Rd.
Coronado National Forest
(520) 749-2327

Saguaro National Park
3693 S. Old Spanish Trail
(520) 733-5153

Tucson Botanical Gardens
2150 N. Alvernon Way
(520) 326-9686

▶ SHOPPING

Foothills Mall
7401 N. La Cholla Blvd.
(520) 219-0650

4th Avenue Shopping District
Antiques, galleries, and unique shops
4th Ave. near E. University Blvd.
(520) 624-5004

La Encantada
Upscale stores and restaurants
2905 E. Skyline Dr.
(520) 299-3556

Old Town Artisans
Regional and Native American art and jewelry
201 N. Court Ave.
(520) 623-6024

Park Place Mall
Department stores and specialty shops
5870 E. Broadway Blvd.
(520) 748-1222

Tucson Mall
Department stores and specialty shops
4500 N. Oracle Rd. at Wetmore Rd.
(520) 293-7330

▶ VISITOR INFORMATION

Metropolitan Tucson Convention and Visitors Bureau
100 S. Church Ave.
Tucson, AZ 85701
(520) 624-1817 or (800) 638-8350
www.visittucson.org

DIVERSION

Tubac, Arizona's oldest European settlement and once the site of a Spanish *presidio*, or fort, is now a thriving arts community. Only 45 minutes south of Tucson via I-10 east to I-19, exit 34. (520) 398-0007

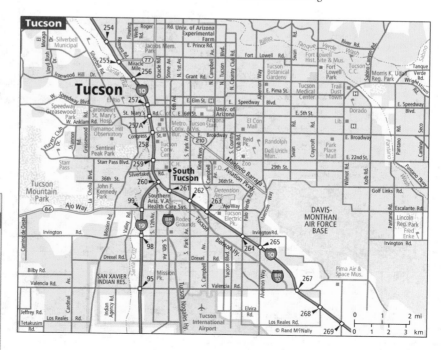

TULSA, Oklahoma

Philbrook Museum of Art

The cultural heart of the prairie, Tulsa has turned its oil wealth into fine arts museums and outstanding architecture. Enhanced gardens at the Philbrook Museum provide a lush setting for this Italianate villa and its collections of art. The art of the American West is the focus of the Gilcrease Museum. At the Oklahoma Jazz Hall of Fame in the popular Greenwood District, visitors recapture the days when artists such as Louis Armstrong and Dizzy Gillespie performed there. More than 50 rides and attractions keep thrill seekers happy at 50-year-old Bell's Amusement Park. *Tax: 13.517% hotel, 8.517% sales. For local weather, call (918) 743-3311.*

DON'T MISS DRIVE

For 10 miles, take Riverside Drive as it follows along the Arkansas River past flowering trees that were present before the city was built and along Zink Lake, where drivers might catch a glimpse of crew teams practicing and fishermen casting.

► SELECTED ATTRACTIONS

Bell's Amusement Park
Log rides, games, Ferris wheels, mini-golf
3901 E. 21st St.
(918) 744-1991

Discoveryland!
Outdoor amphitheater
5529 S. Lewis Ave., Sand Springs
(918) 742-5255

Gilcrease Museum
Art, artifacts, and archives of the American West
1400 N. Gilcrease Museum Rd.
(918) 596-2700 or (888) 655-2278

International Linen Registry Museum and Gift Shop
Collection of ancient linens
4107 S. Yale Ave.
(918) 622-5223

Mary K. Oxley Nature Center
5701 E. 36th St. at Mohawk Park
(918) 669-6644

Oklahoma Aquarium
300 Aquarium Dr., Jenks
(918) 296-3474

Oklahoma Jazz Hall of Fame
322 N. Greenwood Ave.
(918) 596-1001 or (800) 348-9336

Philbrook Museum of Art
2727 S. Rockford Rd.
(918) 749-7941 or (800) 324-7941

Tulsa Zoo and Living Museum
6421 E. 36th St. N., Mohawk Park
(918) 669-6600

Will Rogers Memorial
Tribute to great roper, pundit, actor, and writer
1720 W. Will Rogers Blvd., Claremore
(918) 341-0719

Woolaroc Museum and Wildlife Preserve
Art and artifacts of the Southwest
45 miles north off US 75, Bartlesville
(918) 336-0307

► SHOPPING

Cherry Street District
Quaint shops in historic neighborhood
E. 15th St. between Peoria and Utica Aves.

The Farm Shopping Center
Uptown shopping in village square setting
51st St. and S. Sheridan Rd.
(918) 622-3860

Tulsa Promenade
Eclectic mix of retailers
41st and S. Yale in midtown Tulsa
(918) 627-9282

Utica Square Shopping Center
Upscale shops and restaurants
21st and S. Utica Ave.
(918) 742-5531

Woodland Hills Mall
Department stores and specialty shops
71st St. and S. Memorial Dr.
(918) 250-1449

► VISITOR INFORMATION

Tulsa Convention and Visitors Bureau
2 W. 2nd St., Williams Tower II, Ste. 150
Tulsa, OK 74103
(918) 585-1201 or (800) 558-3311
www.visittulsa.com

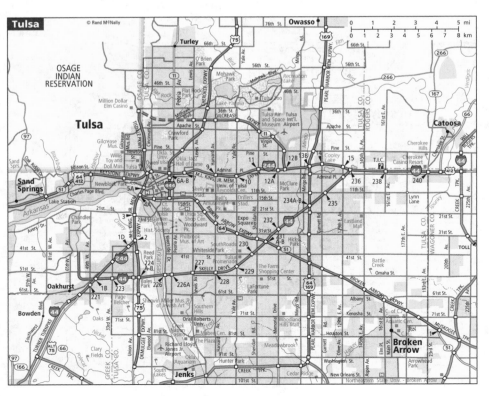

VANCOUVER, British Columbia, Canada

Tucked between ocean waters and steep mountainsides, Vancouver's natural beauty makes it the jewel of western Canada. The city's recreational heart is Stanley Park, a vast playground with formal gardens, miniature train, barnyard, athletics fields, seawall walk, and a forest wilderness easy to get lost in. Vancouver is also rich in fine cuisine, such as the seafood on offer at C Restaurant, where diners can enjoy 180-degree views of the water. Nightclubbers head to the newly trendy Yaletown neighborhood near False Creek. Ferries and water taxis make it easy to get around —this city is surrounded by water on three sides. *Tax: 10% hotel, 10% liquor, 7% goods and services, 7% provincial services. For local weather, call (604) 664-9010.*

Vancouver skyline

► SELECTED ATTRACTIONS

Bloedel Floral Conservatory
Indoor botanical garden
33rd Ave. and Cambie St. in Queen
Elizabeth Park
(604) 257-8584

Chinese Cultural Centre
Exhibits and Chinatown walking tours
50 E. Pender St.
(604) 658-8850

Dr. Sun Yat-Sen Classical Chinese Garden
578 Carrall St.
(604) 662-3207

Gastown
1880s district and steam clock
Bounded by Water, Seymour, Cordova, and
Columbia Sts.
(604) 683-5650

Grouse Mountain
Skiing and year-round recreation
6400 Nancy Greene Way, North Vancouver
(604) 984-0661

H. R. MacMillan Space Centre
1100 Chestnut St.
(604) 738-7827

Minter Gardens
52892 Bunker Rd., Rosedale
(604) 794-7191 or (888) 646-8377

Museum of Anthropology
6393 NW Marine Dr. at the University of
British Columbia
(604) 822-5087

Stanley Park
Gardens, seawall walk, and beaches
2099 Beach Ave.
(604) 257-8400

Vancouver Aquarium Marine Science Center
845 Avison Way in Stanley Park
(604) 659-3474

Vancouver Maritime Museum
1905 Ogden Ave. in Vanier Park
(604) 257-8300

► SHOPPING

Granville Island
Public market and unique shops
1661 Duranleau St.
(604) 666-7535

Metropolis at Metrotown
Department stores and specialty shops
4800 Kingsway, Burnaby
(604) 438-4700

Pacific Centre Mall
Department stores and specialty shops
910–609 Granville St.
(604) 688-7235

Robson Street
Specialty shops, restaurants, and services
Robson St. from Howe St. to Jervis St.
(604) 669-8132

► VISITOR INFORMATION

Greater Vancouver Convention and Visitors Bureau
200 Burrard St., Ste. 210
Vancouver, BC V6C 3L6 Canada
(604) 682-2222
www.tourismvancouver.com

► DIVERSION

Drive out to Whistler in the breathtaking Blackcomb Mountains for great downhill skiing. Off the slopes, visit a spa, shop, or gallery hop. Less than 100 miles north off BC 99. (604) 932-5922

► DON'T MISS DRIVE

Slip into the soothing waters of Harrison Hot Springs, which bubble all year long. Take Trans-Canada Hwy. 1 east to Rosedale, then BC 9 to Harrison. (604) 796-5581

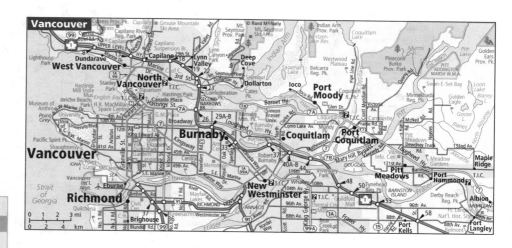

WASHINGTON, D.C.

Smithsonian Institute Building (The Castle)

The great monuments and museums of the nation's capital serve as a welcome reminder of the great American purpose: liberty and justice for all. The National Mall, the greensward stretching from the Lincoln Memorial to the Capitol, is edged by fine institutions including the National Air and Space Museum and the National Gallery of Art, as well as moving tributes to the nation's past such as the Jefferson and Vietnam Veterans memorials. Free tours of the White House can be arranged in advance through members of Congress. Increased security measures may slow down or restrict general access to some public buildings. *Tax: 14.5% hotel, 5.75% sales, 10% food and beverage. For local weather, call (703) 260-0107.*

▶ SELECTED ATTRACTIONS

Arlington National Cemetery
Arlington, VA
(703) 607-8000

Corcoran Gallery of Art
500 17th St. NW
(202) 639-1700

Franklin Delano Roosevelt Memorial
Tidal Basin West
(202) 426-6841

International Spy Museum
Exhibits on the craft, practice, history, and role of espionage
800 F St. NW
(202) 393-7798

Jefferson Memorial
Tidal Basin in E. Potomac Park
(202) 426-6841

Korean War Veterans Memorial
French Dr. SW at the Lincoln Memorial
(202) 426-6841

Library of Congress
Largest library in the world
101 Independence Ave. SE
(202) 707-5000

Lincoln Memorial
23rd St. NW and Constitution Ave.
(202) 426-6841

Mount Vernon
Home of George Washington
8 miles south of Alexandria, VA on George Washington Memorial Pkwy.
(703) 780-2000

National Air and Space Museum
6th St. and Independence Ave. SW
(202) 633-1000

National Gallery of Art
4th St. and Constitution Ave. NW
(202) 737-4215

continued on page 118

▶ DON'T MISS DRIVE

Independence Avenue and Constitution Avenue border the National Mall, with its plethora of monuments and museums. They also pass by the U.S. Capitol.

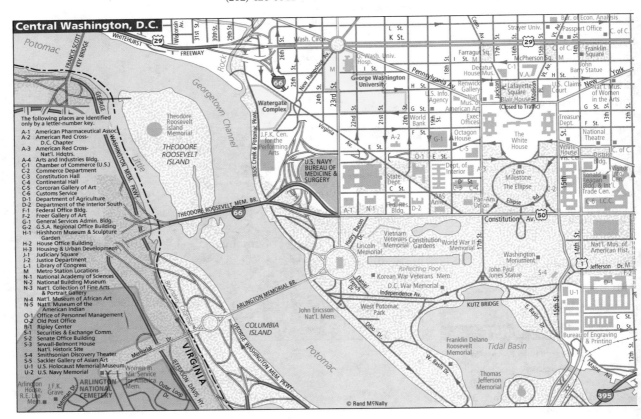

Central Washington, D.C.

The following places are identified only by a letter-number key.

A-1 American Pharmaceutical Assoc.
A-2 American Red Cross-
      D.C. Chapter
A-3 American Red Cross-
      Nat'l. Hdqtrs.
A-4 Arts and Industries Bldg.
C-1 Chamber of Commerce (U.S.)
C-2 Commerce Department
C-3 Constitution Hall
C-4 Continental Hall
C-5 Corcoran Gallery of Art
C-6 Customs Service
D-1 Department of Agriculture
D-2 Department of the Interior South
F-1 Federal Office Bldg.
F-2 Freer Gallery of Art
G-1 General Services Admin. Bldg.
G-2 G.S.A. Regional Office Building
H-1 Hirshhorn Museum & Sculpture
      Garden
H-2 House Office Building
H-3 Housing & Urban Development
J-1 Judiciary Square
J-2 Justice Department
L-1 Library of Congress
M   Metro Station Locations
N-1 National Academy of Sciences
N-2 National Building Museum
N-3 Nat'l. Collection of Fine Arts
      & Portrait Gallery
N-4 Nat'l. Museum of African Art
N-5 Nat'l. Museum of the
      American Indian
O-1 Office of Personnel Management
O-2 Old Post Office
R-1 Ripley Center
S-1 Securities & Exchange Comm.
S-2 Senate Office Building
S-3 Sewall-Belmont House
      Nat'l. Historic Site
S-4 Smithsonian Discovery Theater
S-5 Sackler Gallery of Asian Art
U-1 U.S. Holocaust Memorial Museum
U-2 U.S. Navy Memorial

© Rand McNally

When in D.C., do as the tourists do—visit the monuments

Tributes to moments of American history and to those who have led the country are depicted in monuments and memorials in and around the capital. These include:

African American Civil War Memorial
Sculpture commemorating more than 208,000 African American Civil War soldiers.
1200 U St. NW
(202) 667-2667
www.afroamcivilwar.org

FDR Memorial
Multi-acre site that explores the 12 years of Franklin Delano Roosevelt's presidency.
1850 W. Basin Dr. SW
(202) 426-6841
www.nps.gov/fdrm

Jefferson Memorial
Statue of Thomas Jefferson in a rotunda encircled by passages of his writings, including the Declaration of Independence.
E. Basin Dr. SW
(202) 426-6841
www.nps.gov/thje

Korean War Veterans Memorial
Wall etched with 2,500 photographic images of military support personnel flanking a sculpture of foot soldiers.
French Dr. SW at the Lincoln Memorial
(202) 426-6841
www.nps.gov/kowa

Lincoln Memorial
19-foot marble statue of Abraham Lincoln that overlooks the Reflecting Pool, Washington Monument, and U.S. Capitol.
West Potomac Park at 23rd St. NW
(202) 426-6841
www.nps.gov/linc

National Law Enforcement Officers Memorial
Marble walls show the names of officers killed in the line of duty dating back to 1792.
Judiciary Square
(202) 737-3213
www.nleomf.com

National World War II Memorial
First national memorial dedicated to all who served during World War II.
East end of the Reflecting Pool between the Lincoln Memorial and Washington Monument
(202) 426-6841
www.nps.gov/nwwm

Theodore Roosevelt Island
Island of forest and wetlands that honors President Roosevelt's vision as an early champion of conservation (accessible by footbridge).
Off north-bound lane of George Washington Memorial Parkway
(703) 289-2500
www.nps.gov/this

Vietnam Veterans Memorial
Black granite walls display the 58,245 names of Americans missing or killed in the Vietnam conflict (Frederick Hart's life-size bronze sculpture of three servicemen is adjacent to the Wall).
Constitution Ave. and Henry Bacon Dr. NW
(202) 426-6841
www.nps.gov/vive

Vietnam Women's Memorial
Glenna Goodacre's bronze statue of three servicewomen and a wounded soldier.
21st St. and Constitution Ave. NW
(202) 426-6841
www.nps.gov/vive/memorial/women.htm

Washington Monument
Obelisk dedicated in 1885 to George Washington (one of the tallest masonry structures in the world).
15th St. and Constitution Ave. NW
(202) 426-6841
www.nps.gov/wamo

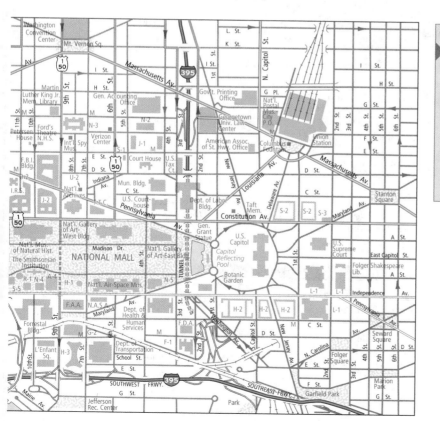

DIVERSION

Drive out to 800-acre Great Falls Park, part of the George Washington Memorial Parkway. Great Falls is known for its scenic beauty. Cross the Potomac River on Arlington Memorial Bridge to connect with the parkway.

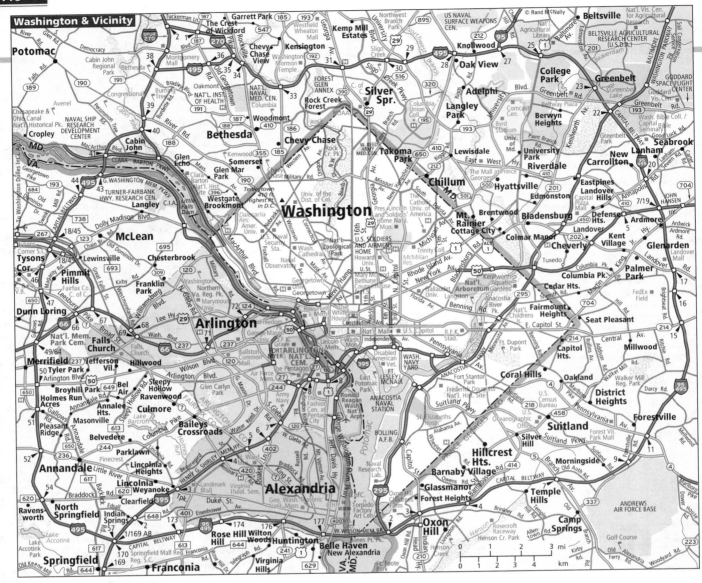

Washington, D.C. attractions continued

National Museum of the American Indian
4th St. & Independence Ave. SW
(202) 633-1000

National Museum of Natural History
10th St. and Constitution Ave. NW
(202) 633-1000

National Zoological Park
3001 Connecticut Ave. NW
(202) 633-4800

Smithsonian Institution Building
"The Castle"
1000 Jefferson Dr. SW
(202) 633-1000

United States Capitol
National Mall at 1st St. NW
(202) 225-6827

**United States Holocaust
Memorial Museum**
100 Raoul Wallenberg Pl. SW at
Independence Ave.
(202) 488-0400

Vietnam Veterans Memorial
Constitution Ave. at Henry Bacon Dr. NW
(202) 426-6841

Washington Monument
National Mall at 15th St. NW and
Constitution Ave.
(202) 426-6841

White House
*Tours available on a limited basis for groups of
10 or more through members of Congress*
1600 Pennsylvania Ave. NW
(202) 456-7041

SHOPPING

Fashion Centre at Pentagon City
1100 S. Hayes St., Arlington, VA
(703) 415-2400

Mazza Gallerie
Neiman Marcus and other specialty stores
5300 Wisconsin Ave. NW
(202) 966-6114

Old Post Office Pavilion
Unique shops and boutiques
1100 Pennsylvania Ave. NW
(202) 289-4224

The Shops at Georgetown Park
Specialty shops and galleries
3222 M St. NW
(202) 298-5577

Tysons Corner Center
Department stores and specialty shops
1961 Chain Bridge Rd., McLean
(703) 893-9400

VISITOR INFORMATION

**Washington, D.C. Convention and
Tourism Corporation**
901 7th St. NW, 4th Floor
Washington, D.C. 20001
(202) 789-7000
www.washington.org

Photo Credits

p. 16 ©Panoramic Images/Getty Images; p. 17 Old Town Plaza, Albuquerque Convention and Visitors Bureau/Ron Behrmann; p. 18 Centennial Olympic Park, ©Digital Vision; p. 19 Atlantic City beach, Atlantic City Convention and Visitors Authority; p. 20 Texas State Capitol, Austin Convention and Visitors Bureau; p. 21 Baltimore Area Convention and Visitors Bureau; p. 22 A Biloxi Shrimping Trip expedition/Mississippi Gulf Coast Convention & Visitors Bureau; p. 23 Boston's Inner Harbor, Greater Boston Convention and Visitors Bureau; p. 25 The Branson Strip, Branson/Lakes Area Chamber of Commerce; p. 26 Eau Claire Market, Tourism Calgary; p. 27 Middleton Place Gardens, Charleston Area Convention and Visitors Bureau; p. 28 Paramount's Carowinds theme park, Charlotte Convention and Visitors Bureau; p. 29 Shedd Aquarium, City of Chicago/Peter J. Shulz; p. 32 Taft Museum of Art, Greater Cincinnati Convention and Visitors Bureau; p. 33 Rock and Roll Hall of Fame and Museum, Convention and Visitors Bureau of Greater Cleveland/Joan Tiefel; p. 34 Short North Arts District, Greater Columbus Convention and Visitors Bureau; p. 35 USS *Lexington* Museum on the Bay, Corpus Christi Convention and Visitors Bureau; p. 36 Dallas skyline, Dallas Convention and Visitors Bureau; p. 38 Sundance Square in Ft. Worth, Ft. Worth Convention and Visitors Bureau; p. 39 Shops at the 16th St. Mall, Denver Metro Convention and Visitors Bureau/Stan Obert; p. 40 ©Detroit Metro Convention and Visitors Bureau; p. 42 Edmonton skyline, Edmonton Tourism; p. 43 The Presidio along the Mission Trail, El Paso Convention and Visitors Bureau/©Brian Knoff; p. 44 Ripley's Aquarium of the Smokies, Gatlinburg Department of Tourism; p. 45 The Cathedral and the Plaza de Armas, ©Dean M. Hengst; p. 46 Fire-knife dancer at the Polynesian Cultural Center, ©Polynesian Cultural Center; p. 47 Battleship USS *Texas,* Greater Houston Convention and Visitors Bureau; p. 48 ©Getty Images, Inc./Jeremy Woodhouse; p. 49 Canal walk in Indianapolis, Indianapolis Convention and Visitors Bureau; p. 51 Lone Sailor statue on waterfront, Rand McNally; p. 52 Nelson-Atkins Museum of Art, Convention and Visitors Bureau of Greater Kansas City; p. 54 Duval Street, Florida Keys Convention and Visitors Bureau; p. 55 The Las Vegas Strip at night, Las Vegas News Bureau; p. 56 Bronze horse statues at Thoroughbred Park, Lexington Convention and Visitors Bureau/©Jeff Rogers; p. 57 River Market District, Little Rock Convention and Visitors Bureau; p. 58 Movie premiere in Hollywood, Los Angeles Convention and Visitors Bureau/©Arnesen Photography; p. 61 Louisville skyline, Louisville Convention and Visitors Bureau; p. 62 Graceland, Memphis Convention and Visitors Bureau; p. 63 Palace of Fine Arts, Mexico Tourism Authority/ ©Edward Ruiz; p. 64 Miami skyline and marina, Greater Miami Convention and Visitors Bureau; p. 65 Milwaukee Art Museum, Greater Milwaukee Convention and Visitors Bureau; p. 66 Minneapolis Sculpture Garden at Walker Art Center, Greater Minneapolis Convention and Visitors Authority; p. 67 Marjorie McNelly Conservatory, Greater Minneapolis Convention and Visitors Authority; p. 68 Bragg-Mitchell Mansion, Mobile Convention and Visitors Corporation; p. 69 Montréal skyline from parc Jean-Drapeau, ©Tourisme Montréal; p. 70 Pier at Barefoot Landing, South Carolina Dept. of Parks, Recreation, and Tourism; p. 71 Country Music Hall of Fame and Museum, Nashville Convention and Visitors Bureau/Timothy Hursley; p. 72 Mardi Gras festivities in the French Quarter, ©1999 New Orleans Metropolitan Convention and Visitors Bureau/Jeff Strout; p. 74 Central Park, ©NYC & Company, Inc./Joseph Pobereskin and p. 77 New York City's theater district ©NYC & Company, Inc./Jeff Greenberg; p. 78 Tall ships in Norfolk Harbor, Norfolk Convention and Visitors Bureau; p. 79 Virginia Marine Science Museum, Virginia Beach Convention and Visitors Bureau; p. 80 Bricktown Canal, Oklahoma City Convention and Visitors Bureau; p. 81 Gene Leahy Pedestrian Mall, Greater Omaha Convention and Visitors Bureau; p. 82 EPCOT Center at Walt Disney World, Orlando/Orange County Convention and Visitors Bureau; p. 83 Changing of the guard at Parliament Hill, ©2001 Ontario Tourism; p. 84 Commonwealth of Pennsylvania/ Commonwealth Media Services; p. 86 Hot-air balloon race over Phoenix, Greater Phoenix Convention and Visitors Bureau/Jessen Associates, Inc.; p. 88 Point State Park, Greater Pittsburgh Convention and Visitors Bureau; p. 89 Portland skyline with Mount Hood, Portland Oregon Visitors Association; p. 90 Providence Tourism Council/Michael Melford; p. 91 Raleigh skyline, Greater Raleigh Convention and Visitors Bureau; p. 92 (tr) Butterfly House at the Museum of Life Science, Durham Convention and Visitors Bureau; p. 92 (bl) North Carolina Botanical Graden, Chapel Hill Convention and Visitors Bureau; p. 93 Nightlife in Reno, Reno-Sparks Convention and Visitors Authority; p. 94 Sunken Garden at Agecroft Hall, Agecroft Hall and Gardens/Dwight Dyke; p. 96 Downtown St. Louis and the Gateway Arch, Courtesy St. Louis Convention & Visitors Commission; p. 97 Beehive House, Salt Lake Convention and Visitors Bureau/Jason Mathis; p. 98 Entrance to Spanish Governor's Palace, San Antonio Convention and Visitors Bureau/Dave G. Houser; p. 99 The Alamo, ©PhotoDisc; p. 100 USS *Ranger,* San Diego Convention and Visitors Bureau; p. 102 Alcatraz and p. 104 Golden Gate Bridge, San Francisco Convention and Visitors Bureau/Glen McLeod; p. 105 San Jose skyline, San Jose Convention and Visitors Bureau; p. 106 El Rancho de las Golondrinas, Santa Fe Convention and Visitors Bureau; p. 107 Pike Place Market, Seattle News Bureau/Nick Gunderson; p. 109 The Florida Aquarium, Tampa Bay Convention and Visitors Bureau/Jeff Greenburg; p. 110 The Pier shopping area in St. Petersburg, St. Petersburg/Clearwater Area Convention and Visitors Bureau; p. 111 Tijuana Cultural Center, San Diego Convention and Visitors Bureau/©Bob Yarbrough; p. 112 Ontario Place theme park, Toronto Convention and Visitors Association; p. 113 Mural in historic downtown Tucson, Metropolitan Tucson Convention and Visitors Bureau/James Randklev; p. 114 Philbrook Museum of Art, Tulsa Metro Chamber of Commerce/Don Sibley; p. 115 Vancouver skyline, Tourism Vancouver; p. 116 Smithsonian Institution Building (The Castle), Washington, D.C. Convention and Visitors Association

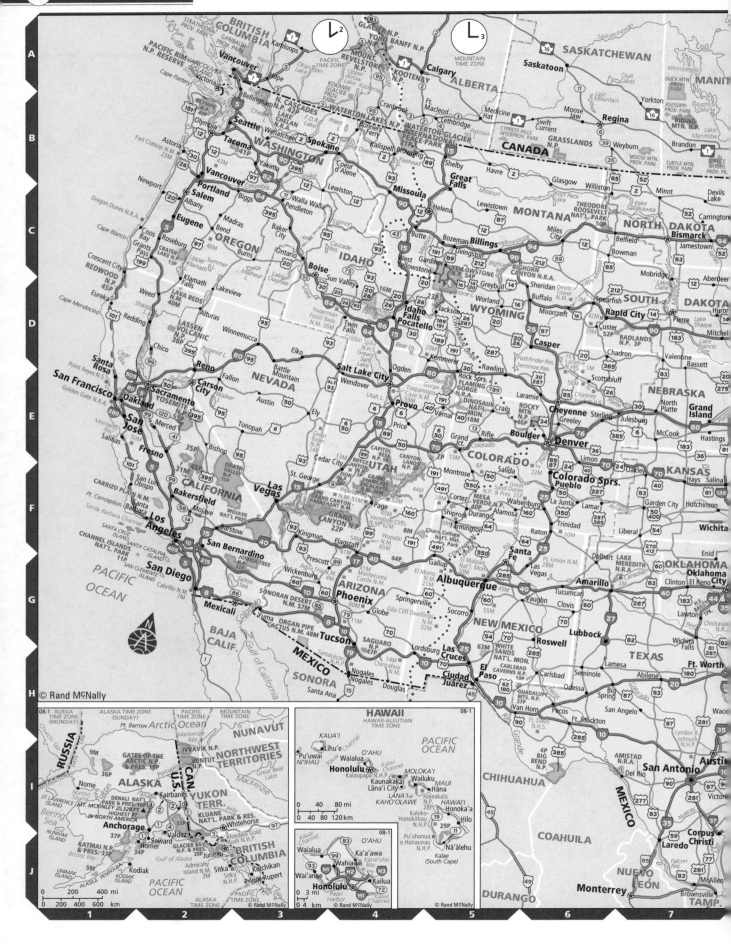

© Rand McNally

Alabama

Population: 4,557,808
Land area: 50,744 sq. mi.
Capital: Montgomery

© Rand McNally

© Rand McNally

Alaska

Population: 663,661
Land area: 571,951 sq. mi.
Capital: Juneau

Cities and Towns

Akiachak	D-3
Akutan	F-1
Alakanuk	C-2
Ambler	E-4
Anchor Point	D-5
Anchorage	E-7
Anderson	D-6
Angoon	E-7
Aniak	D-3
Barrow	C-5
Bethel	D-3
Big Delta	B-3
Buckland	D-5
Cantwell	D-2
Chevak	C-5
Circle	C-5
Circle Hot Springs Station	C-5
College	C-5
Copper Center	E-6
Cordova	E-6
Craig	E-7
Delta Junction	B-3
Dillingham	D-3
Douglas	E-7
Eagle	C-5
Eielson	E-6
Emmonak	C-2
Fairbanks	C-2
Galena	B-5
Gambell	C-1
Glennallen	E-7
Gustavus	E-7
Haines	E-4
Healy	E-4
Homer	E-4
Hoonah	E-7
Hooper Bay	D-2
Hydaburg	F-8
Iditarod	D-3
Juneau	E-7
Kake	F-7
Kaktovik	E-6
Kenai	D-4
Ketchikan	F-8
King Cove	E-2
King Salmon	E-3
Kipnuk	D-2
Kivalina	B-8
Klawock	E-7
Kodiak	E-4
Kotlik	C-2
Kotzebue	E-4
Kwethluk	D-3
Kwigillingok	D-2
Manokotak	D-3
McGrath	C-3
Metlakatla	F-8
Mountain Village	C-2
Naknek	E-3
Nenana	D-2
New Stuyahok	D-3
Nikiski	D-4
Ninilchik	D-5
Noatak	B-2
Nome	B-2
Noorvik	B-3
North Pole	B-4
Nulato	B-5
Palmer	D-5
Perryville	E-2
Petersburg	F-8
Pilot Station	C-2
Point Hope	A-2
Prudhoe Bay	A-4
Quinhagak	D-2
Ruby	B-5
St. Michael	C-2
Sand Point	F-2
Savoonga	B-1
Scammon Bay	C-2
Selawik	B-3
Seward	D-5
Shaktoolik	B-4
Shungnak	F-7
Sitka	E-7
Skagway	D-5
Soldotna	E-4
Stebbins	C-2
Talkeetna	E-7
Tanana	B-3
Teller	B-2
Togiak	D-2
Tok	C-6
Toksook Bay	D-2
Umiat	A-4
Unalakleet	C-3
Unalaska	F-1
Valdez	D-5
Venetie	B-5
Wainwright	A-3
Wasilla	D-5
Willow	D-5
Wrangell	F-8
Yakutat	E-6

For border crossing information, please see p. 177

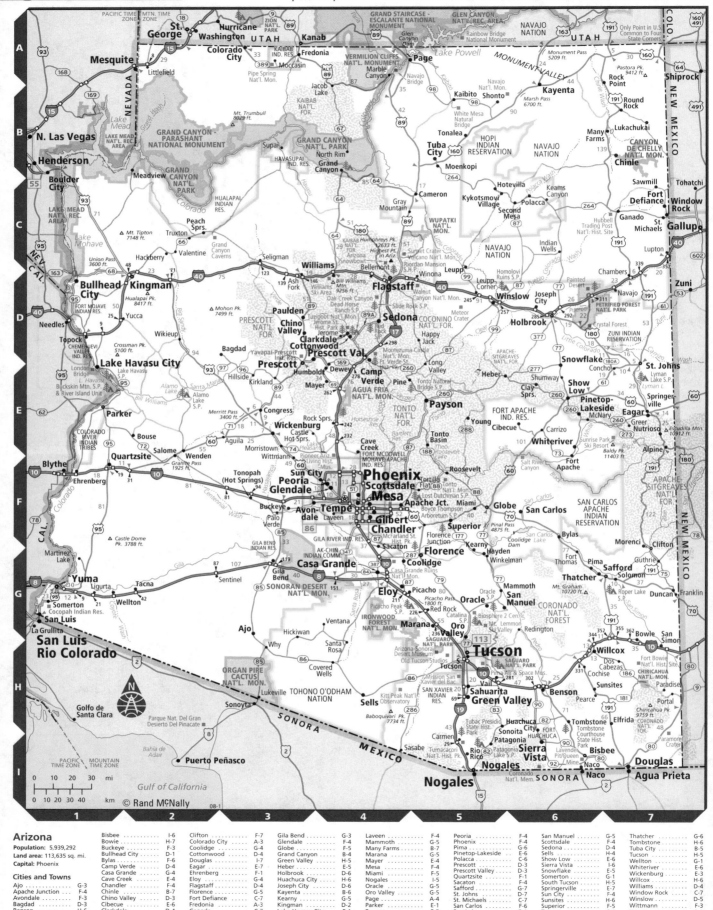

© Rand McNally   08-1

Arizona

Population: 5,939,292
Land area: 113,635 sq. mi.
Capital: Phoenix

Cities and Towns

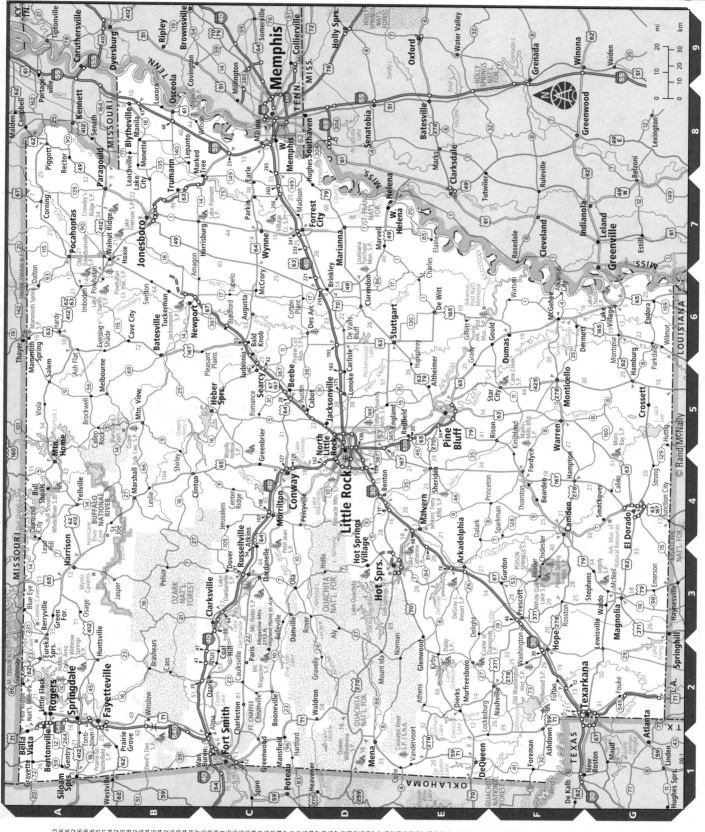

California

Population: 36,132,147
Land area: 155,959 sq. mi.
Capital: Sacramento

Cities and Towns

For border crossing information,
please see p. 177

© Rand McNally

Colorado

Population: 4,665,177
Land area: 103,718 sq. mi.
Capital: Denver

Cities and Towns

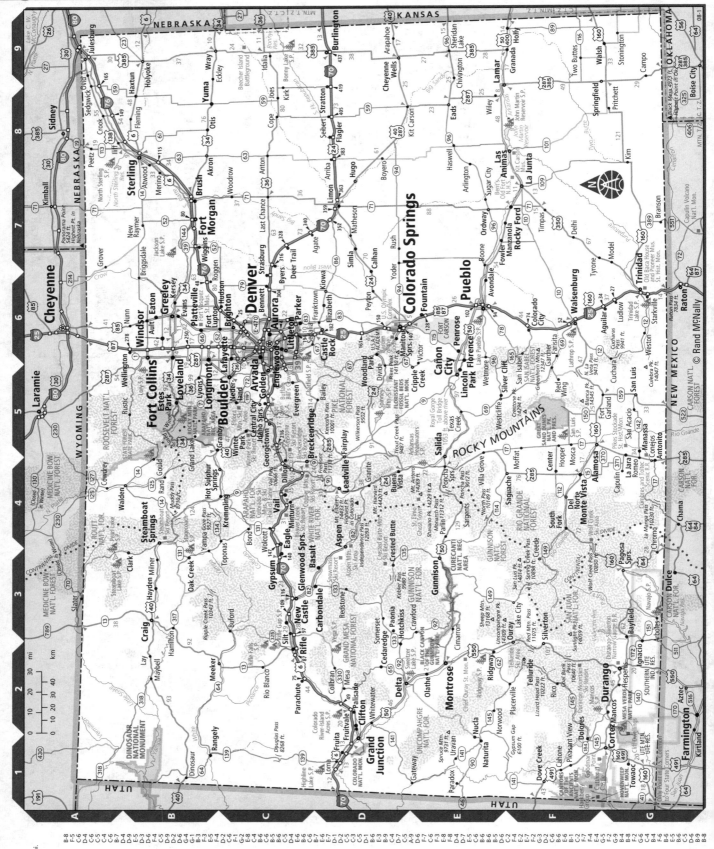

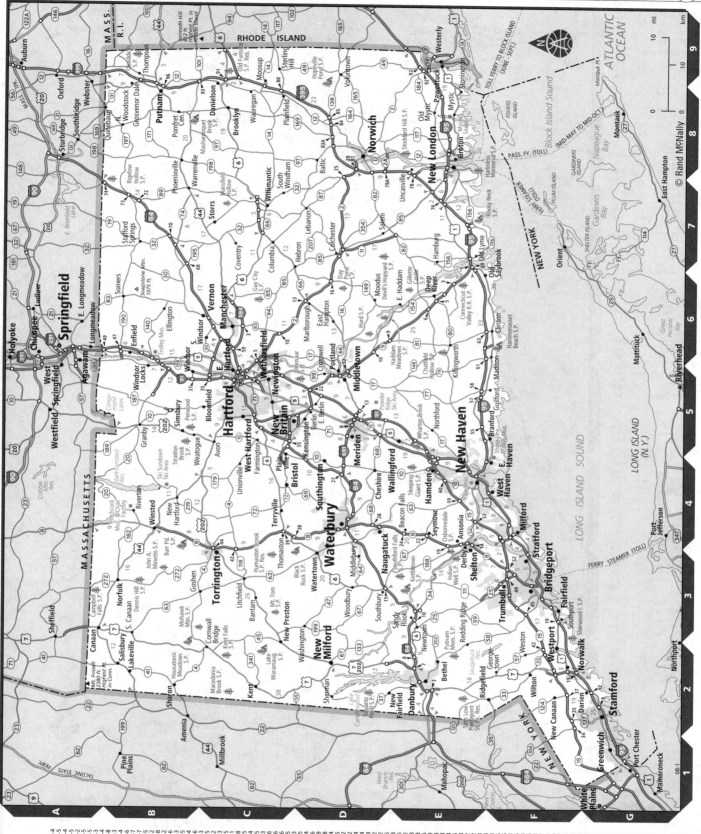

Connecticut

Population: 3,510,297
Land area: 4,845 sq. mi.
Capital: Hartford

Delaware

Population: 843,524
Land area: 1,954 sq. mi.
Capital: Dover

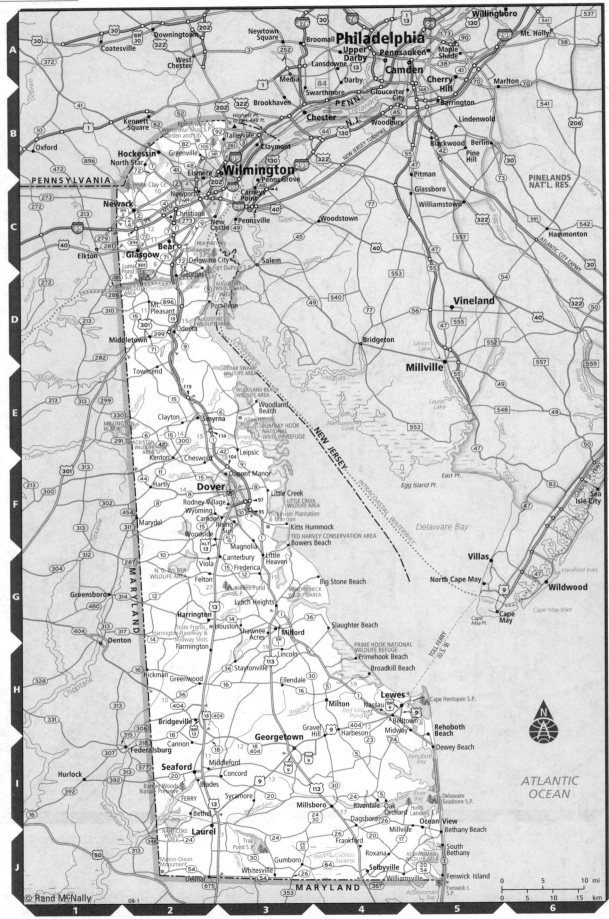

Florida

Population: 17,789,864
Land area: 53,927 sq. mi.
Capital: Tallahassee

Cities and Towns

© Rand McNally

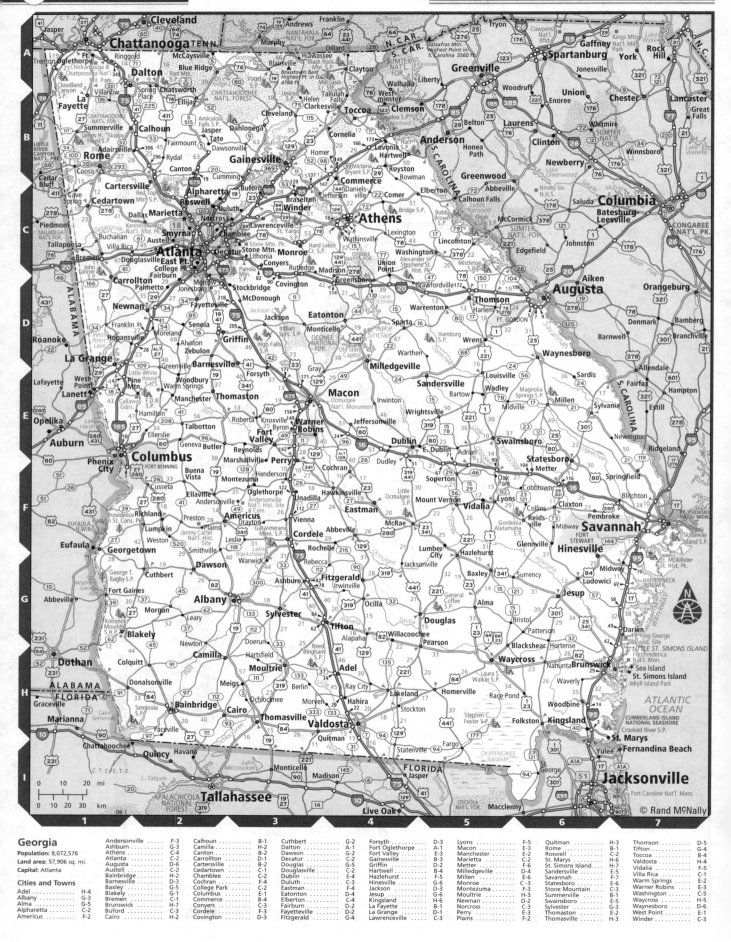

Georgia

Population: 9,072,576
Land area: 57,906 sq. mi.
Capital: Atlanta

Cities and Towns

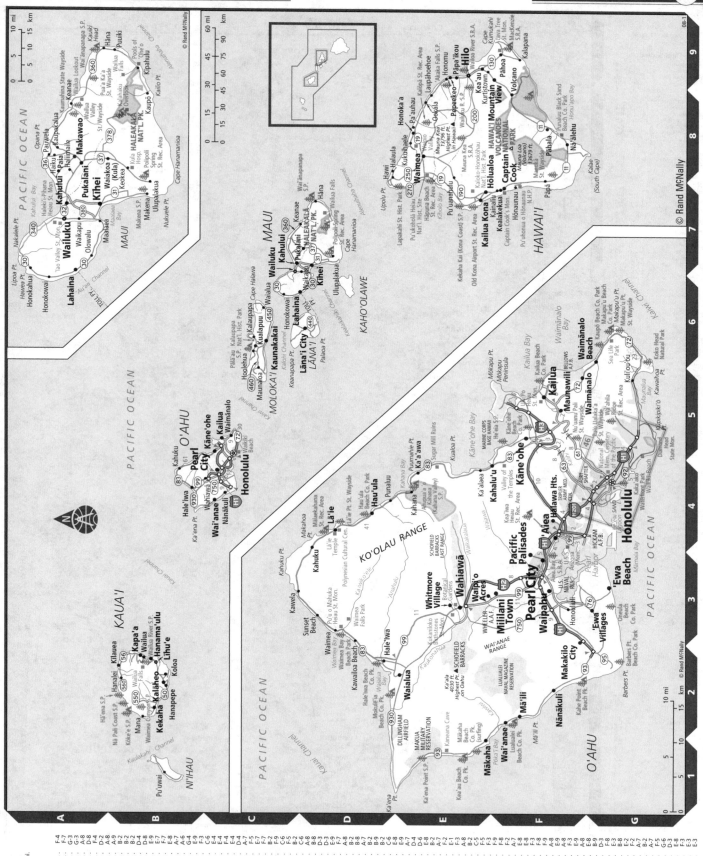

© Rand McNally

Hawaii

Population: 1,275,194
Land area: 6,423 sq. mi.
Capital: Honolulu

© Rand McNally

08-1

For border crossing information, please see p. 177

For border crossing information, please see p. 177

Get more Idaho info at go.randmcnally.com/ID

Idaho

Population: 1,429,096
Land area: 82,747 sq. mi.
Capital: Boise

Cities and Towns

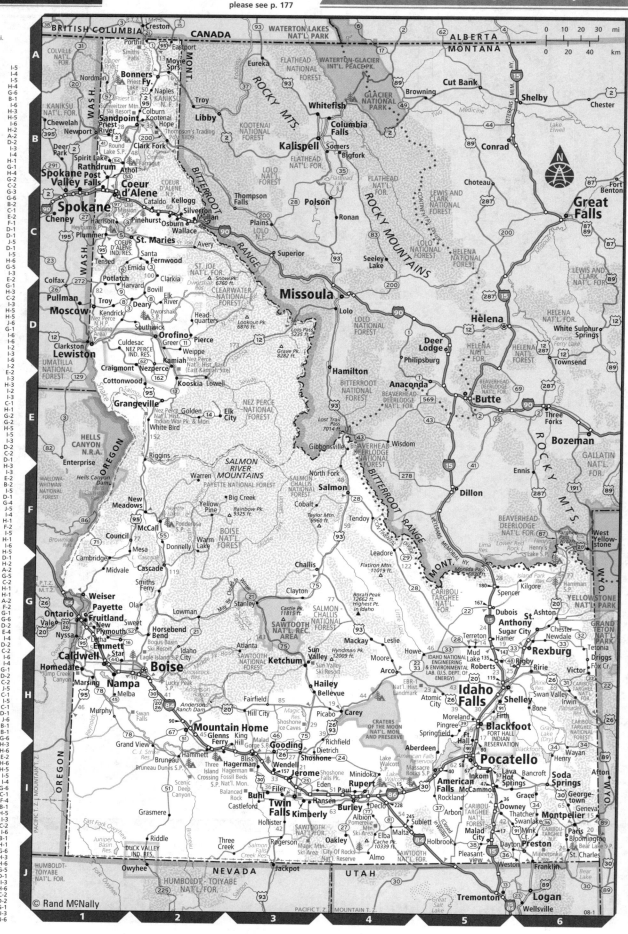

© Rand McNally

08-1

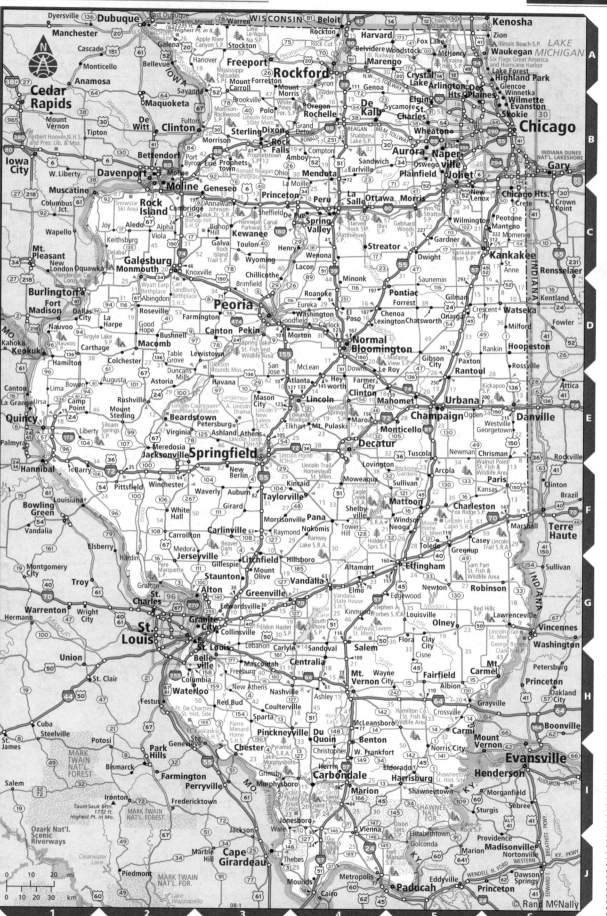

Illinois

Population: 12,763,371
Land area: 55,584 sq. mi.
Capital: Springfield

Cities and Towns

Indiana

Population: 6,271,973
Land area: 35,867 sq. mi.
Capital: Indianapolis

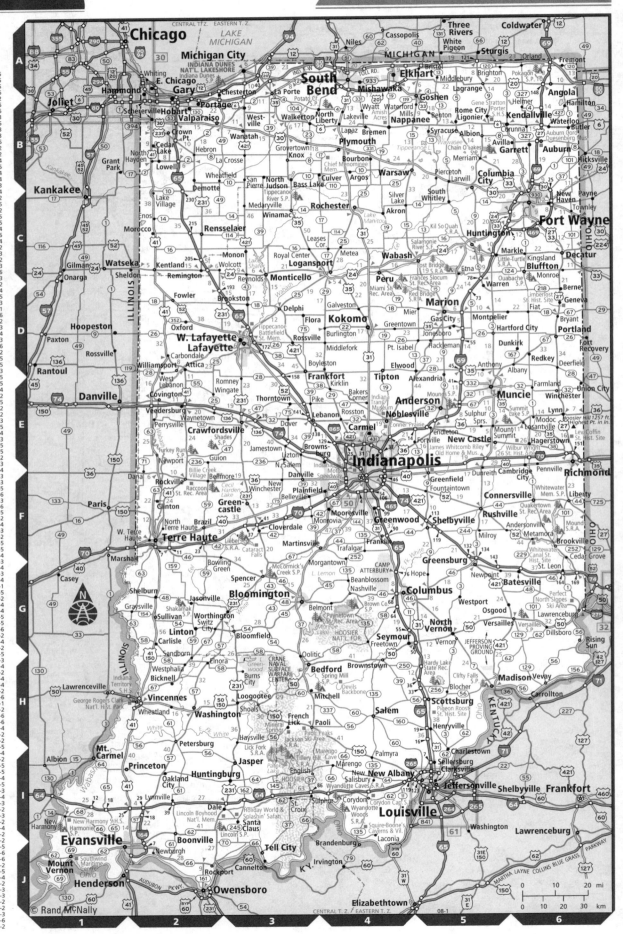

© Rand McNally

Kansas

Population: 2,744,687
Land area: 81,815 sq. mi.
Capital: Topeka

Cities and Towns

City	Grid
Abilene	C-7
Anthony	F-6
Arkansas City	F-7
Ashland	F-4
Atchison	B-9
Atwood	B-2
Augusta	E-7
Baxter Springs	F-10
Beloit	C-6
Belleville	B-6
Burlington	E-9
Caney	F-9
Chanute	E-9
Cherryvale	F-9
Cimarron	E-3
Clay Center	C-7
Coffeyville	F-9
Colby	B-2
Coldwater	F-4
Columbus	F-10
Concordia	B-6
Cottonwood Falls	D-8
Council Grove	C-8
Derby	E-7
Dighton	D-3
Dodge City	E-3
El Dorado	E-7
Ellinwood	D-5
Ellis	C-4
Ellsworth	C-6
Emporia	D-8
Erie	E-9
Eureka	E-8
Fort Scott	E-10
Fredonia	E-9
Garden City	E-2
Garnett	D-9
Girard	E-10
Goodland	B-1
Great Bend	D-5
Greensburg	E-4
Harper	F-6
Herington	C-7
Hiawatha	B-9
Hill City	C-3
Hillsboro	D-7
Hoisington	D-5
Holton	C-9
Howard	E-8
Hugoton	F-2
Humboldt	E-9
Hutchinson	D-6
Iola	E-9
Jetmore	E-4
Johnson	E-1
Junction City	C-7
Kansas City	C-10
Kinsley	E-4
Kirwin	B-4
La Crosse	D-4
Lakin	E-2
Larned	D-4
Lawrence	C-9
Leavenworth	B-10
Leoti	D-2
Liberal	F-2
Lincoln	C-6
Lyndon	C-9
Lyons	D-6
Manhattan	C-8
Mankato	B-5
McPherson	D-7
Meade	F-3
Medicine Lodge	F-5
Minneapolis	C-6
Mound City	D-10
Mulvane	E-7
Neodesha	E-9
Newton	D-7
Norton	B-4
Oakley	C-2
Oberlin	B-3
Olathe	C-10
Osage City	C-8
Osawatomie	D-10
Osborne	C-5
Oskaloosa	C-9
Oswego	F-10
Ottawa	C-9
Paola	C-10
Parsons	F-9
Peabody	D-7
Phillipsburg	B-4
Pittsburg	F-10
Plainville	C-4
Pratt	E-5
Russell	C-5
Sabetha	B-9
St. John	E-5
St. Marys	C-8
Salina	C-6
Scott City	D-2
Sedan	F-8
Seneca	B-8
Sharon Springs	C-1
Shawnee	C-10
Smith Center	B-5
S. Hutchinson	D-6
Sterling	D-6
Sublette	E-2
Syracuse	E-1
Tonganoxie	C-9
Topeka	C-8
Tribune	D-1
Troy	B-9
Ulysses	E-2
WaKeeney	C-4
Wamego	C-8
Washington	B-7
Wellington	E-7
Winfield	E-7
Yates Center	E-9

© Rand McNally

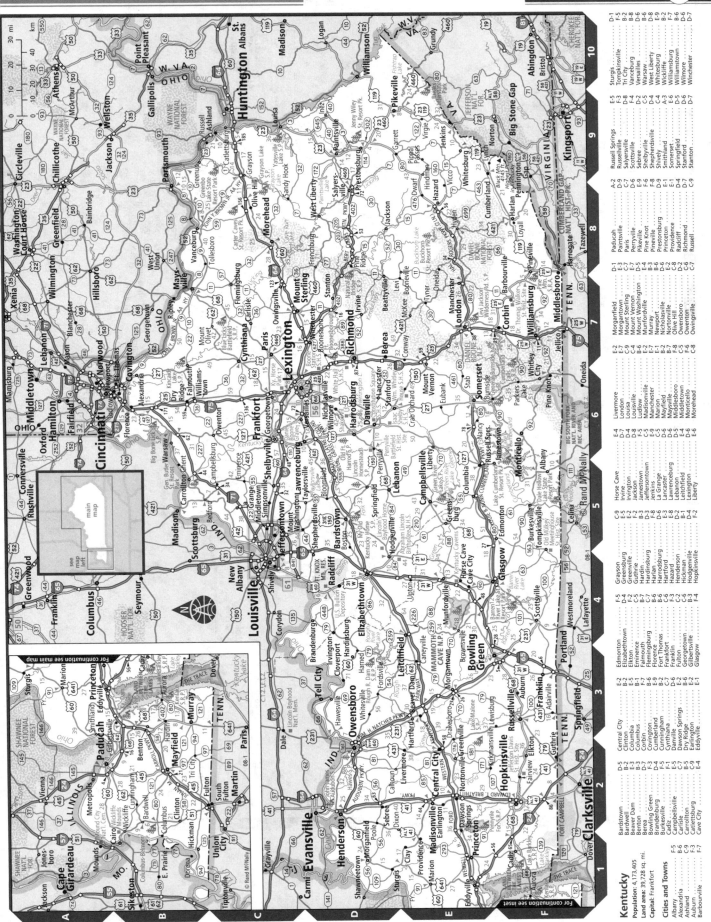

Kentucky

Population: 4,173,405
Land area: 39,728 sq. mi.
Capital: Frankfort

Cities and Towns

Albany	F-5
Alexandria	B-6
Ashland	C-9
Auburn	F-3
Barbourville	F-7

Bardstown	D-5
Bardwell	B-2
Beaver Dam	B-3
Berea	D-7
Bowling Green	F-3
Brandenburg	C-5
Buckner	F-1
Cadiz	E-5
Campbellsville	E-5
Carlisle	C-7
Carrollton	B-5
Cave City	C-9

Central City	D-5
Clinton	B-2
Columbia	B-3
Corbin	D-7
Covington	F-3
Cumberland	E-9
Cunningham	F-1
Cynthiana	F-5
Danville	C-7
Dawson Springs	B-5
Dry Ridge	C-9
Eddyville	E-4

Edmonton	F-5
Elizabethtown	B-2
Elkton	B-1
Eminence	F-7
Falmouth	C-5
Flemingsburg	C-7
Florence	B-6
Fort Thomas	C-6
Frankfort	D-6
Franklin	F-3
Fulton	C-2
Georgetown	B-1
Gilbertsville	B-3
Glasgow	F-2

Grayson	F-5
Greensburg	D-4
Greenville	C-5
Guthrie	B-3
Hardinsburg	B-4
Harlan	B-6
Harrodsburg	C-6
Hartford	F-3
Hazard	C-2
Henderson	B-1
Hopkinsville	B-1
Horse Cave	D-4
Hodgenville	B-3
Hopkinsville	F-2

Horse Cave	C-9
Irvine	E-5
Irvington	F-2
Jackson	C-5
Jamestown	B-3
Jeffersontown	F-8
Jenkins	D-6
La Grange	E-3
Lancaster	B-7
Lawrenceburg	E-8
Lebanon	B-1
Lexington	D-4
Liberty	F-2

Livermore	E-4
London	D-7
Louisville	D-8
Ludlow	B-5
Madisonville	C-7
Manchester	E-9
Marion	D-6
Mayfield	C-5
Middlesboro	E-8
Middletown	B-1
Monticello	D-4
Morehead	E-6

Morganfield	E-2
Mount Sterling	E-7
Mount Vernon	C-9
Mount Washington	G-4
Munfordville	B-7
Murray	E-7
Newport	E-1
Nicholasville	B-7
Nortonville	F-8
Olive Hill	E-1
Owensboro	D-7
Owenton	C-9

Paducah	D-1
Paintsville	C-7
Paris	D-6
Perryville	D-5
Pikeville	B-3
Pine Knot	D-4
Pineville	D-6
Prestonsburg	C-8
Princeton	C-2
Providence	B-7
Radcliff	C-8
Richmond	C-7
Russell	C-9

Russell Springs	A-2
Russellville	D-9
Salyersville	D-6
Scottsville	G-4
Sebree	B-3
Shelbyville	F-8
Shepherdsville	D-4
Shively	D-9
Smithland	A-3
Somerset	D-6
Springfield	D-7
Stanford	C-9
Stanton	D-7

Sturgis	D-1
Tompkinsville	F-5
Tri City	F-8
Vanceburg	F-4
Versailles	C-5
Warsaw	D-4
West Liberty	D-8
Whitesburg	D-8
Wickliffe	A-3
Williamsburg	D-5
Williamstown	B-6
Winchester	D-7

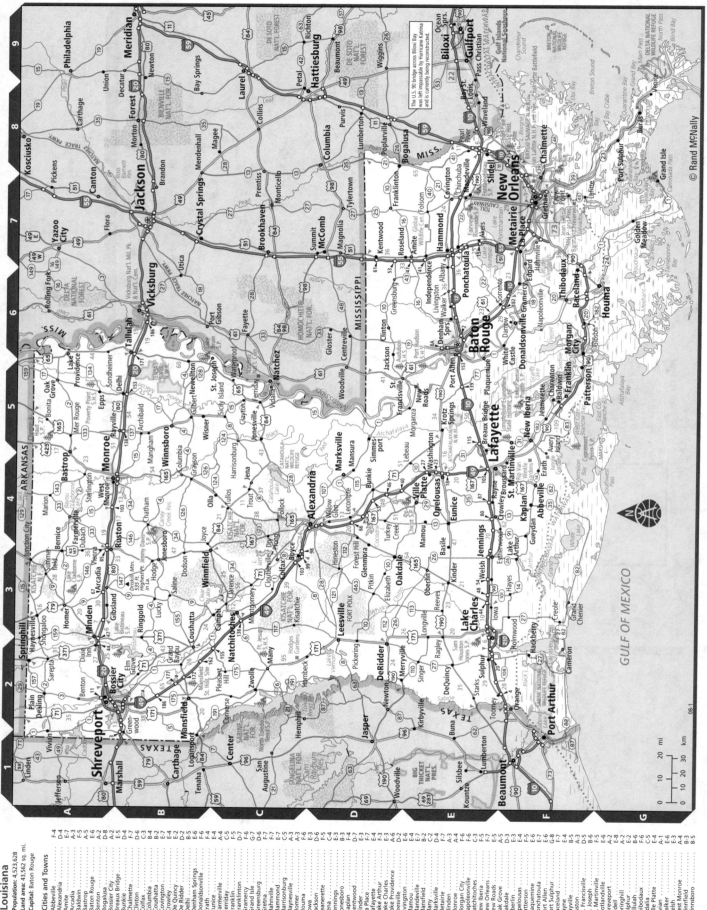

Louisiana

Population: 4,523,628
Land area: 43,562 sq. mi.
Capital: Baton Rouge

For border crossing information, please see p. 177

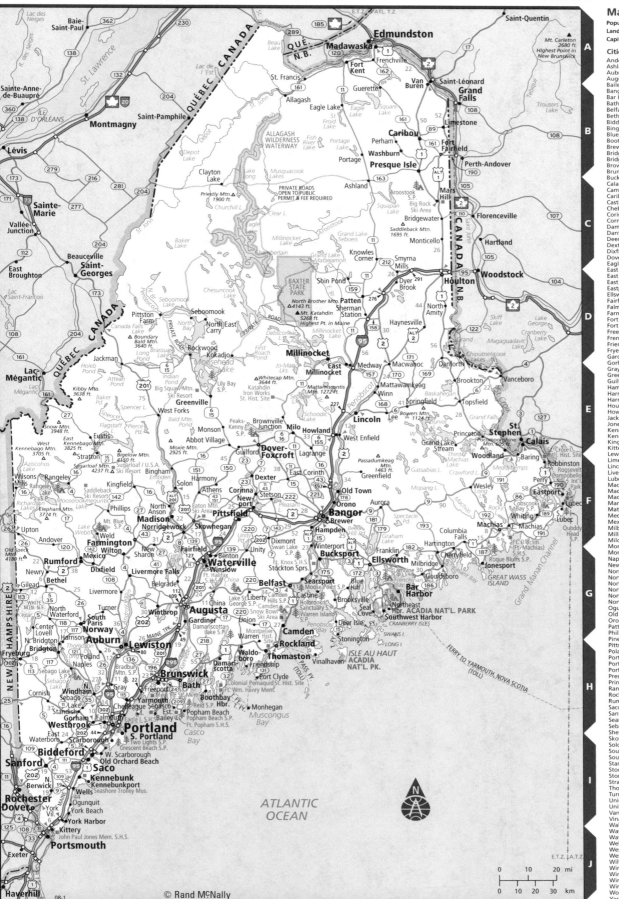

Maine

Population: 1,321,505
Land area: 30,862 sq. mi.
Capital: Augusta

Cities and Towns

Plan a Maryland trip at go.randmcnally.com/MD

Maryland

Population: 5,600,388
Land area: 9,774 sq. mi.
Capital: Annapolis

District of Columbia

Population: 550,521
Land area: 61 sq. mi.

© Rand McNally

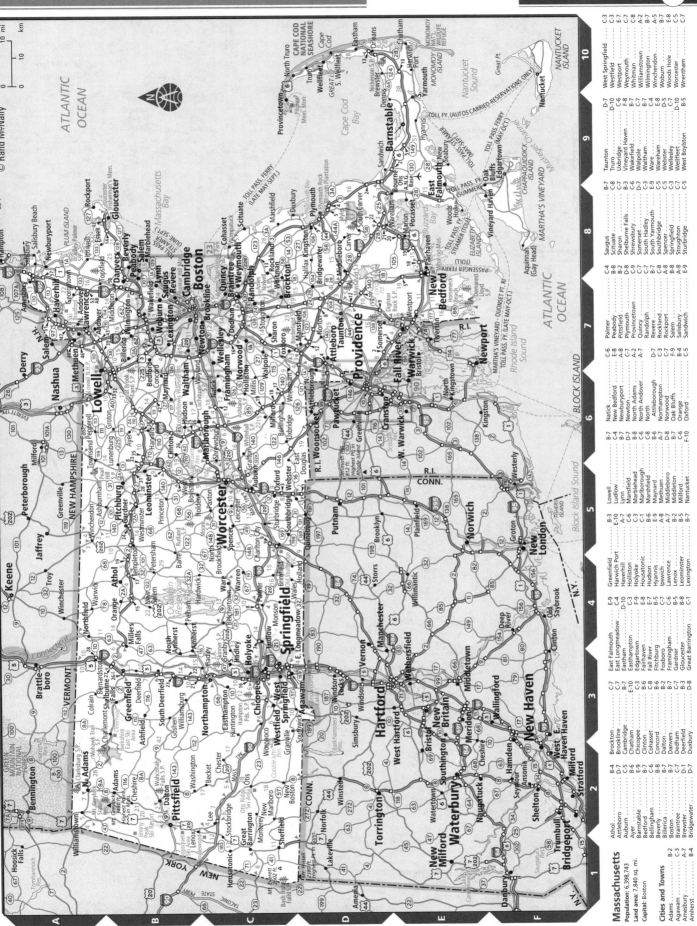

For border crossing information, please see p. 177

Explore Michigan at go.randmcnally.com/MI

Michigan

Population: 10,120,860
Land area: 56,804 sq. mi.
Capital: Lansing

Cities and Towns

Adrian J-4
Albion I-4
Allegan H-2
Alma G-4
Alpena D-5
Ann Arbor I-5
Bad Axe F-6
Baldwin F-2
Battle Creek I-3
Bay City G-5
Bellaire E-3
Benton Harbor I-1
Benton Heights I-2
Berrien Springs J-2
Bessemer B-5
Big Rapids G-3
Birmingham I-5
Boyne City D-3
Brighton I-5
Burton H-5
Cadillac F-3
Caro G-5
Cass City G-5
Cassopolis J-2
Cedar Springs G-3
Centreville J-3
Charlevoix D-3
Charlotte I-3
Cheboygan D-4
Chelsea I-4
Clare F-3
Clio H-5
Coldwater J-3
Corunna H-4
Croswell G-6
Crystal Falls B-6
Davison H-5
Dearborn I-5
Detroit I-5
Dowagiac I-2
East Tawas F-5
Escanaba C-1
Evart F-3
Fenton H-5
Flint H-5
Frankenmuth G-5
Frankfort E-2
Fremont G-2
Garden City E-4
Gaylord D-4
Gladstone C-1
Gladwin F-4
Grand Haven H-2
Grand Ledge H-4
Grand Rapids H-2
Grayling E-3
Greenville H-3
Hancock A-6
Harbor Beach F-6
Harbor Springs D-3
Harrison F-3
Hart G-2
Hastings H-3
Hillsdale J-4
Holland H-2
Holly H-5
Houghton A-6
Howell H-4
Hudson J-4
Hudsonville H-2
Imlay City H-5
Ionia H-3
Iron Mountain C-6
Iron River B-6
Ironwood B-5
Ishpeming B-6
Ithaca G-4
Jackson I-4
Jonesville I-4
Kalamazoo I-2
Kalkaska E-3
L'Anse B-6
Lake City F-3
Lansing H-4
Lapeer H-5
Livonia I-5
Ludington F-1
Mackinaw City C-3
Manistee F-2
Manistique C-2
Marlette G-5
Marquette B-6
Marshall I-3
Marysville H-6
Mason H-4
Menominee C-6
Midland G-4
Monroe J-5
Mount Clemens I-6
Mount Pleasant G-3
Munising B-1
Muskegon G-2
Muskegon Heights H-2
Negaunee B-6
New Buffalo J-1
Newberry B-2
Niles J-2
Norway C-6
Ontonagon B-5
Owosso H-4
Paw Paw I-2
Petoskey D-3
Plainwell I-2
Pontiac H-5
Port Huron H-6
Portage I-3
Reed City F-3
Rockford H-3
Rogers City D-4
St. Clair H-6
St. Ignace C-3
St. Johns H-4
St. Joseph I-1
Saline I-5
Sandusky G-6
Sault Ste. Marie B-4
South Haven I-2
Sparta H-2
Standish F-4
Sturgis J-3
Tawas City F-4
Tecumseh I-4
Three Rivers J-2
Traverse City E-2
Trenton I-5
Vassar G-5
Wakefield B-5
Warren I-5
West Branch F-4
Westland I-5
Wyandotte I-5
Wyoming H-2
Ypsilanti I-5
Zeeland H-2

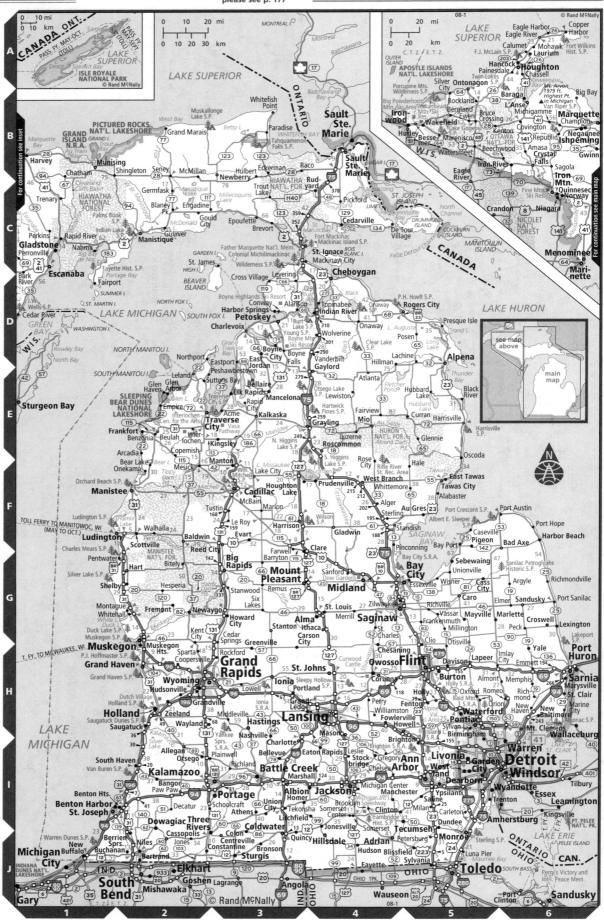

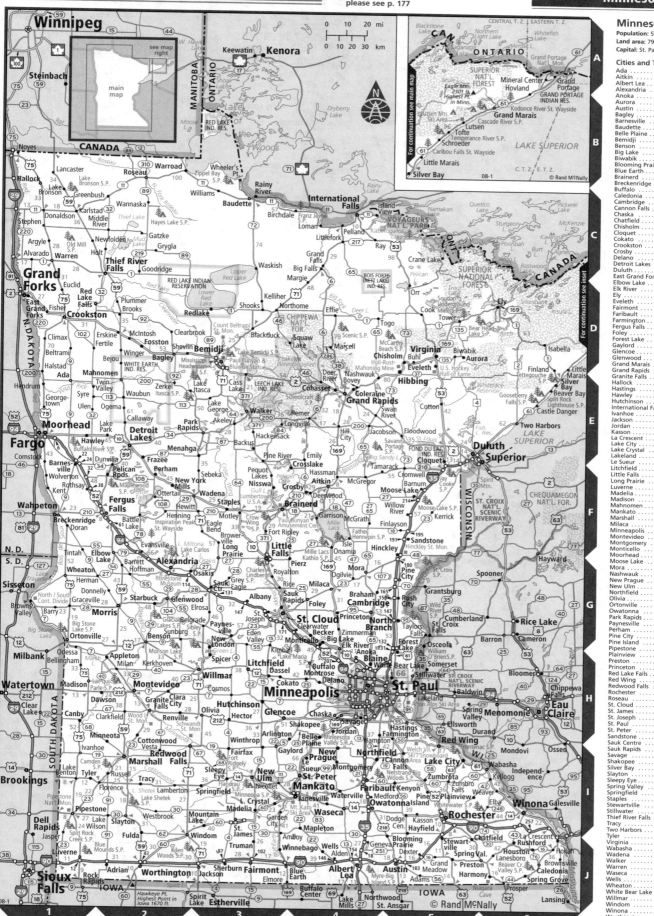

Minnesota

Population: 5,132,799
Land area: 79,610 sq. mi.
Capital: St. Paul

Mississippi

Population: 2,921,088
Land area: 46,907 sq. mi.
Capital: Jackson

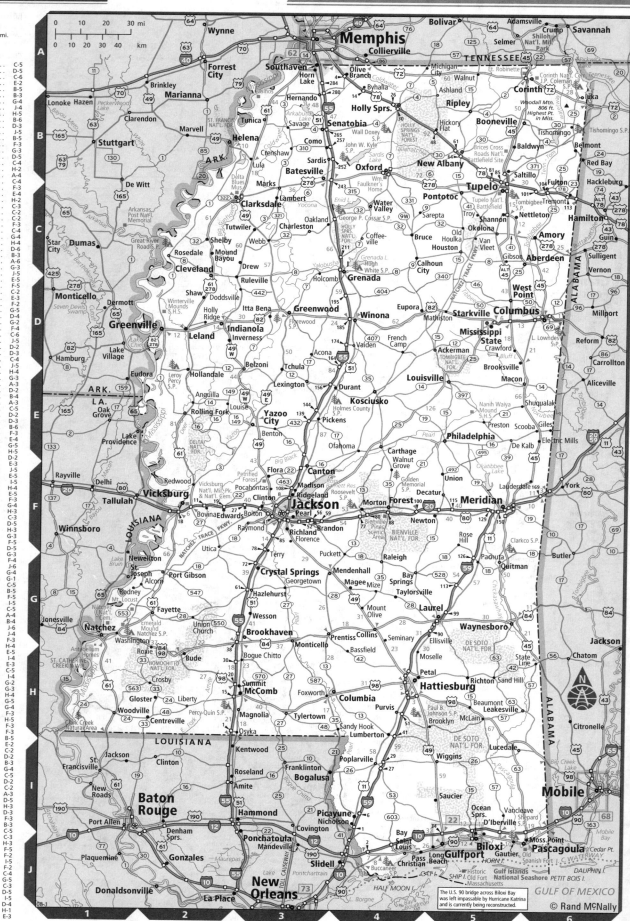

08-1

© Rand McNally

For border crossing information, please see p. 177

Montana

Population: 935,670
Land area: 145,552 sq. mi.
Capital: Helena

Cities and Towns

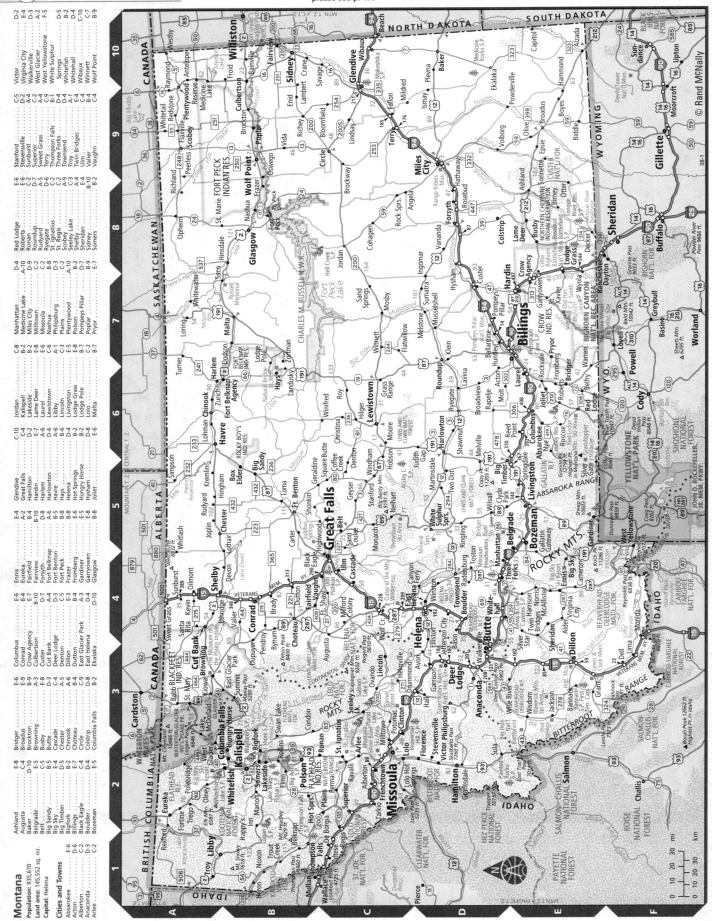

© Rand McNally

© Rand McNally

Nevada

Population: 2,414,807
Land area: 109,826 sq. mi.
Capital: Carson City

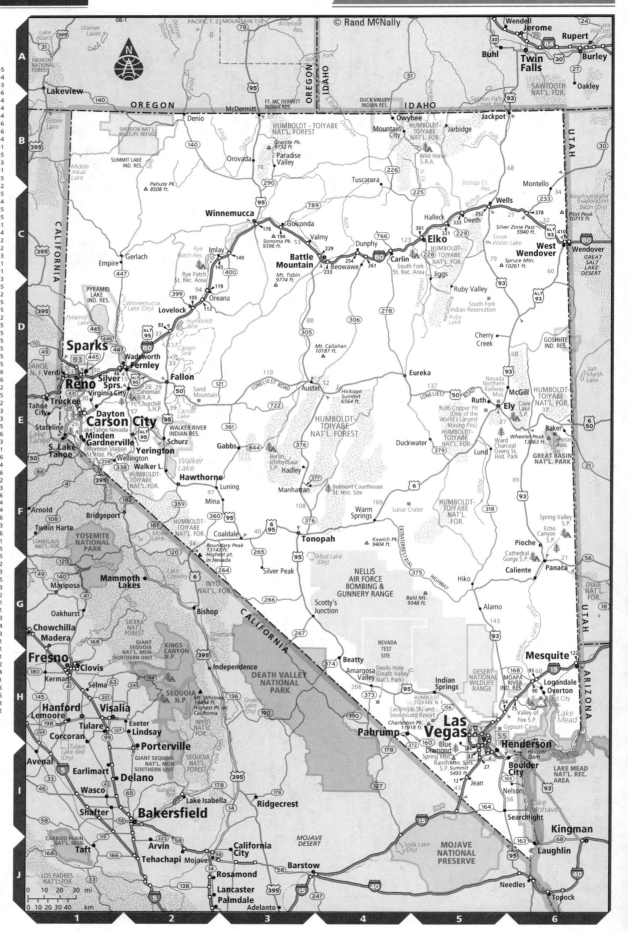

© Rand McNally

New Hampshire

Population: 1,309,940
Land area: 8,968 sq. mi.
Capital: Concord

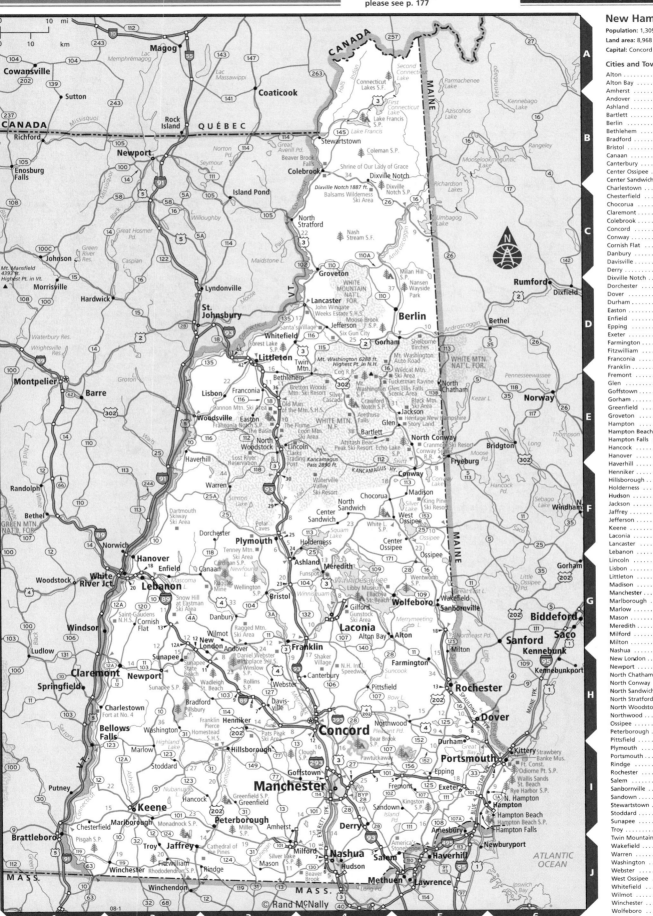

Get more New Jersey info at go.randmcnally.com/NJ

New Jersey

Population: 8,717,925
Land area: 7,417 sq. mi.
Capital: Trenton

Cities and Towns

Absecon H-4
Asbury Park E-5
Atlantic City I-4
Atlantic Highlands G-2
Audubon G-2
Barnegat Light G-5
Bayonne D-5
Beach Haven H-5
Beachwood F-5
Belleville C-5
Belvidere C-3
Berlin G-3
Bernardsville C-4
Blackwood G-2
Bloomfield C-5
Boonton C-4
Bordentown F-3
Bound Brook D-4
Bridgeton H-2
Bridgewater D-4
Brigantine H-4
Browns Mills F-4
Budd Lake C-3
Buena H-3
Burlington F-3
Butler B-4
Caldwell C-5
Camden F-2
Cape May J-3
Cape May Court
  House J-3
Cherry Hill G-2
Clark D-4
Clifton C-5
Cranford D-4
Denville C-4
Dover C-4
Dumont C-5
East Orange C-5
Eatontown E-5
Edison D-4
Egg Harbor City H-4
Elizabeth D-5
Englewood C-5
Ewing E-3
Flemington D-3
Franklin B-4
Freehold E-5
Glassboro G-2
Gloucester City G-2
Hackensack C-5
Hackettstown C-3
Hammonton G-3
High Bridge D-3
Highlands E-5
Hightstown E-4
Hopatcong C-3
Irvington C-5
Iselin D-4
Jamesburg E-4
Jersey City D-5
Keansburg D-5
Lakehurst F-5
Lakewood F-5
Lambertville E-3
Lawrenceville E-3
Linden D-5
Little Silver E-5
Long Branch E-5
Madison C-4
Mahwah B-5
Manville D-4
Margate City I-4
Matawan E-5
Mays Landing H-3
Metuchen D-4
Millville H-2
Morris Plains C-4
Morristown C-4
Mount Holly F-3
Neptune City E-5
Netcong C-3
New Brunswick D-4
New Providence ... C-5
Newark C-5
Newfoundland B-4
Newton B-3
North Bergen C-5
Oakland B-5
Ocean City I-4
Ocean Grove E-5
Old Bridge E-4
Palisades Park C-5
Paramus B-5
Passaic C-5
Paterson C-5
Paulsboro G-2
Penns Grove G-1
Pennsauken F-2
Pennsville G-1
Perth Amboy D-5
Phillipsburg C-2
Plainfield D-4
Pleasantville H-4
Point Pleasant F-5
Princeton E-3
Rahway D-5
Ramsey B-5
Raritan D-4
Red Bank E-5
Ridgewood B-5
Salem H-1
Sayreville D-4
Scotch Plains D-4
Sea Bright E-5
Sea Isle City I-3
Seaside Park F-5
Ship Bottom G-5
Somerdale G-2
Somers Point I-4
Somerville D-4
South River D-4
Sparta B-4
Spring Lake E-5
Stratford G-2
Toms River F-5
Trenton E-3
Tuckerton H-4
Union C-5
Ventnor City I-4
Villas J-3
Vineland H-2
Waldwick B-5
Wanaque B-5
Washington C-3
West Orange C-5
Wildwood J-3
Williamstown G-3
Willingboro F-3
Woodbury G-2
Woodstown G-2
Wrightstown F-4
Wyckoff B-5

© Rand McNally

© Rand McNally

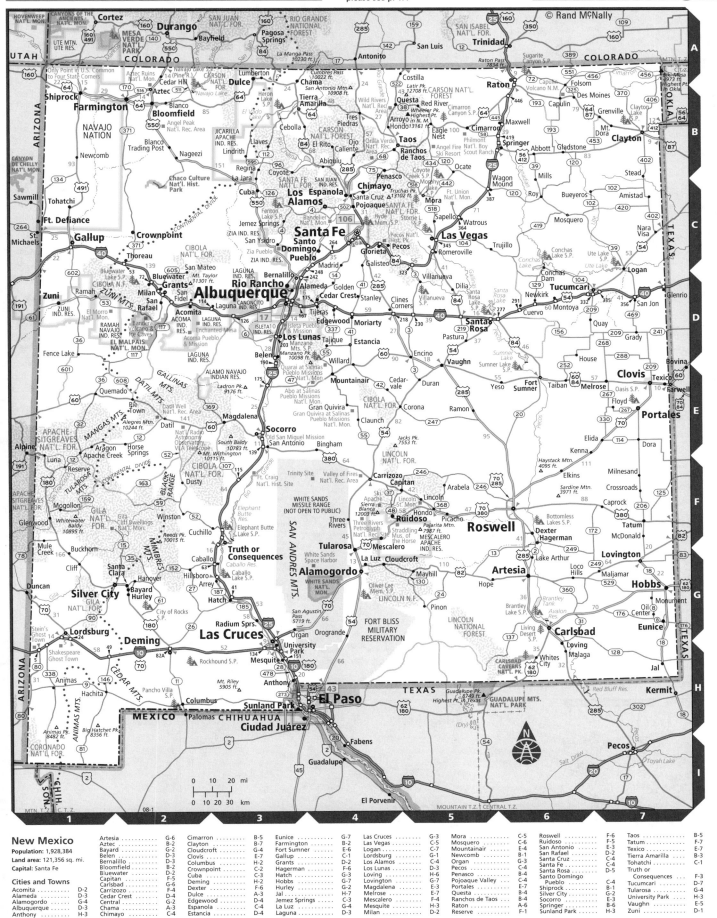

New Mexico

Population: 1,928,384
Land area: 121,356 sq. mi.
Capital: Santa Fe

Cities and Towns

Plan a New York trip at go.randmcnally.com/NY

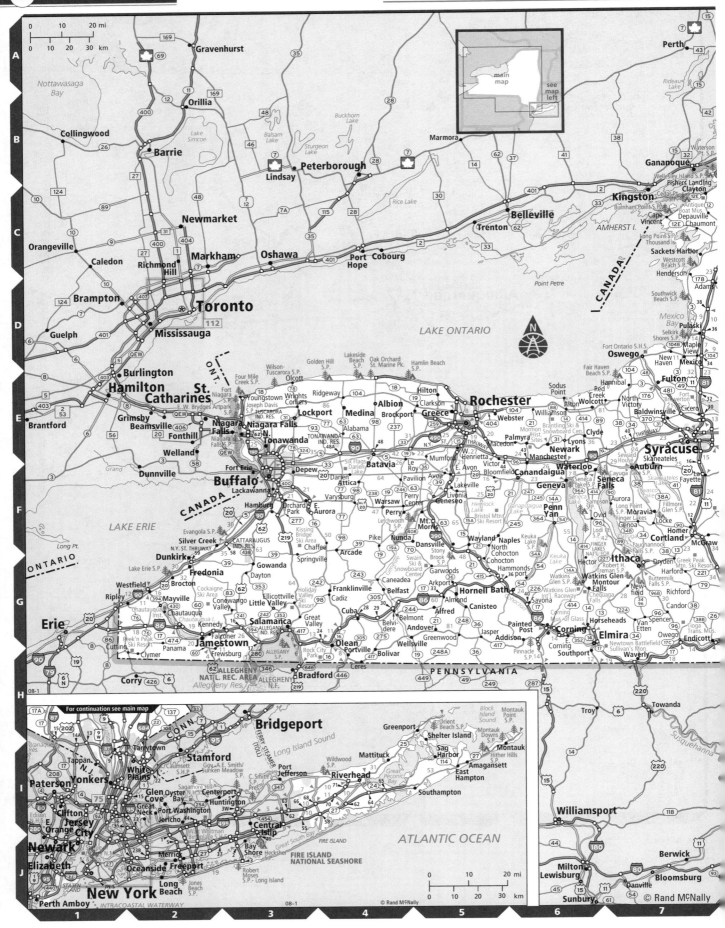

© Rand McNally

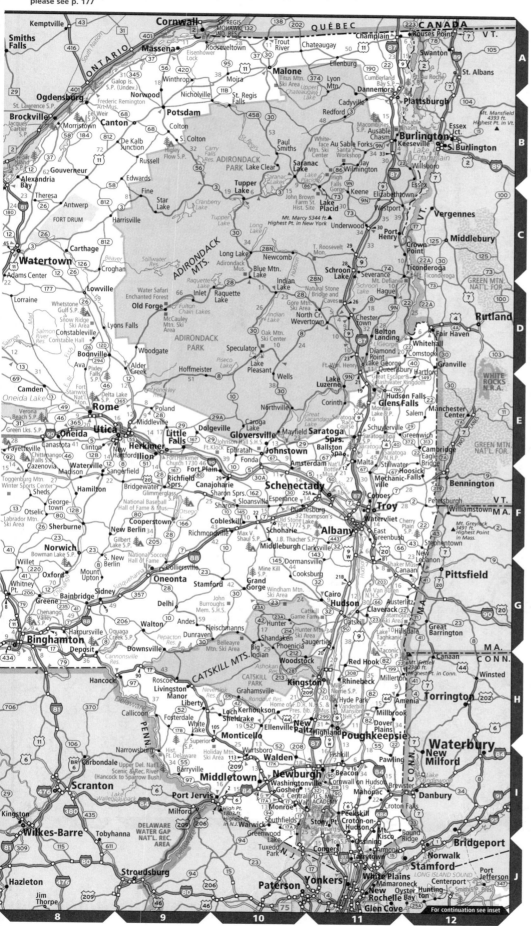

New York

Population: 19,254,630
Land area: 47,214 sq. mi.
Capital: Albany

Cities and Towns

North Carolina

Population: 8,683,242
Land area: 48,711 sq. mi.
Capital: Raleigh

Cities and Towns

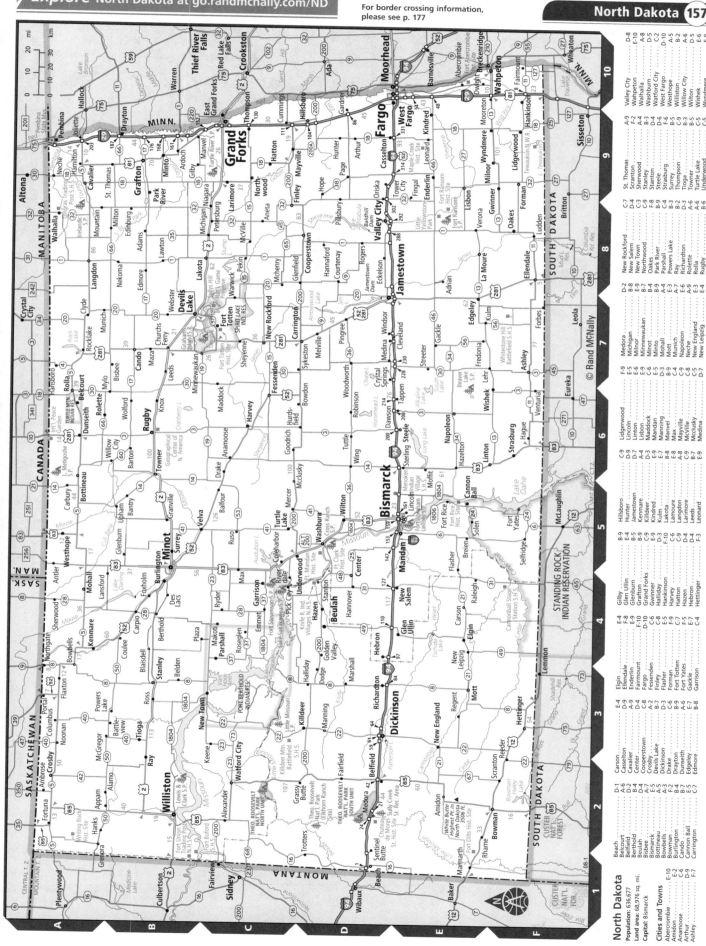

North Dakota

Population: 636,677
Land area: 68,976 sq. mi.
Capital: Bismarck

Cities and Towns

Abercrombie	E-10	
Amidon	E-2	
Anamoose	C-6	
Arthur	D-9	
Ashley	F-7	

Beach	D-1
Belcourt	A-6
Belfield	D-2
Berthold	B-4
Beulah	D-4
Bisbee	B-7
Bismarck	D-5
Bottineau	A-5
Bowbells	A-3
Bowman	F-2
Burlington	B-4
Cando	B-7
Cannon Ball	E-5
Carrington	C-7

Carson	D-4
Casselton	D-9
Cavalier	A-9
Center	D-4
Cooperstown	C-8
Crosby	A-2
Devils Lake	B-7
Dickinson	D-3
Drake	C-6
Drayton	A-9
Dunseith	A-6
Edgeley	E-7
Edmore	B-8

Elgin	E-4
Ellendale	F-8
Enderlin	E-9
Fairmount	F-10
Fargo	D-10
Fessenden	C-6
Finley	C-8
Flasher	E-5
Forman	F-9
Fort Totten	B-7
Fort Yates	E-5
Gackle	E-7
Garrison	B-8

Gilby	B-9
Glen Ullin	D-4
Glenburn	B-5
Grafton	B-9
Grand Forks	B-9
Gwinner	E-9
Halliday	D-3
Hankinson	F-10
Harvey	C-6
Hazelton	E-6
Hazen	D-4
Hebron	D-4
Hettinger	F-3

Hillsboro	C-9
Hunter	C-9
Jamestown	D-7
Kenmare	B-4
Killdeer	C-3
Kindred	D-9
Kulm	E-7
Lakota	B-8
Lamoure	E-8
Langdon	A-8
Larimore	C-9
Leeds	B-7
Leonard	D-9

Lidgerwood	C-9
Lincoln	D-9
Linton	D-7
Lisbon	D-3
Maddock	E-9
Mandan	E-5
Manvel	B-9
Max	C-4
Mayville	C-9
McClusky	C-8
McVille	B-7
Medina	E-9

Medora	F-9
Michigan	E-5
Milnor	E-6
Minnewaukan	C-9
Minot	B-4
Minto	B-9
Mohall	A-4
Mott	B-3
Munich	B-9
Napoleon	C-9
Neche	C-8
New England	C-5
New Leipzig	D-7

New Rockford	D-2
New Salem	B-8
New Town	E-9
Northwood	B-4
Oakes	B-9
Park River	A-4
Parshall	A-5
Powers Lake	E-3
Ray	E-6
Richardton	D-3
Rolla	A-6
Rugby	B-6

St. Thomas	C-7
Scranton	D-4
Sherwood	C-3
Stanley	C-9
Stanton	F-8
Steele	C-4
Surrey	B-3
Thompson	B-2
Tioga	D-3
Towner	A-6
Turtle Lake	B-5
Underwood	C-4

Valley City	D-8
Wahpeton	E-10
Walhalla	A-8
Washburn	D-5
Watford City	D-6
West Fargo	F-6
Westhope	A-5
Williston	B-2
Willow City	A-6
Wilton	D-5
Wishek	C-5
Wyndmere	C-5

© Rand McNally

Ohio

Population: 11,464,042
Land area: 40,948 sq. mi.
Capital: Columbus

Cities and Towns

Place	Grid
Aberdeen	K-3
Ada	E-3
Akron	E-8
Alliance	E-9
Amherst	D-6
Antwerp	C-2
Archbold	C-2
Ashland	E-6
Ashtabula	D-9
Athens	I-7
Aurora	D-8
Austintown	E-9
Barberton	E-8
Barnesville	G-9
Batavia	J-2
Beavercreek	H-3
Bellaire	G-10
Bellefontaine	F-4
Bellevue	D-6
Bethel	J-3
Beverly	H-8
Bexley	G-5
Blanchester	I-3
Bluffton	E-3
Boardman	E-9
Bowling Green	D-4
Bremen	G-6
Bridgeport	G-10
Brilliant	F-10
Brookville	H-2
Brunswick	D-7
Bryan	C-2
Cadiz	F-9
Caldwell	G-8
Cambridge	G-8
Camden	H-1
Canal Fulton	E-8
Canton	E-8
Carey	E-4
Carrollton	F-9
Cedarville	H-3
Celina	F-2
Centerburg	F-5
Chardon	D-8
Cheviot	J-1
Chillicothe	H-5
Cincinnati	J-1
Circleville	G-5
Cleveland	D-8
Cleveland Heights	D-8
Clyde	D-5
Coldwater	F-2
Columbiana	E-9
Columbus	G-5
Columbus Grove	E-3
Conneaut	D-9
Coshocton	F-7
Covington	G-2
Creston	E-7
Crestline	E-5
Crooksville	G-6
Cuyahoga Falls	E-8
De Graff	F-3
Defiance	D-2
Delaware	F-4
Delphos	E-3
Delta	C-3
Deshler	D-3
Dover	F-8
Dresden	F-7
East Cleveland	D-8
East Liverpool	E-10
East Palestine	E-10
Eastlake	D-8
Eaton	H-1
Edgerton	C-2
Elmore	D-5
Elyria	D-7
Englewood	H-2
Euclid	D-8
Fairborn	H-3
Fairfield	I-1
Fairport	D-8
Fincastle	J-3
Forest Park	I-1
Fort Recovery	F-2
Fostoria	D-5
Franklin	H-2
Fredericktown	F-6
Fremont	D-5
Gahanna	G-5
Gallipolis	I-6
Gambier	F-6
Garfield Heights	D-8
Geneva	D-9
Genoa	C-4
Georgetown	K-2
Germantown	H-2
Glouster	H-7
Granville	F-6
Greenfield	I-4
Greenville	G-1
Greenwich	E-6
Hamilton	I-1
Harrison	J-1
Hillsboro	I-4
Holgate	D-3
Hudson	E-8
Huron	D-6
Ironton	K-6
Jackson	I-5
Jamestown	H-3
Jefferson	D-9
Johnstown	F-5
Kent	E-8
Kenton	E-4
Kettering	H-2
Kings Mills	I-2
Lakewood	D-8
Lancaster	G-6
Lebanon	I-2
Lewisburg	H-1
Lima	E-3
Lisbon	E-9
Lodi	E-7
Logan	H-6
London	G-4
Loudonville	E-6
Loveland	I-2
Lucasville	J-5
Madison	D-8
Mansfield	E-6
Marietta	H-8
Marion	F-5
Martins Ferry	G-10
Marysville	F-4
Mason	I-2
Massillon	E-8
Maumee	C-4
McArthur	I-6
McComb	D-3
McConnelsville	H-7
Mechanicsburg	G-4
Medina	D-7
Mentor	D-8
Miamisburg	H-2
Middleport	I-7
Middletown	I-2
Milan	D-6
Milford	I-2
Millersburg	F-7
Minerva	E-9
Minster	F-2
Monroeville	D-6
Montgomery	I-2
Montpelier	C-2
Mount Gilead	F-5
Mount Healthy	I-1
Mount Orab	J-3
Mount Sterling	G-4
Mount Vernon	F-6
Napoleon	D-3
Navarre	E-8
Nelsonville	H-6
New Boston	K-5
New Carlisle	H-3
New Concord	G-7
New Lebanon	H-2
New Lexington	G-6
New London	E-6
New Paris	H-1
New Philadelphia	F-8
New Richmond	J-2
Newark	F-6
Newcomerstown	F-7
Niles	E-9
North Baltimore	D-4
North Ridgeville	D-7
Northridge	H-2
Northwood	D-5
Norwalk	D-6
Norwood	I-2
Oak Harbor	D-5
Oak Hill	J-6
Oberlin	D-6
Ontario	E-5
Orrville	E-7
Ottawa	E-3
Oxford	I-1
Painesville	D-8
Parma	D-7
Paulding	D-3
Peebles	J-4
Perrysburg	D-4
Piketon	I-5
Piqua	G-2
Plain City	G-5
Plymouth	E-5
Poland	E-10
Pomeroy	I-6
Port Clinton	D-5
Portage Lakes	E-8
Portsmouth	K-5
Powhatan Point	G-9
Reading	I-2
Ravenna	D-8
Richwood	F-4
Ripley	K-3
Rittman	E-7
Toronto	F-10
Trenton	I-1
Trotwood	H-2
St. Clairsville	G-9
St. Marys	F-2
Salem	E-9
Salineville	E-9
Sandusky	D-5
Shaker Heights	D-8
Shelby	E-5
Sidney	G-2
Solon	D-8
South Charleston	H-4
South Euclid	D-8
South Lebanon	I-2
South Russell	D-8
Spencerville	F-2
Springfield	G-4
Steubenville	F-10
Stow	E-8
Streetsboro	D-8
Strongsville	D-7
Struthers	E-10
Sugarcreek	F-8
Sunbury	G-5
Sylvania	C-4
Tiffin	E-4
Toledo	C-4
Troy	G-2
Twinsburg	D-8
Uhrichsville	F-8
Union City	F-1
Uniontown	E-8
Upper Sandusky	E-4
Urbana	G-3
Utica	F-6
Van Wert	E-2
Vandalia	H-2
Vermilion	D-6
Versailles	G-2
Wadsworth	E-7
Wapakoneta	F-3
Warren	E-9
Washington Court House	G-4
Wauseon	C-3
Waverly	J-5
Waynesville	H-3
Wellington	D-6
Wellston	J-6
West Liberty	G-3
West Salem	E-7
West Union	J-4
West Unity	C-2
Westerville	G-5
Westlake	D-7
Whitehall	G-5
Willard	E-5
Williamsburg	J-3
Wilmington	I-3
Withamsville	H-2
Woodsfield	G-9
Wooster	E-7
Worthington	G-5
Xenia	H-3
Yellow Springs	H-3
Youngstown	E-10
Zanesville	H-7

© Rand McNally
08-1

Oklahoma

Population: 3,547,884
Land area: 68,667 sq. mi.
Capital: Oklahoma City

Cities and Towns

City	Grid	City	Grid	City	Grid
Ada	D-8	Clinton	C-5	Healdton	E-7
Altus	D-5	Coalgate	D-8	Heavener	C-10
Anadarko	D-6	Collinsville	B-9	Hennessey	C-6
Antlers	E-9	Comanche	E-6	Henryetta	C-9
Apache	D-6	Commerce	A-10	Hobart	D-5
Arapaho	C-5	Cordell	C-5	Holdenville	C-8
Ardmore	E-7	Coweta	B-9	Hollis	D-4
Arnett	B-4	Cushing	C-8	Hooker	A-3
Atoka	D-8	Davis	D-7	Hugo	E-9
Bartlesville	A-8	Dewey	A-8	Idabel	E-10
Beaver	A-3	Dwight	D-7	Jay	A-10
Bixby	B-9	Duncan	D-6	Kingfisher	C-6
Blackwell	B-7	Durant	E-8	Konawa	C-8
Blanchard	D-7	Edmond	C-7	Krebs	D-9
Boise City	A-1	El Reno	C-6	Lawton	D-6
Bristow	C-8	Enid	B-6	Lexington	D-7
Broken Arrow	B-9	Eufaula	C-9	Lindsay	D-7
Broken Bow	E-10	Fairfax	B-7	Lone Grove	E-8
Buffalo	A-4	Fairview	B-5	Madill	E-8
Cache	D-6	Frederick	E-6	Mangum	D-5
Carnegie	D-6	Grove	A-10	Marietta	E-7
Checotah	C-9	Guthrie	C-7	Marlow	D-6
Chandler	C-7	Guymon	A-2	McAlester	D-9
Chelsea	A-9	Haileyville	D-9	Medford	B-6
Cherokee	B-6	Harrah	C-7	Mcloud	A-7
Cheyenne	C-4	Haskell	B-9	Midwest City	C-7
Chickasha	D-6				
Claremore	B-9				
Cleveland	B-8				

City	Grid	City	Grid
Muskogee	C-9	Picher	A-10
Newkirk	B-7	Ponca City	B-7
Nowata	A-9	Poteau	C-10
Okeene	C-6	Prague	C-8
Oklahoma City	C-7	Pryor	B-9
Okmulgee	C-8	Purcell	D-7
Panama	C-10	Sallisaw	C-10
Pauls Valley	D-7	Sand Springs	B-8
Pawhuska	B-8	Sapulpa	B-8
Perkins	C-7	Seminole	C-8
Perry	C-7	Shawnee	C-8

City	Grid	City	Grid
Skiatook	B-8	Tulsa	B-8
Spiro	C-10	Vinita	A-9
Stigler	C-9	Wagoner	B-9
Stillwater	C-7	Walters	E-6
Stroud	C-8	Watonga	C-6
Tahlequah	B-9	Waurika	E-6
Talihina	D-9	Weatherford	C-5
Tecumseh	C-8	Wewoka	C-8
Tishomingo	E-8	Wilburton	D-9
Tonkawa	B-7	Woodward	B-5
		Wynnewood	D-7
		Yukon	C-6

© Rand McNally

08-1

© Rand McNally

Oregon

Population: 3,641,056
Land area: 95,997 sq. mi.
Capital: Salem

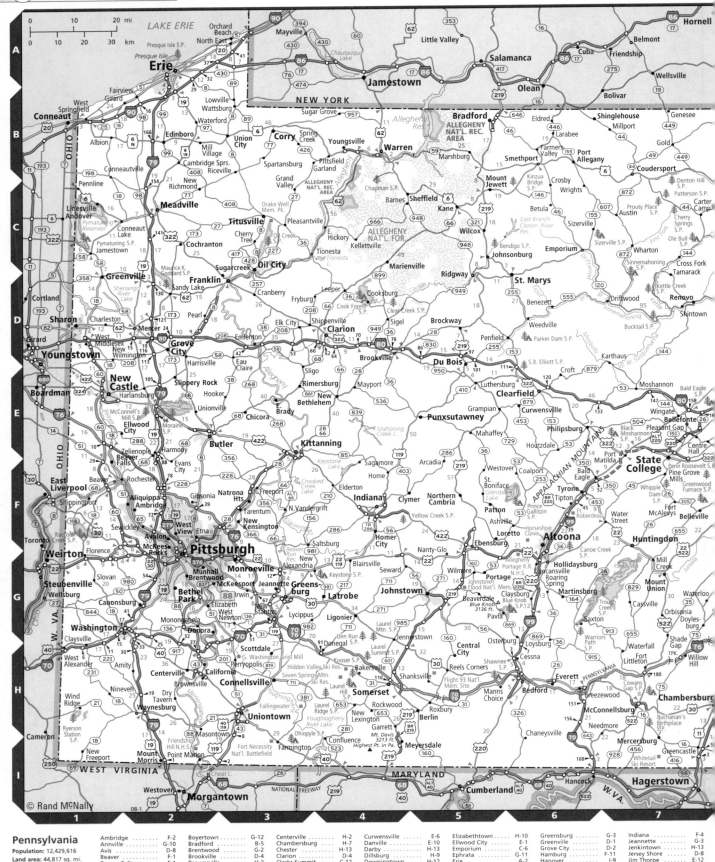

© Rand McNally

Pennsylvania

Population: 12,429,616
Land area: 44,817 sq. mi.
Capital: Harrisburg

Cities and Towns

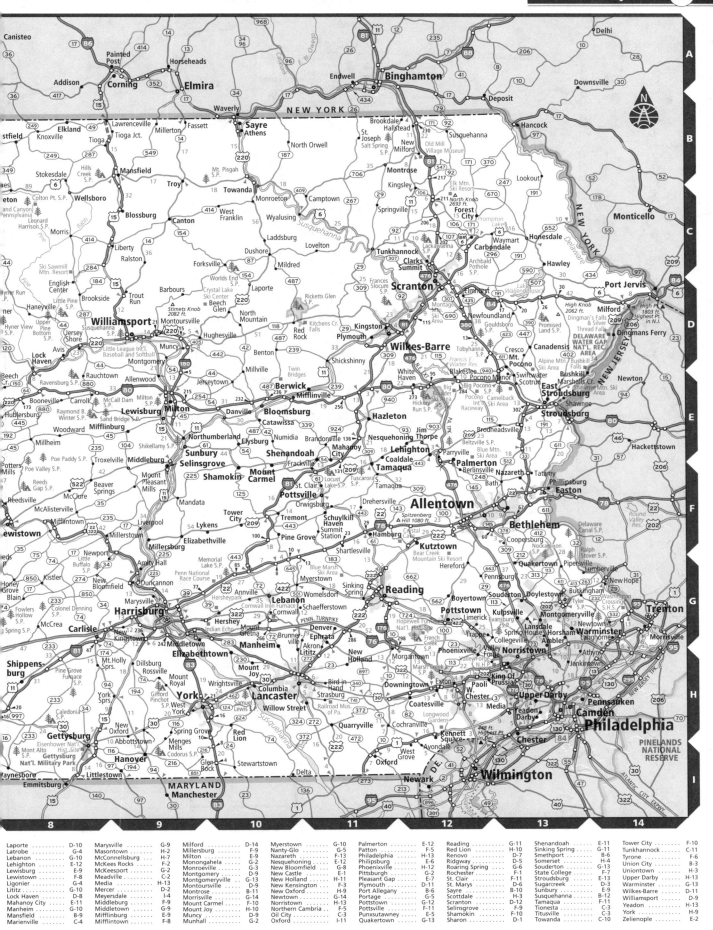

Get more Rhode Island info at go.randmcnally.com/RI

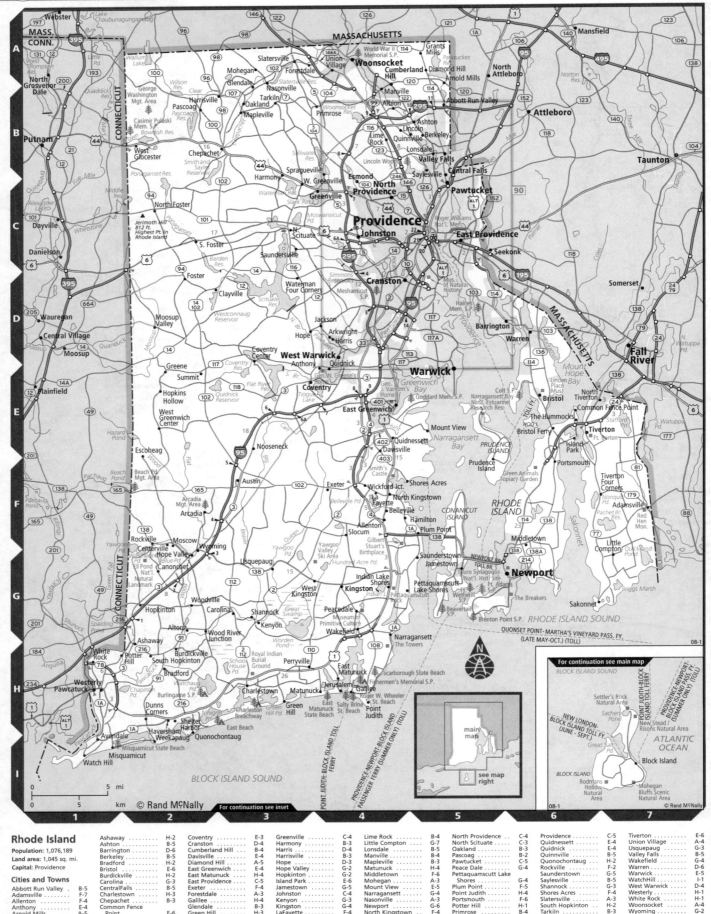

Rhode Island

Population: 1,076,189
Land area: 1,045 sq. mi.
Capital: Providence

Cities and Towns

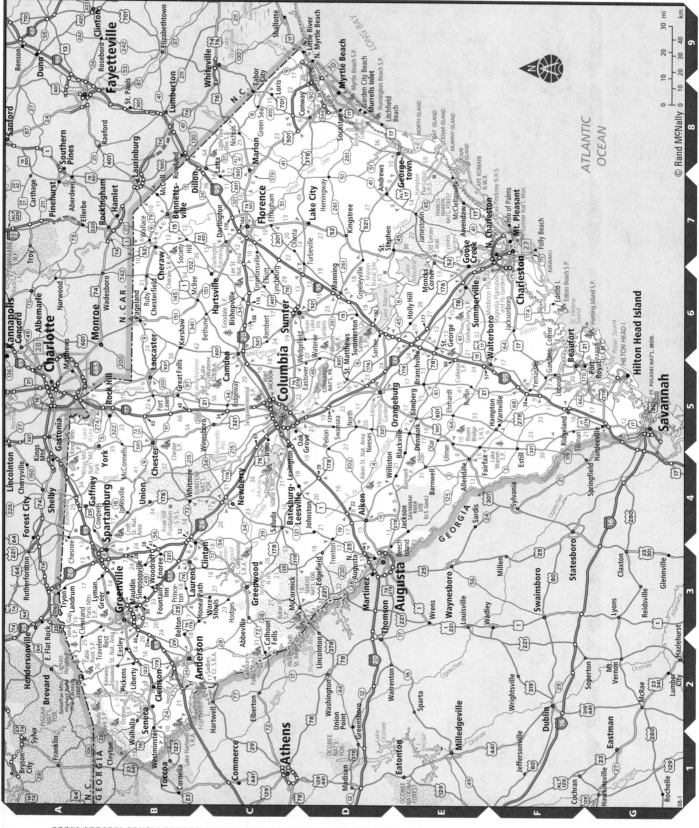

South Dakota

Population: 775,933
Land area: 75,885 sq. mi.
Capital: Pierre

Cities and Towns

Aberdeen	B-8
Alexandria	D-8
Arlington	C-9
Armour	E-8
Avon	F-8
Belle Fourche	C-1
Beresford	E-10
Bison	C-9
Blunt	B-4
Bonesteel	B-8
Bowdle	B-10
Bridgewater	B-8
Bristol	B-8
Britton	D-8
Bryant	E-8
Buffalo	F-8
Burke	C-1
Castlewood	E-10
Chamberlain	C-9
Cherry Creek	A-3
Clark	E-7
Clear Lake	B-6
Colman	B-8
Colome	C-9
Custer	B-2
De Smet	C-9
Deadwood	A-2
Dell Rapids	D-2
Doland	D-6
Dupree	D-7
Eagle Butte	C-9
Edgemont	D-7
Elkton	C-4
Esteline	C-10
Ethan	C-9
Eureka	E-6
Faith	D-6
Faulkton	D-2
Flandreau	C-9
Fort Pierre	D-10
Fort Thompson	D-6
Gannvalley	E-4
Gregory	C-9
Groton	C-4
Hecla	E-3
Herreid	C-9
Highmore	E-5
Hill City	A-6
Hoven	D-2
Howard	B-6
Huron	C-1
Ipswich	B-7
Iroquois	D-6
Isabel	B-7
Kadoka	B-6
Kennebec	E-6
Kimball	B-8
Kyle	A-6
Lake Andes	C-6
Lake Preston	D-2
Lead	C-1
Lemmon	B-6
Lennox	D-9
Leola	B-7
Madison	D-9
Martin	E-4
McIntosh	A-4
McLaughlin	B-4
Mellette	E-1
Milbank	F-10
Miller	C-9
Mission	E-8
Mitchell	A-8
Mobridge	B-3
Mount City	A-5
Mount Vernon	D-8
Murdo	A-7
New Underwood	D-9
Newell	E-4
Oglala	A-4
Olivet	A-5
Onida	B-10
Parker	E-3
Parmelee	D-8
Piedmont	E-5
Pierre	E-8
Pine Ridge	A-6
Plankinton	D-8
Platte	D-2
Presho	C-2
Rapid City	C-2
Redfield	C-6
Roscoe	C-6
Rosebud	E-9
Roslyn	E-9
St. Francis	D-4
Salem	C-2
Scotland	C-5
Selby	D-3
Sioux Falls	D-8
Sisseton	E-7
Spearfish	D-6
Stickney	D-6
Sturgis	B-8
Summit	B-5
Timber Lake	E-5
Tripp	E-5
Tyndall	A-10
Veblen	E-9
Vermillion	E-9
Viborg	E-9
Wagner	A-6
Wall	E-10
Watertown	A-9
Waubay	B-9
Webster	B-9
Wessington Sprs.	D-7
White Lake	E-5
White River	E-8
Willow Lake	F-8
Wilmot	A-9
Winner	E-8
Wolsey	E-9
Woonsocket	B-9
Yankton	F-9

© Rand McNally

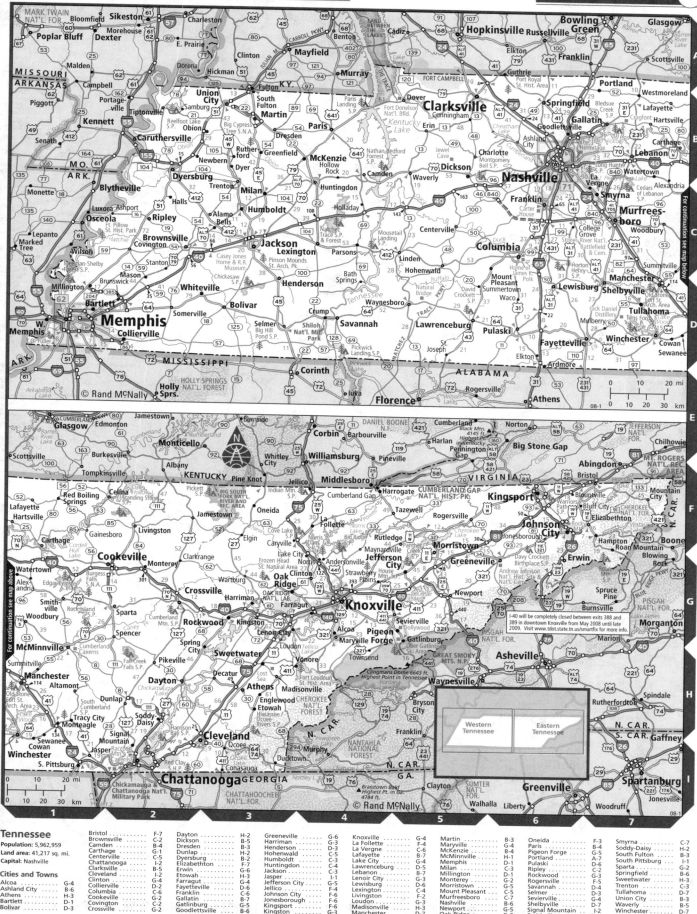

Tennessee

Population: 5,962,959
Land area: 41,217 sq. mi.
Capital: Nashville

Cities and Towns

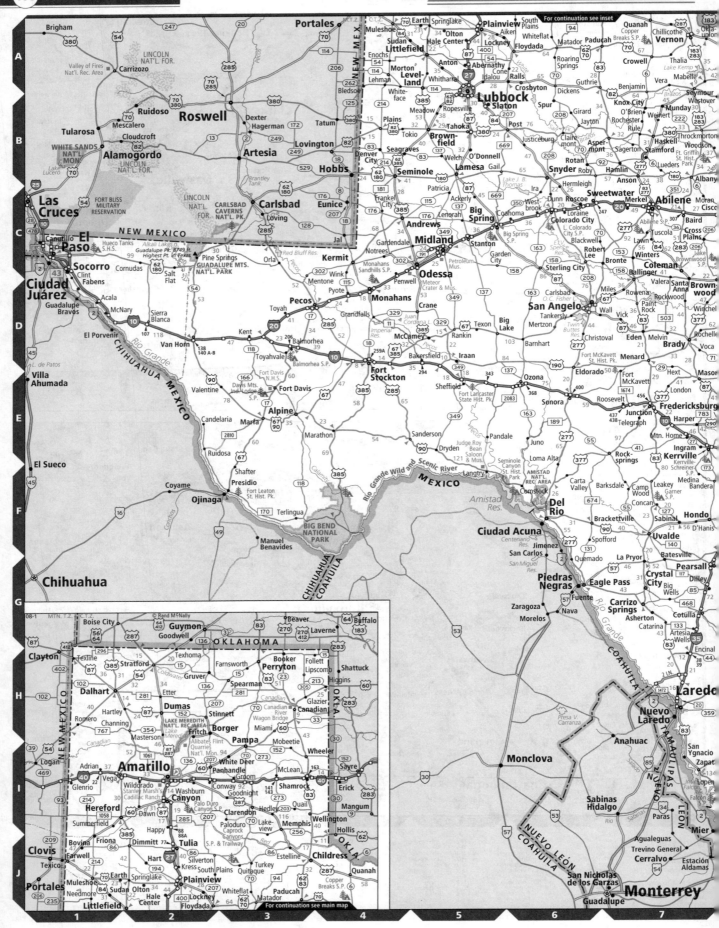

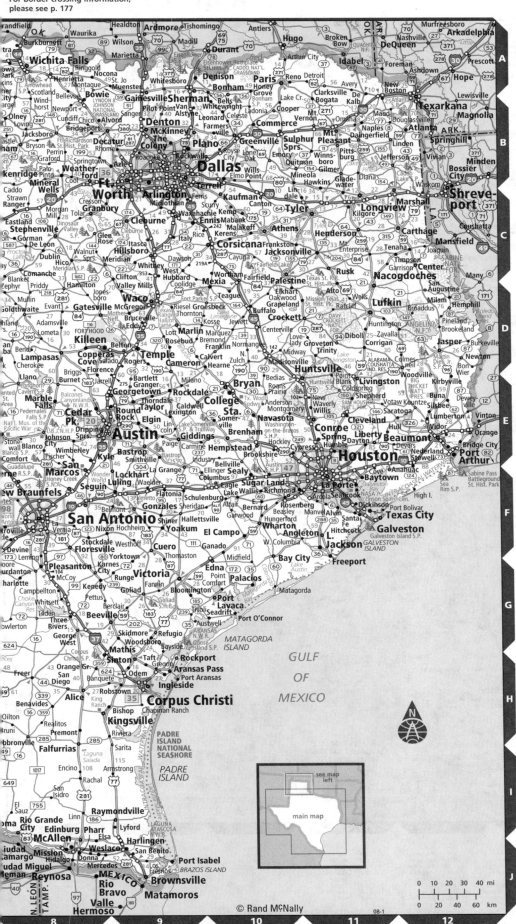

Texas

Population: 22,859,968
Land area: 261,797 sq. mi.
Capital: Austin

Cities and Towns

Abilene	C-7
Albany	B-7
Alice	H-8
Alpine	E-3
Alvin	F-11
Amarillo	I-2
Anahuac	F-11
Andrews	C-4
Angleton	F-11
Anson	B-7
Archer City	B-8
Arlington	B-9
Aspermont	B-7
Athens	C-10
Austin	E-9
Baird	C-7
Ballinger	D-7
Bandera	F-7
Bastrop	E-9
Baytown	F-11
Bay City	F-10
Beaumont	E-12
Beeville	G-9
Bellville	E-10
Belton	D-9
Big Lake	C-5
Big Spring	C-5
Boerne	F-8
Bonham	A-10
Borger	H-2
Brackettville	F-6
Brady	D-7
Breckenridge	B-8
Brenham	E-10
Brownfield	B-5
Brownsville	J-9
Brownwood	D-8
Bryan	E-10
Burkburnett	A-8
Burnet	E-8
Caldwell	D-9
Cameron	D-9
Canadian	H-3
Canton	C-10
Canyon	I-2
Carrizo Springs	G-7
Carthage	C-12
Cedar Park	E-8
Center	C-12
Centerville	D-10
Childress	J-3
Clarendon	I-3
Clarksville	A-11
Cleburne	C-9
Coldspring	E-11
Coleman	C-7
College Station	E-10
Colorado City	C-6
Columbus	C-8
Comanche	C-8
Conroe	E-11
Cooper	B-10
Copperas Cove	D-8
Corpus Christi	H-9
Corsicana	C-10
Cotulla	G-7
Crane	D-5
Crockett	D-11
Crosbyton	A-6
Crowell	A-7
Crystal City	G-7
Cuero	F-9
Daingerfield	B-11
Dalhart	H-1
Dallas	B-9
Decatur	B-9
Del Rio	F-6
Denison	A-9
Denton	B-9
Denver City	B-4
Dimmitt	J-2
Donna	J-8
Dumas	H-2
Eagle Pass	G-6
Eastland	C-8
Edinburg	J-8
Edna	G-10
El Campo	F-10
El Paso	C-1
Eldorado	D-6
Emory	B-10
Ennis	C-9
Fairfield	C-10
Falfurrias	H-8
Farwell	J-1
Floresville	F-8
Floydada	A-6
Fort Davis	E-3
Fort Stockton	D-4
Fort Worth	B-9
Franklin	D-10
Fredericksburg	E-8
Freeport	F-11
Friona	J-1
Gainesville	A-9
Galveston	F-11
Garden City	C-5
Gatesville	D-9
George West	G-8
Georgetown	E-9
Gilmer	B-11
Glen Rose	C-8
Goldthwaite	D-8
Goliad	G-9
Gonzales	F-9
Graham	B-8
Granbury	C-8
Greenville	B-10
Groesbeck	D-10
Groveton	D-11
Hallettsville	F-9
Hamilton	D-8
Harlingen	J-9
Haskell	B-7
Hebbronville	H-8
Hemphill	D-12
Hempstead	E-10
Henderson	C-11
Henrietta	A-8
Hereford	J-1
Hillsboro	C-9
Hondo	F-7
Houston	F-11
Humble	E-11
Huntsville	E-11
Jacksboro	B-8
Jacksonville	C-11
Jasper	D-12
Jayton	B-6
Jefferson	B-12
Johnson City	E-8
Jourdanton	G-8
Junction	E-7
Karnes City	G-8

Kaufman	C-10
Kermit	C-4
Kerrville	E-7
Kilgore	C-11
Killeen	D-9
Kingsville	H-8
Kountze	E-12
La Grange	E-9
La Porte	F-11
Lake Jackson	F-11
Lamesa	B-5
Lampasas	D-8
Laredo	H-7
Leakey	F-7
Levelland	A-5
Liberty	E-11
Linden	B-12
Littlefield	A-5
Livingston	E-11
Llano	E-8
Lockhart	F-9
Longview	C-11
Lubbock	B-5
Lufkin	D-11
Madisonville	A-1
Marfa	E-3
Marlin	D-9
Marshall	C-11
Mason	E-7
Matador	A-6
McAllen	J-8
McKinney	B-9
Memphis	I-3
Menard	D-7
Mercedes	I-8
Meridian	D-9
Mertzon	D-6
Miami	H-3
Midland	C-5
Mineral Wells	B-8
Mission	J-8
Monahans	C-4
Montague	A-8
Morton	A-4
Mount Pleasant	B-11
Mount Vernon	B-11
Muleshoe	A-4
Nacogdoches	D-11
Nederland	E-12
New Braunfels	F-8
Newton	D-12
Odessa	C-4
Orange	E-12
Ozona	E-6
Paducah	A-6
Paint Rock	D-7
Palestine	C-10
Palo Pinto	B-8
Pampa	H-3
Panhandle	H-2
Pearsall	G-7
Pecos	D-3
Perryton	H-3
Pharr	J-8
Pittsburg	B-11
Plains	B-4
Plainview	A-5
Plano	B-9
Pleasanton	G-8
Port Lavaca	G-10
Post	B-6
Quanah	A-7
Quitman	B-11
Rankin	D-5
Raymondville	I-9
Refugio	G-9
Richmond	F-10
Rio Grande City	I-8
Robert Lee	C-6
Robstown	H-9
Roby	B-6
Rockport	H-9
Rocksprings	E-7
Rockwall	B-10
Rosenberg	F-10
Round Rock	E-9
Rusk	C-11
San Angelo	D-6
San Antonio	F-8
San Augustine	D-12
San Benito	J-9
San Diego	H-8
San Marcos	F-8
San Saba	D-8
Sanderson	E-4
Seguin	F-8
Seminole	A-4
Seymour	A-7
Sherman	A-9
Sierra Blanca	D-2
Silverton	J-2
Sinton	H-9
Snyder	B-6
Socorro	C-1
Sonora	E-6
Spearman	H-3
Stamford	B-7
Stanton	C-5
Stephenville	C-8
Sterling City	C-6
Stinnett	H-2
Stratford	H-2
Sugar Land	F-11
Sulphur Springs	B-10
Sweetwater	C-6
Tahoka	B-5
Taylor	E-9
Temple	D-9
Terrell	B-10
Texarkana	B-12
Texas City	F-11
The Colony	B-9
Three Rivers	G-8
Throckmorton	B-7
Tilden	G-8
Tulia	J-2
Tyler	C-11
Uvalde	F-7
Van Horn	D-2
Vega	A-7
Vernon	A-7
Victoria	G-9
Vidor	E-12
Waco	D-9
Waxahachie	C-9
Weatherford	B-8
Wellington	I-3
Weslaco	J-8
Wharton	F-10
Wheeler	I-3
Wichita Falls	A-8
Woodville	D-12
Zapata	I-7

© Rand McNally

08-1

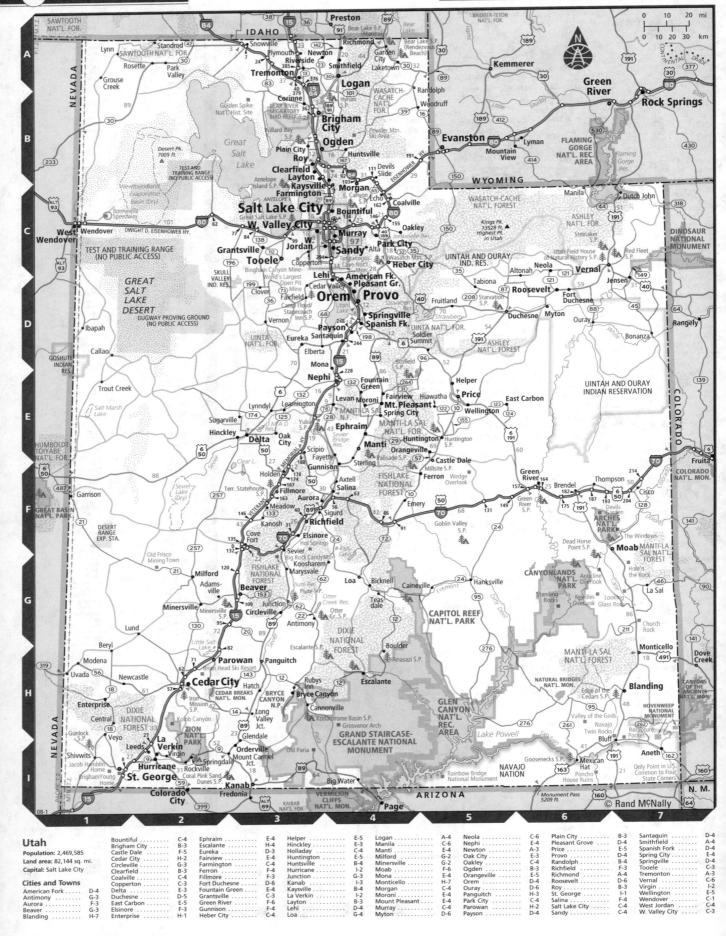

Utah

Population: 2,469,585
Land area: 82,144 sq. mi.
Capital: Salt Lake City

Cities and Towns

© Rand McNally

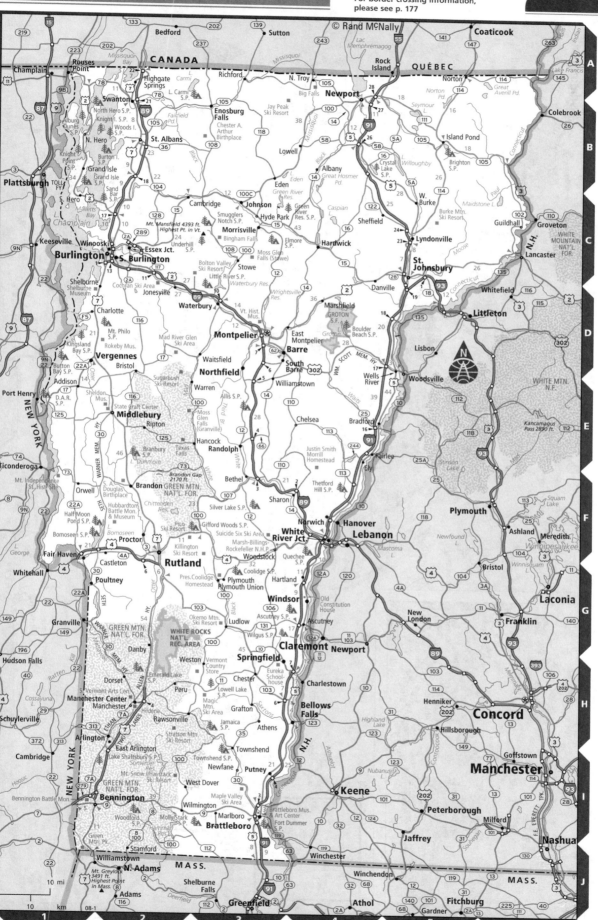

Vermont

Population: 623,050
Land area: 9,250 sq. mi.
Capital: Montpelier

▶ **Explore** Virginia at go.randmcnally.com/VA

Virginia

Population: 7,567,465
Land area: 39,594 sq. mi.
Capital: Richmond

Cities and Towns

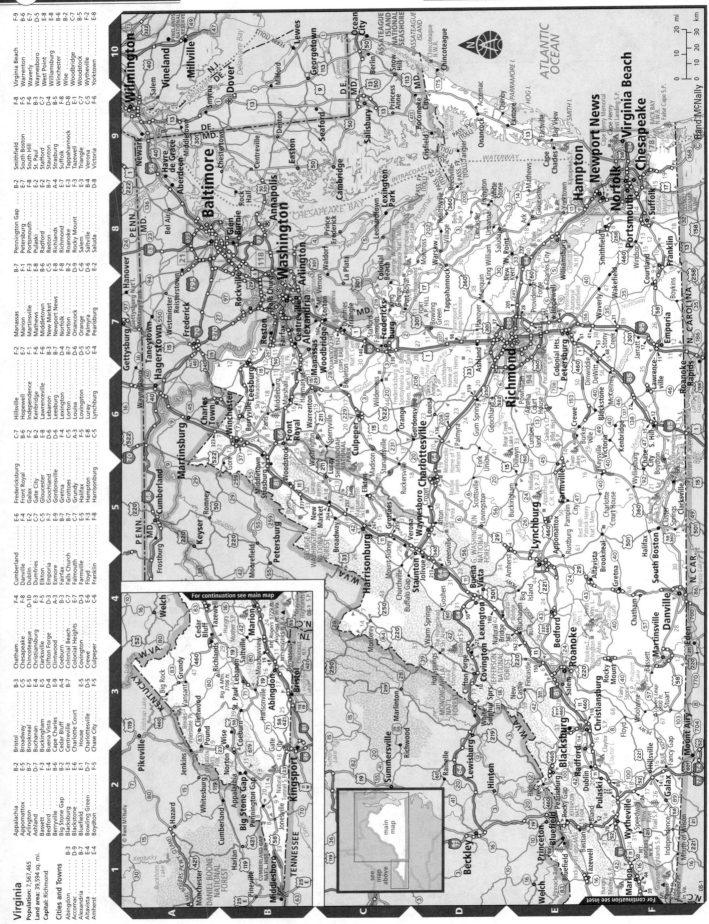

© Rand McNally

For continuation see inset

For continuation see main map

main map

see map above

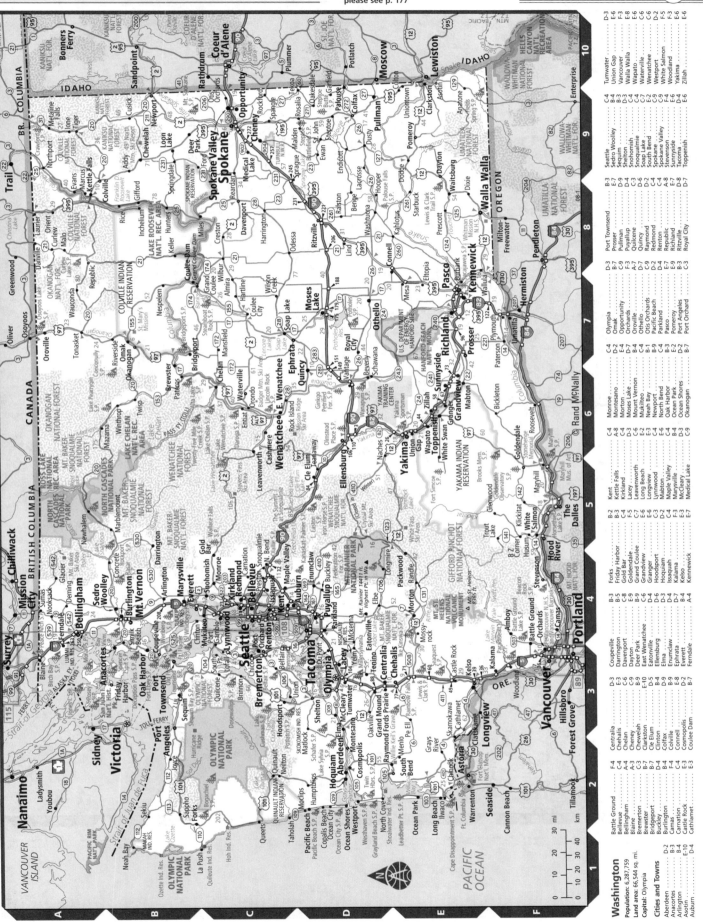

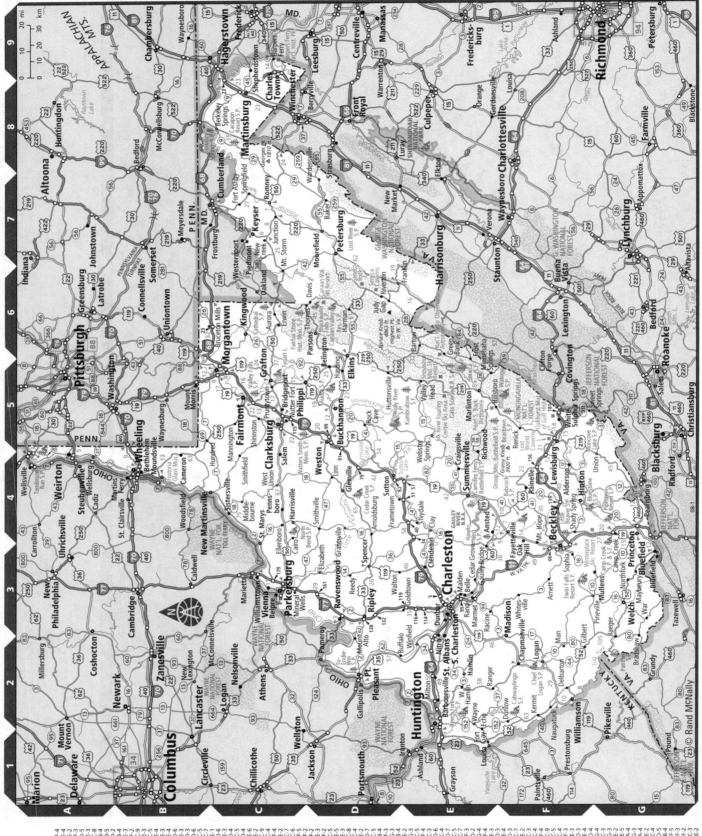

© Rand McNally

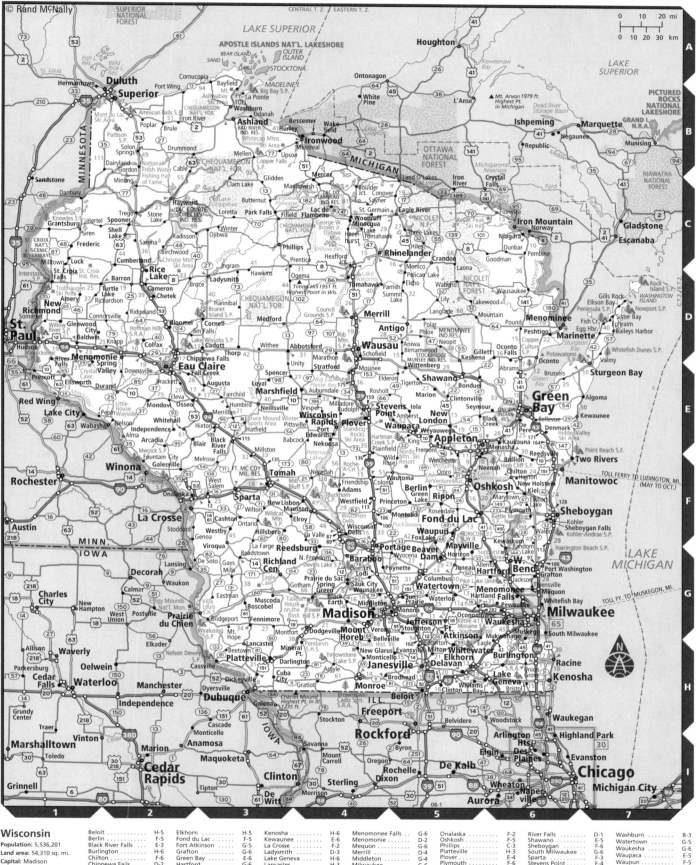

Wisconsin

Population: 5,536,201
Land area: 54,310 sq. mi.
Capital: Madison

Cities and Towns

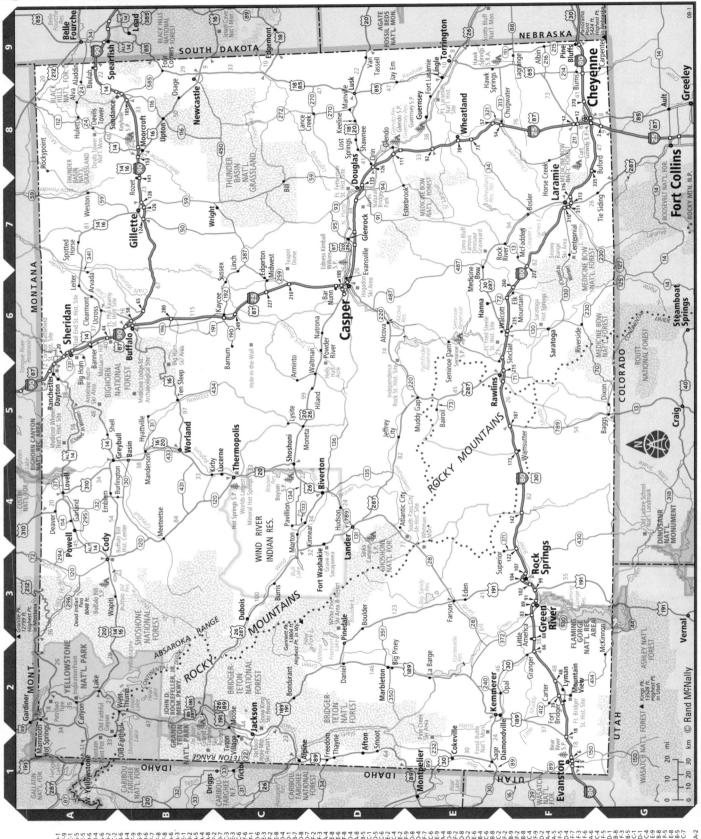

© Rand McNally

Border Crossing
Information

With advance planning, crossing the border to Mexico or Canada can be easier than you think.

Citizenship Documents

A U.S. passport or proof of citizenship, such as an original or certified birth certificate and photo identification (such as a driver's license) is required for entry into Mexico or Canada. Naturalized U.S. citizens should carry citizenship papers; permanent residents of the United States must bring proof of residency and photo identification.

Traveling with Kids

For children under the age of 18, parents should be prepared to provide evidence, such as a birth certificate or adoption decree, to prove they are indeed the parents. Single or divorced parents and parents traveling without spouses should carry a letter of consent from the absent parent or guardian to bring a child across either border. Mexico requires the letter to be original and notarized. Divorced parents should also bring copies of their custody decree. Adults who are not the parents or guardians of the children they are traveling with must have written permission from the parents or guardians to supervise the children.

Traveling with Pets

U.S. visitors may bring a dog or cat to Mexico with a pet health certificate signed by a registered veterinarian and issued within 72 hours of entry and a vaccination certificate for rabies, distemper, hepatitis, pip, and leptospirosis. A permit fee is charged at the time of entry. All dogs and cats three months and older are required to have a current rabies vaccination certificate that should identify the pet and indicate the trade name of the licensed rabies vaccine, serial number and duration of validity in order to enter Canada. Pit bulls are not permitted to enter Ontario.

Re-entry to the U.S.

Proof of both citizenship and identity is required for entry into the United States. Be able to provide proof of U.S. citizenship via a U.S. passport, or a certified copy of your birth certificate, a Certificate of Naturalization, a Certificate of Citizenship, or a Report of Birth Abroad of a U.S. citizen. To prove your identity, present either a valid driver's license, or a government identification card that includes a photo or physical description.

By January 1, 2008, the Western Hemisphere Travel Initiative will require all U.S. citizens to carry a passport or other secure document in order to enter or re-enter the United States. This initiative will be rolled out in two phases:

- December 31, 2006: Requirement applied to all air and sea travel to or from Canada, Mexico, Central and South America, the Caribbean, and Bermuda.
- December 31, 2007: Requirement extended to all land border crossings.

In 2006, the government began producing a secure, alternative passport card for U.S. citizens in border communities who frequently cross to Mexico or Canada. The biometric card will meet the requirement for this initiative and help expedite travel through ports of entry.

Border Crossing Waits

Allow plenty of time. The average time for customs clearance is 30 minutes, but this varies greatly depending on traffic flow and security issues.

Mexico Only

Driving in Mexico

According to U.S. Department of State, tourists traveling beyond the border zone must obtain a temporary import permit or risk having their car confiscated by Mexican customs officials. To acquire a permit, you must submit evidence of citizenship, title for the car, a car registration certificate, driver's license, and a processing fee to either a Banjercito (Mexican Army Bank) branch located at a Mexican Customs office at the port of entry, or at one of the Mexican consulates in the U.S. Mexican law also requires posting a bond at a Banjercito office to guarantee departure of the car from Mexico within a period determined at the time of application. Carry proof of car ownership (the current registration card or a letter of authorization from the finance or leasing company). Auto insurance policies, other than Mexican, are not valid in Mexico. A short-term liability policy is obtainable at the border.

Tourist Cards

Tourist cards are valid up to six months, require a fee, and are required for all persons, regardless of age, to visit the interior of Mexico. Cards may be obtained from Mexican border authorities, Consuls of Mexico, or Federal Delegates in major cities. Cards are also distributed to passengers en route to Mexico by air.

For additional information on traveling in Mexico, contact the Mexican Embassy in Washington, D.C.: (202) 736-1000; www.embassy ofmexico.org or go to the U.S. Department of State website, www.travel.state.gov/travel/tips/regional/regional_1174.html.

Canada Only

Driving in Canada

Drivers need proof of ownership of the vehicle or documentation of its rental, a valid U.S. driver's license, and automobile insurance.

Fast Pass for Frequent Travelers

For frequent travelers, the United States and Canada have instituted the NEXUS program, which allows pre-screened, low-risk travelers to be processed with little or no delay by U.S. and Canadian border officials. Approved applicants are issued photo identification and a proximity card, and they can quickly cross the border in a dedicated traffic lane without routine customs and immigration questioning (unless they are randomly selected).

For additional information on traveling in Canada, contact the Canadian Embassy in Washington, D.C.: (202) 682-1740; www.canadianembassy.org or go to the U.S. Department of State website, travel.state.gov/travel/tips/regional/regional_1170.html.

Duty-free Defined

Duty-free shops are shops where taxes on commercial goods are neither collected by a government, nor paid by an importer. For example, a Swiss watch purchased in a jewelry store in Mexico may cost you $250, a price that includes the duty and taxes that the importer paid to import it. The same watch purchased in a duty-free shop may only cost $175. That's because as long as the item stays in the duty-free shop, or exits the country with the purchaser, it has not been formally imported into the country. There has been no duty charged on it, and the duty-free shop owner has been able to pass on that savings. Its price is free of duty.

If you exceed your personal exemption, when you bring purchases home to the U.S from any shops, including those called duty-free, you will have to pay duty.

Source: U.S. Customs and Border Protection

Food Police

To protect community health and preserve domestic plant and animal life, many kinds of foods either are prohibited from entering the United States or require an import permit.

1. Every fruit or vegetable must be declared and presented for inspection, no matter how free of pests it appears to be. Failure to declare all food products can result in civil penalties.

2. Bakery goods and cured cheeses are generally admissible.

3. Permission to bring meats, livestock, poultry, and their by-products into the United States depends on the animal disease condition in the country of origin.

- Fresh meat is generally prohibited from most countries.
- Canned, cured, or dried meat is severely restricted from some countries.

Contact the U.S. Department of Agriculture, Animal Plant Health Inspection Services for more detailed information.

Source: U.S. Customs and Border Protection

Insider's Tips

1. Get the U.S. Customs and Border Protection booklet "Know Before You Go" before your next trip. (202) 354-1000 or (877) 227-5511; or download it at www.customs.ustreas.gov/xp/cgov/travel/vacation/kbyg/.

2. Currency: Exchange rates are often more favorable at ATMs and banks than at hotels and stores.

3. Duty-free: The duty-free personal exemption is $800, but there are some exceptions, depending on the country visited, how long you were there and whether the items are gifts or for personal use. See www.cbp.gov/xp/cgov/travel/vacation/kbyg/duty_free.xml for more information.

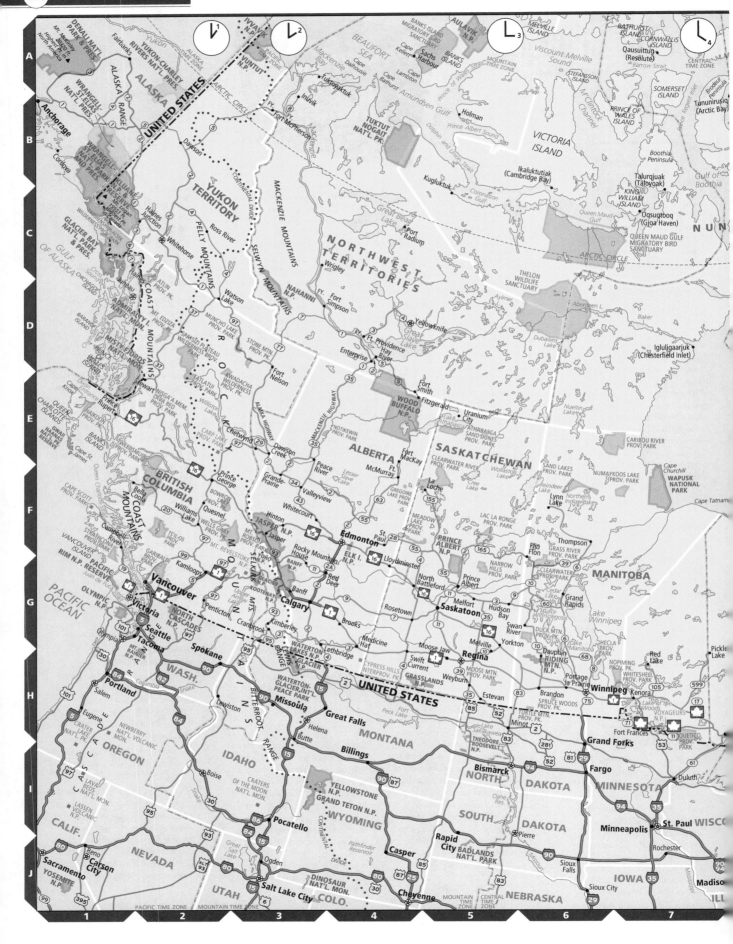

08-1

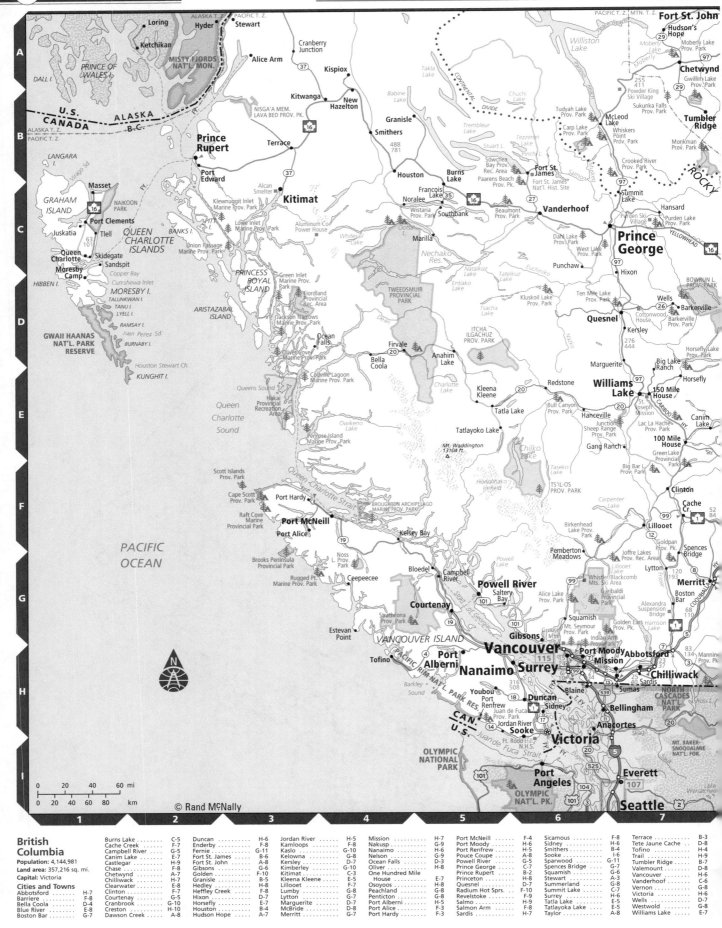

© Rand McNally

British Columbia

Population: 4,144,981
Land area: 357,216 sq. mi.
Capital: Victoria

Cities and Towns

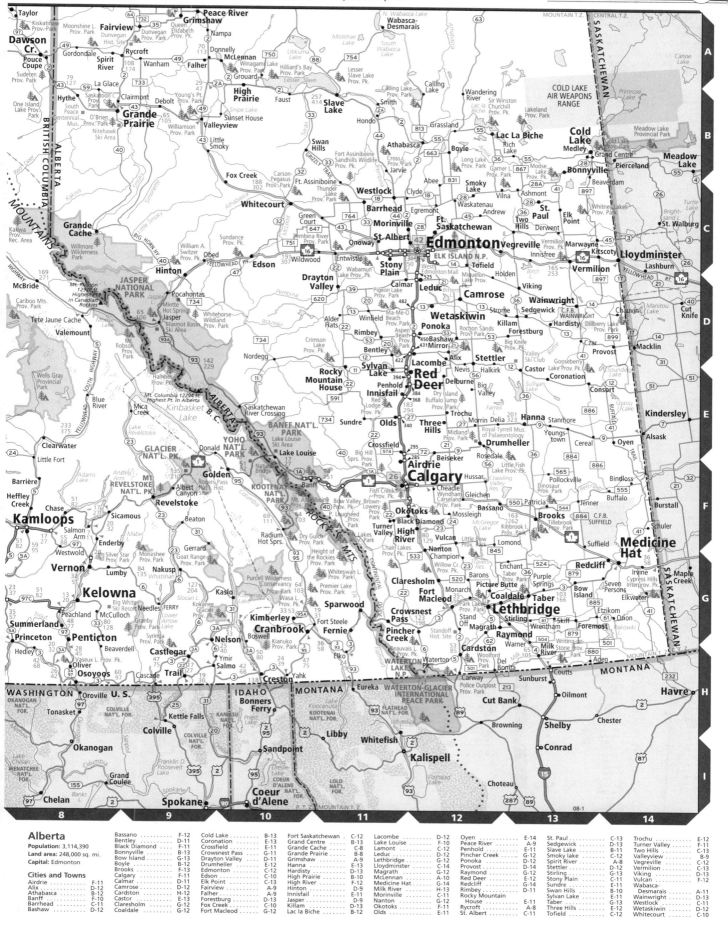

08-1

Manitoba

Population: 1,155,492
Land area: 213,729 sq. mi.
Capital: Winnipeg

Cities and Towns

Saskatchewan

Population: 995,490
Land area: 228,445 sq. mi.
Capital: Regina

Cities and Towns

© Rand McNally

0 20 40 mi
0 20 40 60 km

MANITOBA
SASKATCHEWAN
ONTARIO
UNITED STATES
N. DAK.
MINN.

LAKE WINNIPEG
Lake Winnipegosis
Lake Manitoba

Winnipeg
Brandon
Thompson
Flin Flon
The Pas
Dauphin
Portage la Prairie
Selkirk
Steinbach
Morden
Winkler
Swan River
Yorkton
Melville
Estevan
Roseau
Warroad

Pelican Narrows
Sandy Bay
Creighton
Channing
Snow Lake
Wabowden
Pipun
Cross Lake
Herb Lake
Herb Lake Landing
Dunlop
Ponton
Tyrrell
Wekusko
Cranberry Portage
Cormorant
Wanless
Norway House
Warren Landing
Grand Rapids
Easterville
Overflowing River
Westray
Cumberland House
Prospector
Finger
Moose Lake
Berens River
Hudson Bay
Westgate
Mafeking
Novra
Bowsman
Minitonas
Duck Bay
Camperville
Skownan
Birch River
Lenswood
Cowan
Kenville
Durban
Benito
Pine River
Garland
Winnipegosis
Meadow Portage
Hilbre
Grahamdale
Moosehorn
Hodgson
Dallas
Fisher River
Fisher Branch
Riverton
Arborg
Gimli
Grand Beach
Winnipeg Beach
Matlock
Selkirk
Beausejour
Whitemouth
Falcon Lake
Werner Lake
Carrot River
Arborfield
Crooked River
Prairie River
Bertwell
Somme
Bjorkdale
Porcupine Plain
Usherville
Kelvington
Wadena
Okla
Preeceville
Margo
Sturgis
Amsterdam
Norquay
Pelly
Canora
Kamsack
Gorlitz
Theodore
Jasmin
Willowbrook
Ituna
Yorkton
Roblin
Grandview
Inglis
Russell
Angusville
Rossburn
Oakburn
Elphinstone
Erickson
Binscarth
Solsgirth
Shoal Lake
Birtle
Beulah
Miniota
Crandall
Oak River
Rivers
Minnedosa
Neepawa
Gladstone
MacGregor
Austin
Carberry
Carman
Sanford
Morris
St-Pierre-Jolys
St. Malo
Steinbach
Niverville
Dominion City
Emerson
Pembina
Melville
Bredenbury
Langenburg
Stockholm
Esterhazy
Rocanville
Whitewood
Broadview
Grenfell
Wolseley
Moosomin
Virden
Elkhorn
Hargrave
Reston
Sinclair
Pipestone
Deleau
Souris
Wawanesa
Griswold
Holland
Treherne
Somerset
Baldur
Glenboro
Killarney
Boissevain
Deloraine
Melita
Hartney
Minto
Ninette
Cartwright
Crystal City
Clearwater
Pilot Mound
Manitou
Morden
Winkler
Gretna
Altona
Letellier
Estevan
Bienfait
Oxbow
Carnduff
Carievale
Bowbells
Mohall
Bottineau
Dunseith
Rolla
Langdon
Cavalier
Walhalla
Hallock
Greenbrush
Roseau
Warroad
Karlstad

Riding Mountain National Park
Duck Mountain Provincial Park
Porcupine Provincial Forest
Swan-Pelican Provincial Forest
Grass River Prov. Park
Spruce Woods Prov. Park
Atikaki Provincial Park
Whiteshell Provincial Park
Nopiming Provincial Park
Grand Beach Prov. Park
Hecla/Grindstone Prov. Park
Paint Lake Provincial Park
Cormorant Provincial Forest
Moose Creek Prov. Forest
Sandilands Provincial Forest
Baldy Mtn. 2729 ft. Highest Pt. in Manitoba
Wildcat Hill 2565 ft.
Spirit Mtn. 2585 ft.
Ketchum Hill 2500 ft.
08-1

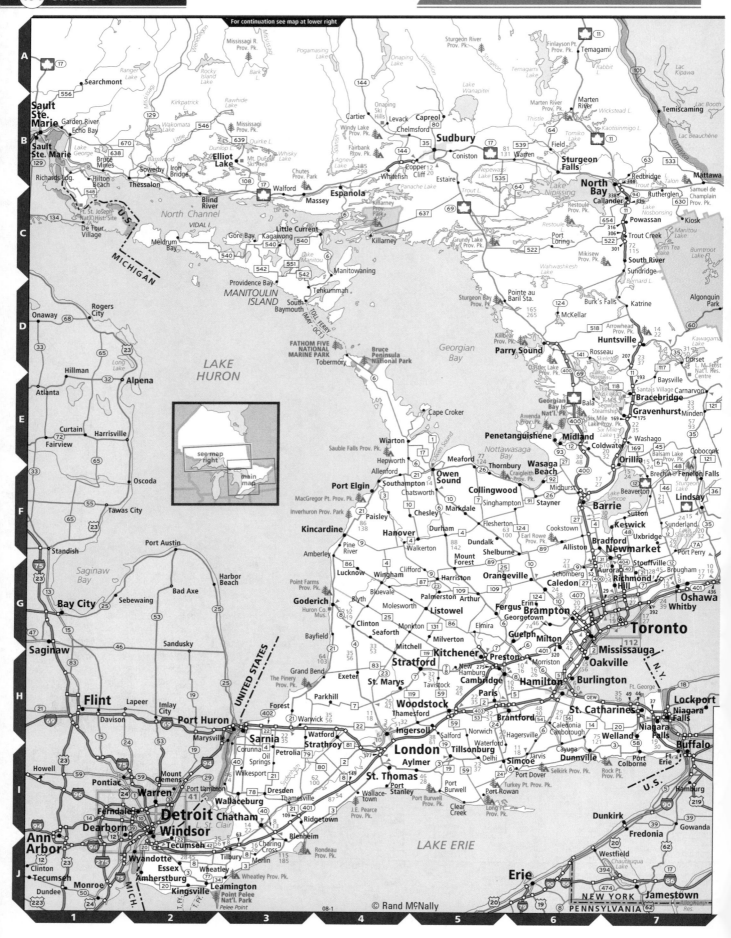

For continuation see map at lower right

© Rand McNally

08-1

NEW YORK
PENNSYLVANIA

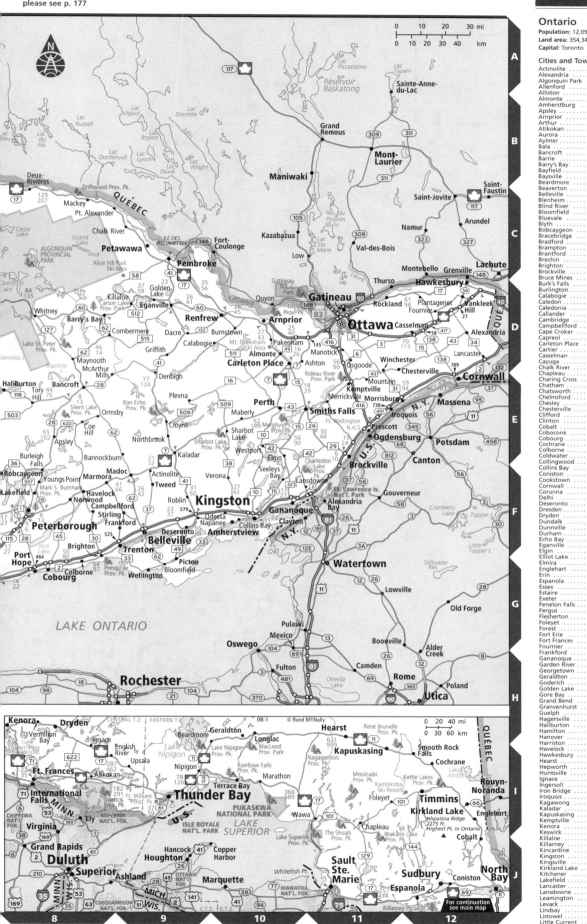

For border crossing information, please see p. 177

Ontario

Population: 12,096,627
Land area: 354,342 sq. mi.
Capital: Toronto

Cities and Towns

Québec

Population: 7,443,491
Land area: 527,079 sq. mi.
Capital: Québec City

New Brunswick

Population: 750,183
Land area: 27,587 sq. mi.
Capital: Fredericton

Cities and Towns

Acadie Siding	E-5
Adamsville	E-5
Alma	G-6
Anagance	F-5
Bathurst	C-5
Belledune	C-5
Big Cove	E-6
Blackville	E-5
Blissfield	E-5
Boiestown	E-4
Bouctouche	E-6
Campbellton	C-4
Canaan	F-6
Cap-Pele	F-6
Cape Tormentine	F-7
Caraquet	C-6
Chatham	D-5
Chipman	F-5
Coles Island	F-5
Cross Creek	F-4
Dalhousie	C-4
Doaktown	E-5
Eastport	E-4
Edmundston	D-2
Escuminac	D-6
Florenceville	E-3
Fredericton	F-4
Grand Falls (Grand Sault)	D-3
Hammondvale	G-5
Hampton	G-5
Harcourt	E-5
Hartland	F-3
Harvey	F-4
Hillsborough	F-5
Jemseg	F-5
Juniper	E-3
Kedgwick	C-3
Keswick Ridge	F-4
Kouchibouguac	E-6
Lameque	C-6
Lawrence Station	G-3
Long Creek	F-4
Lutes Mountain	F-6
Memramcook	F-6
Millville	F-3
Minto	F-5
Miramichi	D-5
Moncton	F-6
Nashwaak Bridge	F-4
Neguac	D-5
Newcastle	D-5
Nictau	D-3
North Head	H-4
Oromocto	F-4
Perth-Andover	E-3
Plaster Rock	E-3
Pointe-Sapin	E-6
Pointe-Verte	C-5
Port Elgin	F-6
Renous	E-5
Rexton	E-6
Richibucto	E-6
Riverside-Albert	F-6
Rogersville	E-5
Sackville	F-6
St. Andrews	G-3
St. Croix	G-3
St. George	G-4
Saint John	G-5
St. Martins	G-5
St-Quentin	D-3
St. Stephan	G-3
Salisbury	F-6
Shediac	F-6
Shippagan	C-6
Sussex	G-5
Sussex Corner	G-5
Thomaston Corner	G-4
Tracy	G-4
Upper Hainesville	F-3
Welsford	G-4
Woodstock	F-3
Youngs Cove	F-5

Newfoundland and Labrador

Population: 519,270
Land area: 144,353 sq. mi.
Capital: St. John's

Cities and Towns

Baie Verte	B-11
Bay de Verde	C-12
Bishop's Falls	C-11
Bonavista	C-12
Brig Bay	A-10
Buchans	C-10
Burgeo	C-10
Channel-Port aux Basques	C-9
Corner Brook	C-10
Daniel's Harbour	B-10
Deer Lake	C-10
Englee	B-11
Gander	C-11
Goobies	C-12
Grand Bank	D-11
Grand Falls-Windsor	C-11
Harbour Breton	D-11
Lark Harbour	C-10
Marystown	D-11
Placentia	D-12
Port Blandford	C-11
Roddickton	B-11
Rose-Blanche-Harbour le Cou	C-9
St. Alban's	C-11
St. Anthony	A-11
St. John's	C-12
St. Lawrence	D-11
Torbay	C-12
Trout River	B-10

Nova Scotia

Population: 934,392
Land area: 20,594 sq. mi.
Capital: Halifax

Cities and Towns

Advocate Harbour	G-6
Albany Cross	H-6
Amherst	F-6

Annapolis Royal	H-5
Antigonish	G-9
Apple River	G-6
Baddeck	F-10
Barrington Passage	J-5
Bass River	G-7
Big Pond	F-10
Bridgetown	H-5
Bridgewater	I-6
Brookfield	G-7
Brooklyn	H-7
Canso	G-10
Carleton	I-5
Centreville	H-5
Chester	H-6
Cheticamp	E-10
Clementsport	H-5
Clyde River	J-5
Corberrie	I-5
Dartmouth	H-7
Digby	H-5
East Bay	F-11
Earltown	G-7
Elmsdale	H-7
Glace Bay	F-11
Glenholme	G-7
Goldboro	G-9
Goldenville	G-9
Grand River	F-10
Greywood	H-5
Guysborough	G-9
Halifax	H-7
Halls Harbour	G-6
Hebron	I-5
Indian Brook	E-10
Ingonish	E-11
Ingonish Beach	E-10
Inverness	E-10
Joggins	G-6
Kentville	H-6
Larrys River	G-9
Liverpool	I-6
Lockeport	J-5
Louisbourg	F-11
Lunenburg	I-6
Maccan	F-6
Mahone Bay	I-6
Margaree Forks	E-10
Margaree Harbour	E-10
Mavillette	I-4
Middle Musquodoboit	H-7
Middlefield	I-6
Middleton	H-6
Mill Village	I-6
Moser River	H-8
Mulgrave	G-9
Musquodoboit Harbour	H-7
Neil's Harbour	E-11
New Germany	H-6
New Glasgow	G-8
New Ross	H-6
New Waterford	E-11
Newport Station	H-6
North Sydney	F-11
Nyanza	F-10
Oxford	F-7
Parrsboro	G-6
Peggys Cove	H-7
Picton	G-8
Pleasant Bay	E-10
Port Hastings	F-9
Port Hawkesbury	G-10
Port Hood	F-9
Pubnico	J-5
Renous	I-6
Sable River	I-6
St. Peters	G-10
Salmon River	I-5
Sand Point	G-10
Shag Harbour	J-5
Sheet Harbour	H-8
Shelburne	J-5
South Brookfield	I-6
Southampton	G-6
Springhill	G-6
Stewiacke	G-7
Sunnybrae	G-8
Sydney	F-11
Sydney Mines	E-11
Tatamagouche	G-7
Tiverton	I-4
Truro	G-7
Upper Musquodoboit	G-8
Upper Rawdon	H-7
Vaughan	H-6
Wedgeport	J-5
Westport	I-4
Weymouth	I-5
Whycocomagh	F-10
Windsor	H-6
Wolfville	G-6
Yarmouth	I-5

Prince Edward Island

Population: 136,998
Land area: 2,185 sq. mi.
Capital: Charlottetown

Cities and Towns

Alberton	E-6
Belle River	F-8
Borden-Carleton	F-7
Campbellton	E-6
Cavendish	E-7
Charlottetown	F-7
Georgetown	F-8
Kensington	E-7
Montague	F-8
Murray Harbour	F-8
Portage	E-6
Rocky Point	F-7
St. Peters	E-8
Souris	E-8
South Lake	E-9
Summerside	E-7
Tignish	D-6
West Point	E-6

For border crossing information, please see p. 177

For border crossing information, please see p. 177

Mexico

Population: 97,483,412
Land area: 758,450 sq. mi.
Capital: Mexico City

Cities and Towns

Acaponeta	D-5
Acapulco	F-6
Acayucan	E-8
Aguascalientes	D-5
Arriaga	F-8
Atixco	E-7
Autlán de Navarro	E-5
Bahía Kino	B-3
Bermejillo	C-5
Buenaventura	B-4
Campeche	E-9
Cancún	D-10
Chapotón	E-9
Chetumal	E-10
Chihuahua	B-4
Chilpancingo	F-6
Cholula	E-7
Cintalapa	E-5
Ciudad Camargo	B-5
Ciudad del Carmen	E-9
Ciudad Juárez	A-4
Ciudad Madero	D-7
Ciudad Mante	D-6
Ciudad Obregón	B-4
Ciudad Valles	D-6
Ciudad Victoria	C-6
Coatzacoalcos	E-8
Colima	E-5
Cozumel	D-10
Cuauhtémoc	B-4
Cuernavaca	E-6
Culiacán	C-4
Durango	C-5
El Fuerte	B-4
El Sueco	B-4
Ensenada	A-2
Fresnillo	C-5
Gómez Palacio	C-5
Guadalajara	E-5
Guamúchil	C-4
Guanajuato	D-6
Guaymas	B-3
Guerrero	B-4
Guzmán	E-5
Hermosillo	B-3
Hidalgo del Parral	C-4
Huajuapan de León	E-7
Iguala	E-6
Irapuato	D-6
Jiménez	C-5
Juan Aldama	C-5
La Paz	C-3
La Pesca	D-6
León	D-6
Linares	C-6
Loreto	C-3
Los Mochis	B-4
Manzanillo	E-5
Matamoros	C-7
Matehuala	D-6
Mazatlán	C-4
Mérida	D-9
Mexicali	A-1
Mexico City	E-6
Monclova	C-6
Monterrey	C-6
Morelia	E-6
Navojoa	B-3
Nogales	A-3
Nueva Rosita	B-6
Nuevo Casas Grandes	A-4
Nuevo Laredo	B-6
Oaxaca	E-7
Ojinaga	B-5
Orizaba	E-7
Pachuca	E-6
Parras	C-5
Piedras Negras	B-6
Pitiquito	A-3
Poza Rica	E-6
Puebla	E-7
Puerto Ángel	F-7
Puerto Escondido	F-7
Puerto Morelos	D-10
Puerto Peñasco	A-2
Puerto Vallarta	E-5
Punta Prieta	B-2
Querétaro	D-6
Reynosa	C-6
Río Lagartos	D-9
Rosario	C-4
Sabinas	B-6
Sabinas Hidalgo	B-6
Sahuaripa	B-4
Salamanca	D-6
Saltillo	C-6
San Blas	C-3
San Carlos	A-2
San Felipe	A-2
San Fernando	B-2
San Francisco del Orco	C-7
San José del Cabo	C-3
San Luis Potosí	A-2
Santa Ana	E-6
Santa Bárbara	B-3
Santa Rosalía	C-4
Santo Domingo	C-6
Tehuantepec	F-8
Tampico	D-7
Tapachula	F-8
Taxco	E-6
Tepic	E-5
Tepehuanes	D-6
Tijuana	A-1
Tlaxcala	E-7
Toluca	E-6
Tónichi	B-3
Topolobampo	B-3
Torreón	C-5
Tuxpan	D-7
Tuxtla Gutiérrez	F-8
Uruapan del Progreso	E-6
Veracruz	E-8
Villahermosa	E-8
Xalapa	E-7
Zacatecas	D-5
Zihuatanejo	F-6

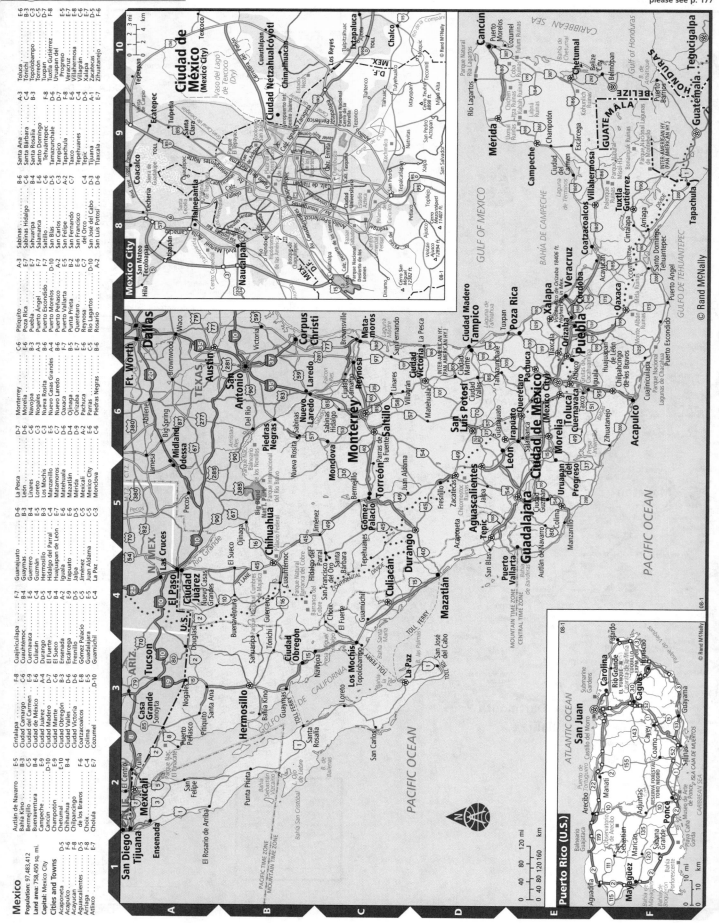

Ciudad de México (Mexico City)

Mexico City

Puerto Rico (U.S.)

© Rand McNally

Tourism Concierge

On the road or before you go, log on to the official tourism website of your destination. These websites offer terrific ideas about organizing a visit and often include calendars of special events and activities. Prefer calling? Most states offer toll-free numbers.

United States

Alabama Bureau of Tourism & Travel
(800) 252-2262
www.800alabama.com

Alaska Travel Industry Association
(907) 929-2200
www.travelalaska.com

Arizona Office of Tourism
(866) 239-9712
www.arizonaguide.com

Arkansas Department of Parks & Tourism
(800) 628-8725
www.arkansas.com

California Travel & Tourism Commission
(800) 862-2543*
(916) 444-4429
www.visitcalifornia.com

Colorado Tourism Office
(800) 265-6723
www.colorado.com

Connecticut Tourism
(800) 282-6863
www.ctbound.org

Delaware Tourism Office
(866) 284-7483
(302) 739-4271
www.visitdelaware.com

Visit Florida
(888) 735-2872
www.visitflorida.com

Georgia Office of Tourism
(800) 847-4842
www.georgiaonmymind.org

Hawaii Visitors & Convention Bureau
(800) 464-2924
www.gohawaii.com

Idaho Tourism
(800) 847-4843
www.visitid.org

Illinois Bureau of Tourism
(800) 226-6632
www.enjoyillinois.com

Indiana Tourism Division
(888) 365-6946
www.enjoyindiana.com

Iowa Tourism Office
(800) 345-4692*
(888) 472-6035
(515) 242-4705
www.traveliowa.com

Kansas Travel & Tourism
(800) 252-6727
www.travelks.com

Kentucky Department of Travel
(800) 225-8747
(502) 564-4930
www.kentuckytourism.com

Louisiana Office of Tourism
(800) 334-8626
www.louisianatravel.com

Maine Office of Tourism
(888) 624-6345
(225) 342-8100
www.visitmaine.com

Maryland Office of Tourism
(800) 634-7386
www.visitmaryland.org

Massachusetts Office of Travel & Tourism
(800) 227-6277
(617) 973-8500
www.massvacation.com

Travel Michigan
(888) 784-7328
www.michigan.org

Minnesota Office of Tourism
(800) 657-3700
(651) 296-5029
www.exploreminnesota.com

Mississippi Division of Tourism
(800) 927-6378
(601) 359-3297
www.visitmississippi.org

Missouri Division of Tourism
(800) 810-5500
(573) 751-4133
www.visitmo.com

Travel Montana
(800) 847-4868
(406) 841-2870
www.visitmt.com

Nebraska Division of Travel & Tourism
(877) 632-7275
(800) 228-4307
(402) 471-3796
www.visitnebraska.org

Nevada Commission on Tourism
(800) 638-2328
www.travelnevada.com

New Hampshire Division of Travel and Tourism Development
(800) 386-4664
(603) 271-2665
www.visitnh.gov

New Jersey Office of Travel & Tourism
(800) 847-4865
(609) 777-0885
www.visitnj.org

New Mexico Department of Tourism
(800) 733-6396
www.newmexico.org

New York State Tourism
(800) 225-5697
(518) 474-4116
www.iloveny.com

North Carolina Division of Tourism
(800) 847-4862
(919) 733-8372
www.visitnc.com

North Dakota Tourism Division
(800) 435-5663
(701) 328-2525
www.ndtourism.com

Ohio Division of Travel & Tourism
(800) 282-5393
www.discoverohio.com

Oklahoma Tourism & Recreation Department
(800) 652-6552
www.travelok.com

Oregon Tourism Commission
(800) 547-7842
www.traveloregon.com

Pennsylvania Center for Travel & Marketing
(800) 847-4872
www.visitpa.com

Rhode Island Tourism Division
(888) 886-9463
(800) 556-2484
(401) 222-2601
www.visitrhodeisland.com

South Carolina Department of Parks, Recreation & Tourism
(888) 727-6453*
(803) 734-1700
www.discoversouthcarolina.com

South Dakota Department of Tourism
(800) 732-5682
(605) 773-3301
www.travelsd.com

Tennessee Department of Tourist Development
(800) 462-8366*
(615) 741-2159
www.tnvacation.com

Texas Tourism Division
(800) 888-8839*
www.traveltex.com

Utah Travel Council
(800) 200-1160
(801) 538-1030
www.utah.com

Vermont Department of Tourism and Marketing
(800) 837-6668
www.vermontvacation.com

Virginia Tourism Corporation
(800) 321-3244
(800) 847-4882
www.virginia.org

Washington State Tourism
(800) 544-1800
www.experiencewashington.com

Washington, D.C. Convention & Tourism Corporation
(800) 422-8644*
(202) 789-7000
www.washington.org

West Virginia Division of Tourism
(800) 225-5982
www.callwva.com

Wisconsin Department of Tourism
(800) 432-8747
www.travelwisconsin.com

Wyoming Travel & Tourism
(800) 225-5996
www.wyomingtourism.org

Canada

Travel Alberta
(800) 252-3782
www.travelalberta.com

Tourism British Columbia
(800) 435-5622
www.hellobc.com

Travel Manitoba
(800) 665-0040
www.travelmanitoba.com

Tourism New Brunswick
(800) 561-0123
www.tourismnbcanada.com

Newfoundland & Labrador Department of Tourism
(800) 563-6353
(709) 729-2830
www.gov.nf.ca/tourism

Nova Scotia Department of Tourism & Culture
(800) 565-0000
novascotia.com

Ontario Travel
(800) 668-2746
www.ontariotravel.net

Prince Edward Island Tourism
(888) 734-7529
www.peiplay.com

Tourisme Québec
(877) 266-5687
www.bonjourquebec.com

Tourism Saskatchewan
(877) 237-2273
www.sasktourism.com

Mexico

Mexico Tourism Board
(800) 446-3942
www.visitmexico.com

*To request travel materials only

Mile Markers
Mileage Chart

This handy chart offers more than 2,500 mileages covering 77 North American cities. Want more mileages? Visit go.randmcnally.com/MC and type in any two cities or addresses.

City	Atlanta, GA	Billings, MT	Boston, MA	Charlotte, NC	Chicago, IL	Cincinnati, OH	Cleveland, OH	Dallas, TX	Denver, CO	Detroit, MI	Houston, TX	Indianapolis, IN	Kansas City, MO	Los Angeles, CA	Memphis, TN	Miami, FL	Milwaukee, WI	Minneapolis, MN	New Orleans, LA	New York, NY	Omaha, NE	Philadelphia, PA	Phoenix, AZ	Pittsburgh, PA	Portland, OR	St. Louis, MO	Salt Lake City, UT	San Francisco, CA	Seattle, WA	Tulsa, OK	Washington, DC	Wichita, KS
Albany, NY	1014	2076	166	777	820	727	478	1682	1814	648	1770	791	1287	2833	1230	1407	921	1236	1441	153	1274	238	2544	472	2927	1040	2206	2953	2899	1433	365	1477
Albuquerque, NM	1406	994	2247	1629	1341	1397	1606	644	439	1591	890	1290	783	799	1014	1960	1424	1222	1170	2019	979	1939	463	1649	1385	1041	626	1097	1456	650	1886	593
Amarillo, TX	1121	971	1962	1344	1056	1112	1321	359	424	1306	605	1005	604	1084	729	1675	1139	1043	885	1734	716	1654	748	1649	1666	756	911	1382	1737	365	1601	417
Atlanta, GA		1890	1100	243	712	463	715	791	1415	723	797	529	810	2205	393	661	811	1132	468	896	1000	816	1862	686	2604	556	1883	2503	2675	798	635	972
Baltimore, MD	673	1960	407	436	704	523	379	1366	1693	532	1454	592	1088	2681	914	1080	805	1120	1125	203	1158	102	2345	251	2811	841	2090	2837	2783	1234	38	1278
Billings, MT	1890		2242	2247	1247	1547	1598	1429	555	1534	1676	1433	1078	1239	1606	2551	1176	843	1954	2067	896	2017	1206	1716	891	1333	549	1179	821	1238	1961	1064
Birmingham, AL	148	1839	1185	391	661	467	719	647	1364	727	671	478	759	2058	246	783	760	1081	342	981	949	901	1722	753	2553	505	1832	2356	2624	651	743	825
Bismarck, ND	1558	417	1828	1610	833	1133	1184	1274	709	1120	1521	1019	790	1595	1318	2219	762	429	1709	1653	608	1603	1515	1302	1310	1045	927	1598	1240	1037	1547	802
Boise, ID	2184	621	2673	2349	1702	1959	2029	1704	830	1965	1951	1852	1372	846	1900	2845	1741	1466	2229	2498	1233	2448	995	2147	425	1627	338	648	496	1513	2392	1339
Boston, MA	1100	2242		863	986	893	644	1768	1980	814	1856	957	1453	2999	1316	1483	1087	1402	1527	211	1440	313	2710	586	3093	1206	2372	3119	3065	1599	441	1643
Buffalo, NY	896	1787	461	659	531	438	189	1376	1525	359	1495	502	998	2544	924	1381	632	947	1243	417	985	412	2255	216	2638	751	1917	2664	2610	1144	388	1188
Charleston, SC	321	2196	966	207	911	619	721	1112	1721	850	1113	730	1116	2526	714	580	1010	1325	784	762	1306	661	2183	654	2910	862	2189	2981	2977	1119	525	1306
Charlotte, NC	243	2055	863		770	478	516	1034	1580	645	1040	589	975	2428	617	724	869	1184	711	659	1165	534	2092	449	2769	721	2048	2726	2840	1021	398	1165
Cheyenne, WY	1450	455	1939	1615	968	1225	1295	974	100	1231	1221	1118	638	1102	1166	2111	1007	878	1499	1764	499	1714	906	1413	1155	893	434	1181	1226	783	1658	609
Chicago, IL	712	1247	986	770		293	342	933	1009	278	1089	179	529	2028	536	1373	92	407	927	811	469	761	1804	460	2122	300	1401	2148	2070	693	705	719
Cincinnati, OH	463	1547	893	478	293		252	938	1208	260	1057	112	603	2196	486	1124	392	707	805	660	726	580	1860	290	2379	356	1658	2405	2370	749	524	793
Cleveland, OH	715	1598	644	516	342	252		1190	1336	170	1309	316	812	2355	738	1238	443	758	1057	486	796	436	2069	135	2449	565	1728	2475	2421	958	380	1002
Columbus, OH	574	1606	783	433	352	111	142	1049	1276	204	1168	175	671	2264	597	1155	451	766	916	553	794	473	1928	183	2447	424	1726	2473	2429	817	417	861
Dallas, TX	791	1429	1768	1034	933	938	1190		882	1198	247	882	552	1440	454	1316	1016	991	526	1564	664	1484	1069	1228	2124	633	1403	1741	2195	262	1326	365
Davenport, IA	792	1166	1135	898	175	421	491	915	843	427	1095	314	363	1862	550	1453	214	359	941	960	303	910	1609	609	1956	266	1235	1982	1989	612	854	553
Denver, CO	1415	555	1980	1580	1009	1208	1336	882		1272	1129	1101	605	1022	1097	2076	1048	919	1407	1805	540	1750	809	1460	1250	858	529	1276	1321	691	1694	517
Des Moines, IA	961	997	1304	1067	333	590	660	746	674	596	926	483	194	1693	623	1622	372	243	1014	1129	134	1079	1440	778	1787	350	1066	1813	1820	443	1023	384
Detroit, MI	723	1534	814	645	278	260	170	1198	1272		1317	310	792	2291	746	1367	379	694	1065	639	732	589	2054	288	2385	550	1664	2411	2357	943	533	955
Duluth, MN	1189	861	1459	1241	464	764	815	1145	1073	751	1325	650	593	2092	965	1850	393	157	1356	1284	533	1234	1839	933	1754	681	1465	2042	1684	842	1178	783
El Paso, TX	1426	1178	2394	1669	1488	1544	1753	633	623	1738	753	1437	930	807	1087	1939	1571	1369	1100	2197	1016	2117	436	1796	1627	1188	868	1188	1698	797	1959	740
Fargo, ND	1369	607	1639	1421	644	944	995	1087	901	931	1334	830	603	1785	1131	2030	573	240	1522	1464	421	1414	1707	1113	1500	858	1117	1788	1430	850	1358	725
Flagstaff, AZ	1733	1070	2574	1956	1668	1724	1933	971	613	1918	1217	1617	1110	472	1341	2287	1751	1549	1497	2346	1210	2266	136	1976	1279	1368	520	770	1350	977	2213	920
Houston, TX	797	1676	1856	1040	1089	1057	1309	247	1129	1317		1025	732	1560	573	1190	1179	1171	351	1562	911	1572	1189	1347	2311	837	1650	1941	2442	505	1414	612
Indianapolis, IN	529	1433	957	589	179	112	316	882	1101	310	1025		496	2089	472	1190	278	593	816	729	619	649	1753	359	2272	249	1551	2298	2256	642	593	686
Jackson, MS	383	1817	1424	626	747	692	944	408	1225	952	442	683	737	1850	212	908	837	1119	180	1220	927	1140	1479	982	2467	495	1746	2149	2538	534	982	708
Jacksonville, FL	346	2236	1142	383	1058	795	897	1001	1761	1026	875	875	1156	2431	712	341	1157	1478	546	938	1346	837	2060	830	2950	902	2229	2742	3021	1117	701	1291
Kansas City, MO	810	1078	1453	975	529	603	812	552	603	792	732	496		1626	526	1471	568	439	917	1225	188	1145	1246	855	1792	253	1071	1818	1863	249	1089	190
Knoxville, TN	215	1826	928	229	542	250	502	840	1351	510	928	361	746	2199	388	876	641	956	599	724	936	644	1863	406	2540	492	1819	2611	2623	792	486	936
Las Vegas, NV	1982	966	2726	2205	1755	1956	2082	1220	749	2018	1466	1849	1353	275	1590	2536	1794	1665	1746	2551	1286	2498	292	2208	1021	1606	416	569	1122	1226	2462	1265
Lexington, KY	386	1669	935	401	375	83	335	874	1194	343	993	188	589	2175	422	1047	474	789	741	731	779	645	1839	373	2383	335	1662	2409	2454	728	543	779
Little Rock, AR	531	1513	1453	754	655	623	875	315	966	883	434	591	389	1682	139	1165	745	826	441	1249	577	1169	1346	913	2208	403	1487	1980	2279	275	1011	449
Los Angeles, CA	2205	1239	2999	2428	2028	2196	2355	1440	1022	2291	1560	2089	1626		1813	2746	2067	1938	1907	2824	1559	2738	371	2448	967	1840	689	381	1141	1449	2685	1392
Louisville, KY	415	1595	996	475	297	103	355	835	1120	363	954	114	515	2101	383	1076	396	711	702	763	705	683	1765	393	2309	261	1588	2335	2380	654	617	705
Memphis, TN	393	1606	1316	617	536	486	738	454	1097	746	573	472	526	1813		1027	626	908	392	1112	716	1032	1477	776	2320	284	1599	2111	2391	406	874	580
Miami, FL	661	2551	1483	724	1373	1424	1238	1316	2076	1367	1190	1190	1471	2746	1027		1472	1793	861	1279	1661	1178	2375	1171	3265	1217	2944	3057	3336	1432	1042	1606
Milwaukee, WI	811	1176	1087	869	92	392	443	1016	1048	379	1179	278	568	2067	626	1472		336	1299	912	508	862	1887	561	2069	383	1440	2187	1999	776	806	758
Minneapolis, MN	1132	843	1402	1184	407	707	758	991	919	694	1171	593	439	1938	908	1793	336		1299	1227	379	1177	1685	876	1736	624	1311	2058	1666	688	1121	629
Mobile, AL	329	2003	1429	572	920	726	978	598	1415	986	472	737	923	2028	398	718	1019	1305	143	1225	1113	1145	1657	1009	2657	681	1936	2339	2728	724	964	898
Montréal, QC	1227	1909	324	990	848	829	590	1767	1842	575	1886	879	1362	2861	1315	1632	900	1264	1654	384	1302	463	2632	617	2955	1128	2234	2981	2732	1521	590	1525
Nashville, TN	242	1650	1106	407	472	278	530	663	1175	538	782	289	570	2022	211	903	571	892	527	902	760	822	1686	568	2364	316	1643	2320	2435	615	664	760
New Orleans, LA	468	1954	1527	711	927	805	1057	524	1407	1065	351	816	917	1907	392	861	1017	1299		1323	1007	1243	1536	1095	2649	675	1928	2267	2720	679	1085	890
New York, NY	896	2067	211	659	811	660	486	1564	1805	639	1652	729	1225	2824	1112	1279	912	1227	1323		1265	109	2482	388	2918	978	2197	2944	2890	1371	237	1415
Norfolk, VA	557	2147	577	320	891	601	566	1348	1781	719	1384	713	1176	2729	918	948	992	1307	1055	373	1366	276	2393	438	2970	922	2249	2996	3041	1315	196	1366
Odessa, TX	1147	1204	2122	1390	1244	1292	1509	354	649	1494	546	1193	792	1088	808	1672	1327	1231	882	1918	904	1838	717	1552	1784	944	1025	1469	1855	553	1680	605
Oklahoma City, OK	862	1221	1702	1085	796	852	1061	208	674	1046	455	745	344	1343	470	1496	879	783	733	1474	456	1394	1007	1104	1916	496	1195	1641	1987	105	1342	157
Omaha, NE	1000	896	1440	1165	469	726	796	664	540	732	911	619	188	1559	716	1661	508	379	1107	1265		1215	1346	914	1653	443	932	1679	1724	435	1159	302
Orlando, FL	440	2330	1284	525	1152	903	1039	1095	1855	1163	969	969	1250	2525	806	229	1251	1572	640	1080	1440	979	2154	972	3044	996	2323	2836	3115	1211	843	1385
Philadelphia, PA	816	2017	313	534	761	580	436	1484	1750	589	1572	649	1145	2738	1032	1178	862	1177	1243	109	1215		2402	308	2868	898	2147	2894	2840	1291	136	1335
Phoenix, AZ	1862	1206	2710	2092	1804	1860	2069	1069	809	2054	1189	1753	1246	371	1477	2375	1887	1685	1536	2482	1346	2402		2112	1338	1504	656	752	1486	1113	2349	1056
Pittsburgh, PA	686	1716	586	449	460	290	135	1228	1460	288	1347	359	855	2448	776	1171	561	876	1095	388	914	308	2112		2567	608	1846	2593	2539	1001	252	1045
Portland, ME	1229	2343	117	964	1087	994	745	1897	2081	915	1985	1058	1554	3100	1445	1584	1188	1503	1656	312	1541	414	2811	687	3194	1307	2473	3220	3166	1700	542	1744
Portland, OR	2604	891	3093	2769	2122	2379	2449	2124	1250	2385	2311	2272	1792	967	2320	3265	2069	1736	2649	2918	1653	2868	1338	2567		2047	758	636	174	1933	2812	1759
Rapid City, SD	1521	373	1904	1686	909	1209	1260	1069	400	1396	1316	1095	709	1312	1237	2182	838	609	1628	1729	527	1679	1206	1378	1266	964	644	1391	1196	878	1623	704
Reno, NV	2406	955	2895	2571	1924	2181	2251	1665	1052	2187	1911	2074	1594	473	2122	3067	1963	1834	2193	2720	1455	2670	735	2369	578	1849	522	224	752	1735	2614	1561
Roanoke, VA	430	1917	678	193	663	370	429	1098	1550	558	1186	482	945	2457	646	915	762	1077	857	474	1135	394	2121	365	2739	691	2018	2765	2810	1050	236	1135
St. Louis, MO	556	1333	1206	721	300	356	565	633	858	550	837	249	253	1840	284	1217	383	624	675	978	443	898	1500	608	2047		1326	2073	2118	393	878	443
Salt Lake City, UT	1883	549	2372	2048	1401	1658	1728	1403	529	1664	1650	1551	1071	689	1599	2544	1440	1311	1928	2197	932	2147	656	1846	758	1326		746	829	1212	2091	1038
San Antonio, TX	992	1483	2051	1235	1210	1215	1467	277	936	1475	199	1159	817	1365	731	1385	1293	1256	546	1847	929	1767	994	1505	2100	910	1341	1746	2171	539	1609	630
San Diego, CA	2154	1299	3064	2397	2088	2214	2423	1361	1082	2351	1481	2107	1600	124	1831	2667	2127	1998	1828	2836	1619	2756	354	2466	1091	1858	749	505	1265	1467	2703	1410
San Francisco, CA	2503	1179	3119	2726	2148	2405	2423	1741	1276	2411	1941	2298	1818	381	2111	3057	2187	2058	2267	2944	1679	2894	752	2593	636	2073	746		810	1747	2838	1785
Sault Ste. Marie, ON	1047	1282	943	960	452	584	506	1357	1446	350	1510	537	966	2465	957	1708	404	549	1347	939	906	925	2228	624	2175	724	1838	2585	2105	1197	869	1129
Seattle, WA	2675	821	3065	2840	2070	2370	2421	2195	1321	2357	2442	2256	1863	1141	2391	3336	1999	1666	2720	2890	1724	2840	1486	2539	174	2118	829	810		2004	2784	1830
Shreveport, LA	605	1614	1646	848	851	819	1071	186	1067	1079	239	787	566	1628	335	1130	941	1005	347	1442	752	1362	1257	1109	2309	599	1588	1927	2380	339	1204	550
Sioux Falls, SD	1177	717	1543	1342	569	876	927	849	654	856	1096	769	365	1673	893	1838	498	269	1284	1389	183	1339	1460	1038	1610	620	989	1736	1540	612	1283	487
Spokane, WA	2431	539	2783	2596	1788	2088	2139	1970	1096	2155	2217	1974	1619	1215	2147	3092	1777	1384	2495	2608	1437	2558	1377	2272	352	1874	720	881	282	1779	2502	1605
Springfield, MO	684	1247	1418	849	512	568	777	423	761	762	666	461	169	1630	283	1345	595	606	674	1190	357	1110	1294	820	1961	212	1240	1928	2032	183	1090	263
Tallahassee, FL	270	2143	1301	470	965	733	985	839	1668	993	713	782	1063	2269	550	478	1064	1385	384	1097	1253	996	1898	917	2857	809	2136	2580	2928	955	860	1129
Tampa, FL	458	2348	1340	581	1170	921	1095	1113	1873	1181	987	987	1268	2543	824	273	1269	1590	658	1136	1458	1035	2172	1028	3062	1014	2341	2854	3133	1229	899	1403
Toronto, ON	961	1773	566	766	517	498	296	1436	1511	244	1555	548	1031	2530	984	1488	618	933	1303	528	971	517	2301	323	2624	797	1903	2650	2596	1190	495	1194
Tulsa, OK	798	1238	1599	1021	693	749	958	262	691	943	505	642	249	1449	406	1432	776	688	679	1371	435	1291	1113	1001	1933	393	1212	1747	2004		1271	174
Washington, DC	635	1961	441	398	705	524	380	1326	1694	533	1414	593	1089	2685	874	1042	806	1121	1085	237	1159	136	2349	252	2812	878	2091	2838	2784	1271		1279
Wichita, KS	972	1064	1643	1165	719	793	1002	365	517	955	612	686	190	1392	580	1606	758	629	890	1415	302	1335	1056	1045	1759	443	1038	1785	1830	174	1279	